For Sam Eisenstein,
who has had
his share.

C Kern
4/19/2017

GARY KERN

MISFORTUNE

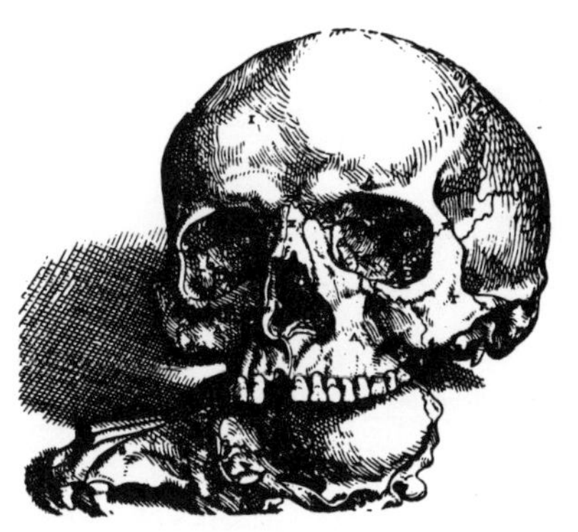

XENOS BOOKS

Second edition, thoroughly revised, 1997

*Cover art and illustrations from
the anatomical studies of Andreas Vesalius.*

Cover design by Karl Kvitko

```
        Library of Congress Cataloging-in-Publication Data

Kern, Gary.
  Misfortune / Gary Kern.
     p.   cm.
  ISBN 0-89370-841-0. -- ISBN 0-89370-941-7 (pbk.)
  1. Kern, Gary--Biography.  2. Authors, American--20th cen-
tury--Biography.   3. Translators--United States--Biography.
I. Title.
PS3561.E573Z468 199088-28071              818'.5409--dc19
                                                  CIP [B]
```

Published by Xenos Books, P.O. Box 52152, Riverside, CA 92517-3152. Tel. (909) 370-2229. Web site: www.xenosbooks.com. Printed in the USA by Van Volumes Ltd., Palmer, MA 01069

CONTENTS

MISFORTUNE

Была ужасная пора,
Об ней свежо воспоминанье...
Об ней, друзья мои, для вас
Начну свое повествованье.
Печален будет мой рассказ.

There was a truly dreadful time,
Of it still fresh is recollection...
Of it, my friends, I'll now begin
To make for you my own narration.
Pathetic is the tale I spin.

Pushkin, *The Bronze Horseman*

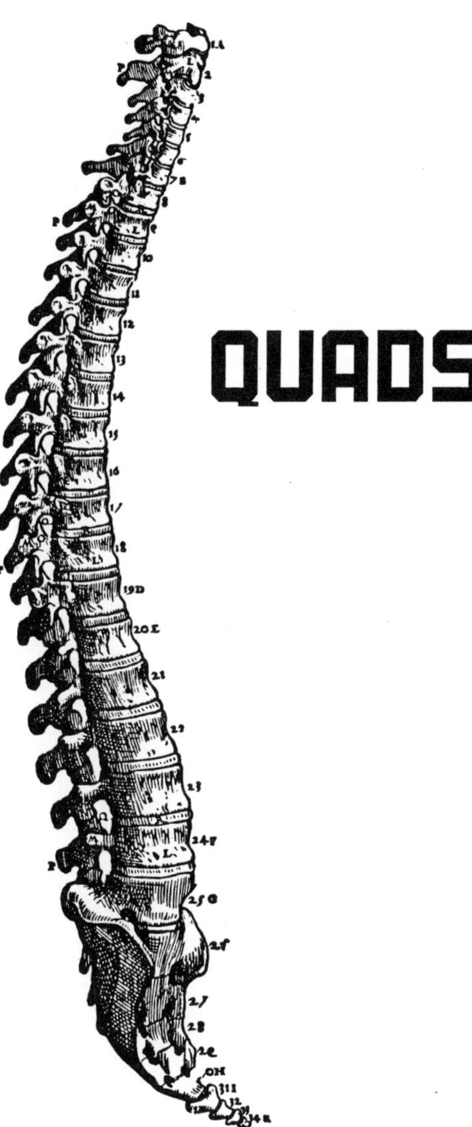
QUADS

ONE

NO-BOOK

uddenly broke. No one rushing to help me out. Notice from the landlord: rent will be raised. No other mail. My proposals, my manuscripts — shelved in offices three thousand miles away. No need to send more. No money. The editors are busy. They're chatting with movie stars, future best sellers. I can live on air. Time to get tough, to take care of myself. Stop being a dreamer. Forget the mailbox, look in the want-ads.

I look, get disgusted. Purposely leave the papers strewn over the floor. A week of old papers scrunched up in the bathroom. I read them in the bathtub, toss them away with contempt, step out on them with sopping wet feet. This will get me nowhere. I'd better get serious. Look for the lesser of evils. But all evils are great: Opportunity for self-motivated individual with unlimited self-confidence who must make $1000 a month. Translate: We need a goon to sell our worthless crap. Or: Mag particle/penetrant inspector. Can there really be such a person, and he's looking through the paper until he finds the ad: Ah, here I am, mag particle/ penetrant inspector. I could drive a bus. No, I couldn't: two years experience required. It turns out I'm overqualified for my profession (for which there are no positions) and unqualified for everything else. Except the sort of jobs I had when I worked my way through college. I could stand them only for that purpose. Now I've gone through, and the jobs are still there. Can't go back.

Another week. I'd really better get serious. Here's one: Prof. Maltz's Psycho-Cybernetics Institute. $60,000 a year. You must be willing to change your outlook. Convince people. Self-improvement techniques. Well, maybe I could fake it for 6 months. Go gung-ho on Maltz's learning machines, make $30,000. Then quit and publish my unpublishable works. Send copies to friends, who wouldn't read them. Two copies each to the Library of Congress — for shelving. (I worked there in my senior year.) O.K., I'll phone. Goddamn it, psycho-cybernetics is the wave of the future. I even know the Greek origins of the words. I can impress Maltz.

Wolfgang and I go to the phone across the street. Wolfgang nonchalantly sprinkles the ivy on the way. I dial. A recording: toll call. All right, I've got a quarter. I dial again, this time putting 1 before the number. The operator comes on: 60¢ for three minutes. The phone is ringing for Maltz. I don't have 60¢. Only 53¢. Ring, ring — hang up fast. I can't afford it. They'd laugh at me in the institute anyway. I'd never even make it to Maltz. I couldn't sell the goddamned psycho-cybernetic contraptions, I'd trip over the wires. I can't do anything... I'm crushed. By 60¢. And just a moment before I was going to make $30,000.

A new ad appears:

AIDE WANTED

For Quadriplegic. Experience preferred. Must be reliable. Good pay.   Must be able to drive. Call 735...

This makes me stop. I read it again. Here's a real change of outlook, none of this gung-ho sales crap. No office, no petty boss insisting on petty routines. No witty chitchat, insipid jokes. A real need. Real work. Good pay. But mainly what is not said: self-sacrifice, spiritual improvement. Nothing else in the paper even comes close. But can I?

Perhaps it's not an accident I failed to get one of those jobs. Just a couple of days ago I picked up a book first read over 20 years ago: *Understanding the Sick and the Healthy.* Franz Rosenzweig had imagined a man stricken with philosophical paralysis, yet after writing the book he himself was stricken with real paralysis. Could there be some connection here? Rosenzweig spoke of a period of life after books. "No-book," he called it. Active participation in life, helping others. I was thinking along these lines, since everything I think and write is "non-commercial," unpublishable and hence private, selfish and of no use to others. The correspondence strikes me as uncanny: Rosenzweig and an ad for a quadriplegic. Perhaps something is telling me: No-book.

I bought something with a food stamp, collected the change. Then dialed again from the pay phone. The operator came on: 25¢ for three minutes. I heard ringing, a click and a distant hello.

"I was interested in the ad for an aide."

"Have you ever worked with a quadriplegic before?"

"No, I have no experience."

"Do you know what a quadriplegic is?"

"Yes, I know."

I thought I might mention the etymology: *quad* — four, *plege* — strike, four strikes and you're out. But I held my peace, no need to be too smart. It turned out I was talking to the man himself, he had a phone-device rigged up. I told him I didn't want to work in an office, I wanted to do something useful. He said experience wasn't necessary, but I'd have to see him first. There were some things that some people found difficult to do.

"Bathing?" I ventured.

"Yes," he picked up, "and I have no control of my bowels. I have a catheter (from the Greek, I thought) and..."

He said something more about bowels, but the operator came on to remind me that three minutes were up. I put in another quarter, and we talked some more. It was decided I should phone tomorrow and arrange to drive out. He was having trouble with his day attendant, didn't really have a night attendant. I would have to borrow the car from my wife. We hung up. The phone started ringing. The operator wanting more money. I laughed at her pleading, which suddenly broke off.

It was premature, but I decided to tell my wife the news. Maybe $500-$600 a month, plus a free room. I could write and translate during the day and attend the quadriplegic (I forgot to ask his name) during the night. She was delighted. Now I could pay child support. My books and things could be stored in the garage. Good material for a novel, she observed. And maybe I could start at low pay, make myself indispensable and then ask for a raise.

"No, I can't go in with the intention of conning the quad."

She laughed. "I guess not, but if you can't con a quad, who can you con?"

We had a good conversation, discussed problems. She was amused by my Maltz phone call. I arranged to borrow the car. I hung up and checked to see if the dime had fallen into the return slot. It hadn't.

TWO

QUAD ONE

I didn't tell the quadriplegic about my weak back. It's been in good shape recently. I should be able to turn him. Nor did I mention the eye problem. Extreme sensitivity to light at night, flashes when I close my eyes. Sometimes kidney-shaped beams of light ahead of me, pain like a needle through the pupil. Early signs of glaucoma, it seems to me. But maybe I'm romanticizing. I have eyestrain, so I imagine the tragedy of a blind artist. Take your pains as they are: they have no special significance.

The next day I phoned, borrowed the car, took off. Already dark, and I don't know the area very well. A couple of hitchhikers — maybe they can guide me. I pull into a restaurant parking lot, they hustle up. A skinny old man with popping blue eyes, an overdressed old woman with a hat. They must be in their sixties. To Corona — to Corona they want to go, they don't know my street. The man tucked a newspaper, folded back to the want-ads, in the pocket of his shiny black suit. What is this, the Depression? Black mountain shapes on both sides of the highway, silence. I let them off by a lighted country store, told them they could phone for a cab from there. No busses seemed to be running. I pulled around and saw them walk away from the store and stick out their thumbs. About ten minutes later, after driving around on unlit roads, peering at buildings without illuminated numbers, I found the apartment complex.

A locked gate, an intercom. I press the button. The same voice. I identify myself. Please wait.

A young man appeared, unlocked the gate. The inner circle: a swimming pool, jacuzzi, ring of neat little doorways.

"Greg's back here," said the man, opened a door.

The apartment was a mess: furniture, metal pieces of equipment, barbells, laundry. We went down the little hall to the bedroom. A medicinal smell, something sweet, sickly. A man lay in bed with a sheet drawn up to his chin. A left hand, palm up, lay to the side of his face, fingers curled. I noticed the shiny yellow-brown skin, the long sideburns and thin, curly moustache. The blue eyes were gleaming.

"This is Greg."

"I'm Gary," I said, and immediately glanced at the television playing to the man in bed.

A pause.

Greg began: "There's not too much to do."

And then he spoke of his problems with attendants. His day attendant was his brother's girlfriend: she had been attentive at first, but lately had been drinking a lot, smoking pot and, I got the impression, whoring around. Just yesterday, she left him lying all afternoon in his own urine. Tom here was only a friend (or neighbor): he was coming by purely on an emergency basis. As for me, I would be the night attendant, move into a little room. The slut would show me what needed to be done and then, if she didn't shape up, would herself be replaced.

"I wonder what's keeping her," he said.

While he was talking, I tried to look Greg in the face. He seemed embarrassed by his condition, made some excuses — "Well, that's how it is." He glanced away at the TV. With a shock I noticed a long pigtail stretched out behind his head on the sheet. Why pigtail, sideburns, moustache? Was he a hippy? On the other hand, must you shear your head and strip yourself when you become a quadriplegic?

Without any coaxing, he told me how it had happened. He was zooming down the highway on his motorcycle. There were no lights, but he could follow the white line. It led right up to a dead end. He shot out into the desert. No pain, just immobility. He watched the stars. Someone caught a glint from the overturned motorcycle in his headlights. This happened two years ago. The suit against Riverside County for faulty highway markings was still in the works.

"He's been on TV," volunteered Tom, who had an ease in talking about Greg that I envied. A program on quadriplegics had followed Greg through rehabilitation procedures, shown the techniques of getting him in and out of bed, etc.

"It sure felt funny, seeing myself on TV like that."

I thought it best to make some preparatory excuses.

"Does the apartment permit dogs?"

"No, no dogs allowed. They even made some people get rid of their cat."

"I've got a dog, Wolfgang. He's beautiful. A husky, with black and white markings. He's been my best friend since my wife threw me out. I'd hate to part with him."

"I don't know."

"Surely they can make an exception. I think Wolfgang would bring a lot of cheer into the place. He's a great dog, doesn't bark or anything."

"Well, maybe," said Greg.

"I don't think so," said Tom.

"I suppose I could leave him in the backyard at my wife's place. She'd be getting child support, so she might be nice about it. But, well, there are a lot of problems..."

Jean and I have an agreement. When we want to get out of something, we can paint the other in the blackest colors. You could say we still have a use for each other.

"I know about wife problems..." said Greg, his pale eyes flashing. Tom laughed out loud and let go a curse. Greg told the story: his wife couldn't handle the accident. They were in their twenties, had been married a couple of years. She tried to help at first, then began complaining, arguing, drinking. She brought a lover into the house, fooled around with him in front of Greg's bed. "I guess it was too much for her," said Greg, looking down into the sheets.

Laughter. Alan King was telling jokes, big buxom women paraded by in red and black cancan outfits. Their breasts bulged, bounced. Greg watched, but seemed not to watch. Probably it was just the color, the motion that occupied him. His eyes seemed not to take in the images.

Tom held a glass over to him with a long straw; he took a few sips.

"Want a cigarette?"

"Yeah."

"Looks like Sally ain't gonna show."

Tom lit him up, held the cigarette between long draws.

Greg had wanted her to show me the ropes. "I have a catheter," he said. "The bag needs to be changed. And there's the excrement. Usually it comes out by itself, and then you have to clean up the mess. But if it doesn't, you have to pull it out. Some people can't do it. Even my own brother, he says he just can't do it."

I didn't know what to say.

"But you probably won't have to bother about that. Only if there's an accident. The night attendant mainly just turns me over twice a night. I can get sores if I'm not turned, the circulation..."

"I can't say if I can do it or not," I finally came out, "but I can give it a try."

"O.K., could you call tomorrow?"

We agreed that I would come back and spend a night, to see how it went. I asked him to check about the dog. A few more minutes of televised boobs, and then I took my leave.

"Thanks," I heard him say.

THREE

GREAT EXPECTATIONS

"I can't do it."

Jean was disappointed. She didn't want to force me into it, yet it seemed I was giving up too easily. Why don't you take a positive attitude? Think of all the ways you could help him. You could clean up the living room, set up your own schedule. The whole feeling of the place could be changed. Wolfgang could stay in the backyard.

I stretched out in my armchair. My apartment was filthy: newspapers on the floor, big balls of dust and dog fur, roaches, ants. Pushkin strode down the high road on the wall before me, his cape flying out, the flash of genius and inspiration in his eye. God, he was great! But here I am, nothing good written, and a bunch of non-commercial ideas. I'm not going to be a genius, I'm not going to be even an ordinary writer, I'm just going to sit here. Wolfgang rested his sleek black head on my leg and looked up with wild hazel eyes. I petted his head and contemplated.

There's something in what Jean says. I could change everything with just a little willpower. No one wants to learn Russian anymore, there's no need to teach him to read Pushkin, but there are a lot of other things I could do. Chess, for example. He need only call out the moves. Lying in bed like that, he's probably developed mental powers — he might be able to play a game in his head. And I could read to him — the classics of English and American literature. Fill the gaps in my own knowledge: Dickens, Stevenson, Cooper, Mark Twain. All good books, and not boring by any means. We could discuss the books, he could request titles from the library. Non-fiction too.

I wonder if I could invent some gadgets for him. A holder for his cup. It could attach to the side of his bed, and the straw would reach up to his lips. Same thing for his cigarette — a long wire with a tray underneath for the ashes. This would be dangerous — smoking in bed. But it would give him a sense of independence, control. And who knows what else I could think up? Probably nothing so complicated as to make his hands or arms move, but maybe something to fit in his mouth and respond to pressure: it could press buttons, turn things on and off. Or just a pencil and electric typewriter. A long paintbrush.

This work would be greater than another novel, certain to be filed away with the standard rejection notices. Besides, a novel isn't excluded. I would have the day to do my work — translating, writing, reading. And I would be getting real-life experience. Maybe that's what I need: my writing's too cerebral, too concocted, cut off from real life. But I shouldn't go in with the intention of gathering material for a book. I have to be honest, help honestly. Each moment must be lived for its own sake, not justified afterwards by a written account. Have the courage to enter the real world: no-book.

But what about the poop? Can I handle some guy's genitals, stick my fingers up his gazoo? That's not the way to think of it: he needs help, these are bodily functions. But I'm not a doctor. The closest I've been to this sort of thing was when I changed my daughters' diapers. And even then, it was easier to change them than the baby boy I got stuck with one day. Another kid's poop is different somehow. I want to face reality, sure, but the reality is that I don't want to do it. I can't tell him so, so I'd better play doctor. The fantasy will permit me to face the reality. Or can it be that I do want to do it, as some sort of test for myself? To prove myself better?

Well, Wolfgang, I don't know. I can't perform a miracle. But I could do a hell of a lot. Not everybody gets a Princeton man as attendant. The level of conversation is bound to go up. Besides, who else will do it? He's lying there in bed, his brother won't do it and his brother's squeeze won't do it, and if I don't do it someone may come along and rip him off. It's like when I first saw you: a few more minutes, and you were headed for the back room. The decompression chamber, the freezer, the grinder — you didn't want to feed a plant, did you, Old Guy?

Wolfgang turned his white snout to the side and walked off from the chair a few paces, circled once and let himself down, crossing his snowy white paws out in front of him. Twitching his eyebrows separately, he flicked his wild hazel eyes up at me.

Sorry I mentioned it, Wolf.

FOUR

THE NIGHT
OF THE THUNDERING HOOVES

All right, then, a one-night stand. If it gets gruesome, pretend to be a doctor. If you want out, blame it on Jean. But give it a real try. Forget the frigging education and all that stuff: you're no better than anybody else. Just be human, helpful. Do what needs to be done.

A short dumpy woman let me in, returned to the whirring vacuum cleaner. Bright light, clean smell. The living room was all straightened up, the boxes removed. Well, that's a job I won't have to do. I walked down the lighted hallway to the room, found Greg seated in his wheelchair with a tray attached. A plate of food on the tray: sliced turkey, stuffing, gravy, peas. A studious dark-haired girl with glasses was spooning it up to him, first touching it to her lips and blowing off the steam. The TV was on.

"How're you doing?"

"Fine."

He looked smaller, propped up in the chair. The chest was wasted, the belly bulging: the muscles didn't hold anything up. The wrists and ankles sticking out of the bathrobe looked like shiny sticks. With his round smiling face, his knotted pigtail and fluffy moustache, he looked Oriental, like a figure in a Japanese painting, performing some unknown ritual. I detected the sweet sweaty smell.

He introduced me to the girl. A temporary attendant: the other one, it seems, had taken off. Yet this girl struck me as expert, in no way constrained, as she fed him and fetched him his pills. There was a nightstand full of bottles and cardboard boxes behind the hospital bed. The cleaning woman, it turned out, was the girl's mother — or somebody else. I may not have heard correctly. Tom was around, phoning a pizza parlor from the hall. The phone could be operated separately, or Greg could press the switch on the voice box placed at the head of the bed. Everyone was busy, moving. I had nothing to do.

I sat down and engaged in small talk. Who I was, who they were, why I wanted the job. We made little comments about the TV, I permitted myself a critical remark or two. Finally supper was over, it was time to show me the ropes. The tray was removed, Greg's bathrobe opened: the girl set to work on the catheter. I saw some kind of white plastic bag, tubing and a rubber sort of thing pulled over the penis. The girl drained the bottom of the bag into a plastic jug, unravelled adhesive tape and pulled off the rubber. I was surprised to see that nothing had been inserted into the penis, as I had expected. I must have remarked on this, and the girl explained that he simply urinated and it went down the tube into the bag. Simple enough, but I didn't feel I understood.

"Would you look at that!"

The girl was holding the head of the penis in her fingers, turning it around. I assumed a medical interest.

"Look how irritated it is!"

"It doesn't look too bad."

"Look here, and here."

Now I could see that the skin was red, peeling. The whole glans was shiny. The girl applied some cream and smoothed it over, then pinched it again and turned it over.

"There's nothing more we can do. It's awfully irritated, Greg. Maybe we shouldn't put a catheter on it tonight. Let it get some air."

"O.K."

"We can use this jug," she said to me, showing me a plastic gallon milk container with the neck cut off and adhesive tape run around the sharp edges.

"Uh, how?"

"We'll just put him in it. But you'll have to check when he starts to go. We can't permit any leaking."

"O.K."

Greg was unstrapped from the chair and hoisted up in a cloth seat attached to a pump. The girl worked the lever, while the cheerful cleaning woman stripped the bed, threw on a big bedpad and a crisp white sheet. Then a big diaper was put on the bed and Greg lowered down onto it. He slowly sprawled out like an inflating raft, while the women bustled about on both sides of the bed. I looked on, as though engaged in learning.

The man lay on his back. The cleaning woman pulled his pigtail up toward the corner. The girl again examined the penis, now standing in a magnificent hard-on almost as far as his navel.

"Gee, it's awfully red."

A conversation began. The women were moving around. Tom appeared, eating pizza. He asked about the TV, switched the channels. Some nighttime soap was on: lipsticked women, jiggling titties. I half-watched, waited. Nothing was happening. People stopped, watched. Time passed.

"Did you ask about the dog?"

"No."

"Didn't have time?"

"No, I was afraid they'd say no."

"They won't let you," Tom piped in.

"Well, I might be able to keep him in my wife's backyard."

Time passed. A beautiful woman was emoting on the screen. She wore a scarlet blouse, pulled open to expose her heaving passions.

"Wow-w-w!" laughed Tom.

"Now don't you boys go talking about that!" scolded the cleaning woman goodnaturedly.

"Man, would you look at that!"

"Uh-huh," said Greg, his head rolled to the side. The great swelling emotion left the room, the commercials came on. The cleaning woman snapped back to life.

"Well, let's cover you up!" she shouted, slapping Greg on the belly. "You're lying there as naked as a jay bird."

And she swished a clean sheet over the huge red erection and folded it at his chest. He smiled politely, an Oriental smile.

In time mother and daughter, or whatever, said adieu, and I was left with the two men. It was decided I should turn Greg on his side while Tom looked on to make sure nothing went wrong. I was instructed to go to the head of the bed, lean over and grab Greg under the arms, then pull him up. As I pulled, I felt the entire weight of his body move into the small of my back. The worst position of all for someone with a bad back, and of course this was dead weight — there was no way he could help. I pulled, pulled — it felt like cords snapping in my spinal rigging.

At last he was high enough. I moved to the side and, following instructions, put his right hand over his chest, threw off the sheet and lifted his knees; then, digging under his back, I tried to turn him on his left side. It didn't work: I was too delicate, not used to handling a body like a sack. A couple more tries, more confidence, and he was turned. I held his shoulder tightly from behind for fear he should roll out onto the floor, but he stayed. Now the steps were very specific: one pillow placed under his left leg, another between his legs, but very carefully, exactly so. The diaper had to be kept smooth underneath. A pillow under his head, exactly so: three times before he approved. The milk jug at his waist, the penis — now shrunk — inserted. The sheet pulled up to his chin, to an exact spot, stretched out precisely as he wanted it. The task took a quarter-hour or more.

Tom decided to go buy a model-airplane kit.

I sat down in the chair before Greg, the TV ahead of us both. I asked if he wanted something to drink. He decided on a rum and coke. In the kitchen I found a well-stocked refrigerator, plenty of coke and a bottle of rum. In the dining room there were samples of the greeting cards he had painted: little foxes and squirrels. Not bad work, every hair had a brushstroke, but the overall effect was cute, commercial. The girl had remarked that Greg had made a deal with somebody, and the cards were locally distributed. So I was not going to bring him painting either.

He sucked on the extra-long straw, asked for a cigarette. We settled down to the TV. I read off a list of programs in the guide, and he chose a cowboy film. Lots of horses and dust, stock phrases. Again, he watched, but didn't watch. There was a distance between him and the set, like a bird watching an airplane.

"She's a nice woman — the cleaning woman."

"She's O.K."

I had expected more enthusiasm. She had changed the cast of the apartment, and she had treated him with a rough familiarity I would have appreciated in his place. The thought occurred to me that people like that were better suited to this type of work — medical stuff in general — than over-sensitive literary types.

"Maybe you could get someone like that to work for you during the day."

"I've had some old women apply for the job, but they couldn't lift me."

"I don't know, some of those old broads are pretty tough."

"Maybe, but they might try to take advantage of you."

I looked at his face. He smiled suggestively: he seemed to have something sexual in mind. I couldn't imagine what.

A bunch of horses galloped over the range, a symphonic orchestra playing at top speed so the underpaid musicians could earn extra money.

"I brought over my chess set," I began.

"I don't know how to play."

"Well, I could teach you. I thought it might be an interesting game for you to know. The moves become very complicated, require a lot of concentration. It's peaceful to sit through a chess game."

"Maybe later?"

"O.K."

The cowboys, dust, whiskey — ornery critters and saloons and boardwalks. These people were all walking around, making money. Or rather, collecting residuals in Beverly Hills. Or mouldering away, down under. Greg finished his drink, wanted another. But first, would I mind scratching his nose? It stands to reason: if you lose the power over all of your limbs, and have feeling only above the neck, your nose is sure to itch. That's life. I scratched it here and there, then took a kleenex and rubbed his eyes, as he requested. Again and again: he felt sure the corners needed to be cleaned. I rubbed until they were perfectly dry: no tears.

So it went: more rum and coke, more cowboys. I mentioned Cuba: rum and coke used to be called *Cuba libre* until Castro came, then it was called *Fidel Castro*. After he took over, the Cubans reverted to calling it *Cuba libre*.

Greg didn't seem interested. I talked about cowboy films, my favorites in childhood. We shared a few stars, but Greg was younger than I: he didn't really know Hopalong, Gene and Roy, not to mention Red Rider. My stock of ordinary-people conversation was quickly being exhausted. Tom returned with the airplane kit and set to work in the kitchen. A grown man making a model airplane.

Greg alerted me to the first voiding. I held the jug close, then when he was finished rushed to the bathroom to empty it. The urine got trapped in the frayed adhesive tape as I poured it out, the bathtub handle was a mystery — how do you turn on the water? But somehow I got water into the jug, after spraying myself, of course, and washed out the vessel. Returned to Greg, I put the jug up just in time.

Another Cuba libre, another cigarette. The nose itched, eyes needed wiping. He wanted me to check the pillows under his legs, something about his feet. To my growing amazement, he was acutely concerned about the placement of his body: he constantly required a general check. I had imagined that a person in his position would regard his body with revulsion, at least with discontent, and would attend to matters of the mind, the spirit. But, on the contrary, the attention to his body was excessive. And reasonably so, as I understood on reflection: without feeling, this body was a bomb, a possible plague that could move up to the mind undetected, and kill the person. Or was it that? In this excessive concern there seemed to be a touch of love.

The movie was over, I scanned the guide. Greg chose another: more cowboys, dust, ornery critters. He watched, didn't watch. Rum and coke. Nose. Corners of the eyes. Ordinary conversation. The jug. The bathroom, faulty handle. Pull the sheet down there, would you? Could you tuck this under my chin? Yeah, I think he's going to plug 'em this time.

Hell, I shouldn't expect to reform a man overnight. It's been only two years since his accident, and I'm a stranger. If I moved in, earned his trust... We could watch something else on occasion. I might read him a book after a while. He does some painting – those beastly little cards, so he has some spark. You can't blame him for drinking, smoking and watching this drek. He's a nice guy, after all.

"How do you like it?"

Tom displayed the model, painted black.

"Not bad."

"Pretty intricate work," I observed, trying to be positive. There's nothing wrong with making a model plane once in your life.

"I'll add it to my collection. I've got a..."

Greg seemed mildly interested as Tom recited the model numbers. They talked about motorcycles too. Perhaps they were old motorcycle buddies. At any rate, they spoke the same language.

"Say, Gary, would you mind – another rum and coke. A bit stronger this time."

"O.K."

Tom went into the small room to sleep. I went in first to remove my sleeping bag, chess set and books, and discovered his girlfriend, blanket pulled up over her bare chest. Oh, sorry. I got my things, Tom came in. Closed the door and went at it. Can you do that? Take care of a quadriplegic and still have sex with your girl at night? Maybe only if you like model airplanes.

Cal Worthington. So help me, if you can find a better car, get a better deal, I'll eat a bug, and that's a fact. Thundering hooves. Rum and coke. Maybe he's getting me to scratch his nose and wipe his eyes to make up for all the attention he's lost. This might be a luxury — his regular attendant has left him flat. Then again, she might have her reasons.

As I returned from the trip to the kitchen, I noticed a smell. No doubt about it: an accident. I informed Greg. Oh no, he said. Well, what should I do? I resolved on a business-like approach. He told me to clean as much as I could with the paper towels on the nightstand. I set to it — not really so different from changing diapers, after all. But the diaper itself was smeared and would have to be removed. I tugged, bundled it up, but coming around to the front learned that the jug had splashed out — he had urinated again. Now he had to be cleaned — he told me where to get the disinfectant. Only the sheet was wet — it would have to be changed. I rolled him around, followed instructions, threw soiled materials in the tub. Then new sheets, new diapers, pads, tugging from over the headboard, snapping spinal cords, pillows under the legs, correct position of the feet, the hands, itching nose. All was back in place again, the hooves clopped through the dust.

A third movie: the late, late one. Again Greg opted for the rawhide. C'mon, boys, we can head 'em off before they reach town! I sipped my own rum and coke, took a long drag on my weed. Greg was bleary, but not tired. He hardly slept, he told me. The sound of the jug — panic! Yes, the penis had come out. A mess. Another complete change. Meanwhile: Cal Worthington. I'll stand on my head, I'll eat a bug, and that's a fact.

Around 6 a.m. I decided to take a rest. Greg had worn me out. I had tried to stay the night with him, to show my good faith, to find something in common. The work was irritating, but not as bad as I feared. The poop — no big deal. The meticulous attention to position — disturbing somehow, but the least I could do. But the cowboy films, the model plane, the range of interests — this was impossible. Not the body, the mind.

I slept till 10. Tom was up, fixing eggs. No, I didn't want any breakfast. I'd better be getting home, my wife wants the car. The two, though polite, hardly spoke to me. As though I didn't belong. Perhaps they knew it was over. Others had tried out for the job.

I took my sleeping bag, chess set and books, stepped out into the sunshine. A woman was invigorating her body in the jacuzzi, a male member of the complex close by. I didn't look.

FIVE

I'VE GOT TO GET OUT

Jean was downcast. She'd already spent the money in her plans, thought of things for the girls. But she had to admit it: it was a bad scene. My grand scheme for reform, enlightenment – snuffed out in one night. He would have to come round by himself, develop interests by himself. I couldn't bring life to him. The cowboy shows might be a transition – or an endless stampede through the nights.

I pedalled back to University Village, Wolf at my side. Dustballs, wolfhair – it was home. A big breakfast, coffee. But I felt funny. Every movement I made was selfish. Reach for this glass, open the refrigerator, pour the orange juice – all for me. Crack the eggs – yes, I'll have some mushrooms, and some sausage – just for me. The coffee – extra strong today, I want it that way. Let's take it over here – I can walk. Sit down here – I can sit. Take a bite – I can do it myself. Every movement of my body – for me.

But Wolfgang. He got a good meal too. And a good slap on his strong shoulders. You'll stick by me, won't you, Wolf – you great big wonderful guy. I went to the bathroom – it felt funny. Is this thing supposed to be used for sex? I can't imagine. After last night, I don't think so. Brush my teeth – again for me. God, what if I had to ask someone else?

Slept all day. Evening already. I know what I have to do.

"Greg?"

"Yeah."

"How're you doing?"

"O.K."

"Greg, I don't think I'm going to be able to take the job. I didn't tell you at the time, but I've got a bad back. It really hurt to pull you up from the head of the bed. That's the worst position, you know. When my back goes out, I double up and can't straighten out for a long time, sometimes days or weeks. The last time took a few months. I'm afraid if I try to move you, I may have a spasm, and this would be dangerous to you. I really need the job, but..."

"That's too bad."

"Yeah, I'm really sorry. My wife would've taken the dog. But I really can't risk the back. I tell you what, though. I might be able to come out sometime. I could teach you chess, after all."

"I don't know. I don't think I'd be very good at it."

"It's an interesting game."

And so on. I begged out, hung up. But I had told the absolute truth. Jean herself said I might land in the hospital if I threw out my back. And after feeling guilty and scoffing at my plans, I looked at it this way. I paid for the gas to drive there twice, I spent a whole night with him free. It isn't a whole lot, but I helped him get through one night. That's more than a lot of other people have done. Maybe I could have been more patient, maybe I awakened and crushed hopes. But the problem was his mind, not his body. He would get up and dance before I ever changed him.

Sorry, Greg.

SIX

MEDITATION ON THE THEME, "IF I WERE A QUAD..."

If I were a quadriplegic, I would have to find a way out. I could dream, dictate, read and take an active part in life, but I could not accept myself as disembodied, or rather, stuck with a huge slug of a body, which I would have to ask others to wash, treat and put in perfect position. I could not accept myself as struck off from those who walk about the earth, condemned not only to be unlike them in mind, but also in body — a monster forever confined to the room, the bed. And to ask one of the walking to serve as my legs, one of the handling to serve as my hands, to suffer tubes and machines and straps without feeling them, to dash forward with quick thoughts while my body, heavy as a seal, lay unmoved. And to curse God every day for picking on me, to repudiate all arguments of special blessing and special mission: to see my condition as meaningless, unfair, a weighty lifelong punishment for a trifle of indiscretion. And to have no one to complain to, no one to make understand: to stifle my groans and choke up my rancor and accept other hands, other eyes, other lives.

First I would have to write about it: the promise that others would understand at a distance. I could endure a few months of another person's care for this purpose, since he would not be serving me so much as my literary project. Then I could get my other works in order, things I had written before the accident: tidy up my posterity. But once the long haul began — nothing ahead but months of struggling with the new life, like a soldier trapped in a broken tank, I would have to find a way out. Help would have to come from outside.

The easiest thing would be to hire a new attendant and tell him to give me an overdose of pills. But this would leave him holding the bag: his word and my corpse. No, I would have to exonerate him. The thing to do is ask for writing materials, and say that I'm writing a confidential letter to my mother, or somebody. Pencil in teeth, paper on writing board, I would state what I plan to do, clear the unsuspecting accomplice. Request a cremation, obliterate the accursed body. Maybe release the eyes to the hospital, if they didn't itch overmuch and would stay sufficiently fresh. Then have the attendant fold up the missive, place it in an envelope and tuck the envelope under my pillow. Later I would ask for the pills, insisting that the huge dosage was normal. The kid would be scared when he found me, but would be relieved of his daily burden. Maybe I should have him put the note in my pajama pocket, in case it should be over-looked otherwise.

Of course, this is just dreaming. If my spine really were broken, my mind would think accordingly. Perhaps still seeing my body, even if the nerves were severed, I would consider myself whole, and try to get on as best I could. A day at a time, if not a step. A new life, new challenges, proof of unlimited courage. God, can the will to live be so strong, so blind? No, the ancients were right — I'm mangled, help me, run me through with the sword!

SEVEN

LITTLE TRAGEDIES

The feeling of guilt would not go away. Nor the rent. Notice in the university newspaper: Aides needed. I dropped by the Special Services Office, filled out the form. Education: highest number. Last job: prof. Willing to do housework, shopping, cooking? Yeah, sure. Bowel care? Well, what the hell? If I say no, why complete the form? Prefer male or female? Prefer? I don't prefer either, but the thought of a crippled female is too horrible. Experience: limited. Salary: open. Remarks: bad back. There, I've paid off my debt to my conscience. It's down on paper that I'm ready and willing. Now I hope no one calls.

For my phone number I listed the radio station. I do an occasional program of classical music there — or used to, until I got fed up with the mumbling phoners asking for rock or disco. Now I do readings on tape: Russian stories, Schopenhauer. That way I can hear a good program at home and shun the public. I told the station manager about my use of the number, and also about my night with Greg. He took his usual sardonic tone.

"You're crazy, Kern. Why did you even apply?"

I gave my reasons.

He laughed and shook his head. It would be better to commit suicide, he said. I asked how he would do it, smirked as he tried to figure it out. When I mentioned Greg's hesitance to hire an old woman, he curled up his lip and shook his head knowingly.

"Quads can have sex, you know."

"C'mon, Clark, they have no feeling."

"But they can get hard, you saw yourself."

"So you think?"

"I know. One of those old mamas would hop right on, swivel herself around, there's a technique to it."

And with the grin of an evil genius expelled from another planet, he told me about a film he had once seen. It was restricted to medical personnel, but he had used a press pass. It seems that... and he told me something so grotesque that I was sure he had made it up. Still, it wasn't anything that the non-handicapped didn't do. Regular people, that is. We spent some time making jokes about quads, trying to gross each other out. I didn't feel ashamed: the reality is such that jokes don't even touch it.

After this, the disaster occurred. A disaster all the more crushing for being trivial, unworthy of complaint. I believe that such disasters happen to people and utterly ruin them, because they despair of ever explaining them to another. These are the disasters that drive men mad, make them leap from windows, because the big disasters come with an aura of self-importance — a big significant weight falls on you, and you labor under the burden heroically. But the little tragedy — it's petty even to mention it. And yet the chipped tooth endangers the root, the strained eye bores into the brain, the ill-considered little word sounds in the ear to the end of your life. The disaster that befell me started with a little screw.

Prehistory. I had called Priscilla (collect), a friend from Princeton days, now the head of the Russian department at her university. She heard my moans and groans about poverty, advised me to ask Carl for work. (Later she sent $100.) Carl, also a friend from graduate-school days, now the founder of a small publishing house specializing in Russian materials, did have something for me: an English-Russian *Lolita* dictionary. (Nabokov wrote *Lolita* first in English, then translated the novel into Russian. A couple of Nabokov freaks in Leningrad compiled a dictionary of his usage, but ineptly, as I later discovered, due to their uncertain English. All of this is germane to the story of the screw, which I am smuggling into my account of quads, because I can't stand it that I should have suffered such an infuriating misfortune for nothing.) Carl wanted me to do a print-ready copy: four columns (English-Russian, English-Russian) of such and such spacing, 57 lines, courier print. Payment: 3 bucks a page.

The event. While typing on my IBM Selectric (purchased in richer days), I noticed the print was smudged. I tried all the knobs and levers — no go. Since I can't afford repairs, I do repairs myself — such as on my TV, which now receives only

UHF. I decided to tighten a few screws. To my delight, the screw behind the element (*i.e.*, the ball) was loose. I tightened it. Wonderful. Just imagine: it was actually loose. To enjoy my victory, I loosened it back to where it had been, then turned it forward again. It snapped, went round and round, didn't hold. The ball hit wrong letters, smudged even worse. I couldn't do Nabokov.

Consequences. IBM charges $47/hr. labor. Rent is $242/mo. I owe a $50 dog fee, hide from the landlord. So the solution: get the stub of the screw out, buy another screw and put it in myself. For a week I tried to remove the stuck stub. I spent two full days grinding a ridge into it with a razor blade. When the ridge was deep enough, I inserted the screw driver and turned with all my might until the metal revolved 360 degrees. But the base of the stub stayed put. Finally an acquaintance who dropped by during my fulminations offered to take the typewriter to a metallist shop: they could drill the stub, insert a plug and unscrew the bugger. The next day he returned with my broken typewriter: the stub wouldn't budge, but the steel foundation underneath (*i.e.*, the carrier) cracked in two. That means nothing in the world, no matter how large, how powerful, could have unscrewed my little screw.

IBM men all wear crisp white shirts, flowery ties and blank expressions. The centers of their eyes are spiral, and their twenty-gallon stomachs hang out over their belts. Their hands are never dirty. I had occasion to view them on repeated visits to the corporation, carrying my machine on my hip and riding the bus, or begging a ride off Clark. The white shirts per-formed swiftly for big business, bogged down on my small account. I heard every excuse in the book: big backlog, repairman out sick, parts out of stock, trouble with the main office. Meanwhile the Nabokov ms. arrived, with an advance from Ardis. I paid the rent, phoned IBM from the station. Excuses, promises. The third week passed. At length, toward the end of February, the machine was ready. The shirts were still crisp, the hands without dirt. The bill: four hours, forty-two minutes, plus parts, $242. Another month's rent. Rice every night.

But now, at long last, to work. I start the Lolita business. First page: 7 hours. Well, wait till I get the hang of it. Second page: 3¼ hours. Still not too good. Next day, fresh start. Third page: less than 3 hours, but by the time I get a drink of orange juice, check everything and start page four — 3 hours. That's it: $1/hr. is the best I can hope for. A forty-seventh of an IBM man. I look ahead through the ms.: scratchy, half-handwritten, half-typed in blotchy ink, but worst of all — without method. A chaos of words without rhyme or reason — even the alphabetical order is flawed. I can't type this without editing, and I can't afford the time. If I complain to Carl, he'll think me an ingrate: he sent me the work as a favor. If I borrow money somewhere for rent and continue typing, I will subsidize the idiot child of two crackpots from Leningrad, who have since come to the USA and found jobs. And so the little tragedy snapped me: I was baffled, distracted, my head was hot, my eyes throbbing, I tossed tears from my cheeks and raised bootless cries to the picture of Pushkin. Wolf hid in the bedless bedroom.

Then Clark left a note on my door. Message at the station. Someone wants me to call.

*****

A sad note to this chapter: Carl Proffer, who made Ardis into the largest publisher of Russian literature in the USA, died prematurely of cancer in 1984. He was a brilliant Slavist, an unassuming overachiever and a good friend, who readily accepted many of my things and tirelessly wrote recommendations for me during my years out of the profession. Among the materials he left behind was a manuscript for a book, The Widows of Russia, *based on conversations with Nadezhda Mandelstam, Elena Bulgakova and other long-suffering wives of persecuted artists. His wife Ellendea published the book and carries on the mission of Ardis. As for the Lolita dictionary, they found someone else to do it.*

EIGHT

QUAD TWO

He was sitting in a wheelchair in front of his bed, completely dressed, with pants, shoes. Heavier than Greg, older. Grey hair, glasses – a rather owlish expression. I noticed he was able to move his forearms irregularly; Greg could move only a finger or two. He spoke decisively, appeared able to stand and walk about: he just happened to be sitting in a chair. His room was larger than that of most students. I saw a TV, a mirror, upper shelves of books, a Dallas Cheerleaders calendar, a big hospital bed and a desk with an IBM typewriter.

We agreed that I should try to lift him. His attendant for the day, a burly fellow with a frontal ridge, bent down and lifted the shoes out from the straps, then reached up under the shirt and undid the velcro chest strap. He stepped back, and I stepped forward, knelt down. The handicapped man put his right arm across my neck. Attempting to keep my back straight, I slipped my left hand behind his back, my right under his knees. I tried then to stand up and felt a weight as solid as a marble block. There was no chance: I couldn't budge him.

While the attendant refastened the straps, we expressed our regrets. He was too heavy, I was too light, and that was that. His regular attendant wanted a break: his grades were low and he needed more time to study. But, well, too bad – we did our best. Unless we could use a lift. What about that? Fine with me. He'd check. Phone in a day or two.

This was a different kettle of fish. The man was not downcast, quite the contrary – upbeat. Working for his Master's, he only needed someone to help him through finals. Then he expected to get a job and move away. Of course, I could hear that thin note of need in his voice, but he disguised it as well as any man. He had his studies, his schedule: no need to educate him, teach him chess. And no need to think of inventions: he was up and about – a motorized wheelchair, a typing splint. I was not called upon to transform his life, only to do little tasks. He could take care of himself.

Back in my apartment. The hot tub. Papers all over the floor. The death mask of Rosenzweig: I hadn't yet finished the book. Things were getting bad. I'd gone in the hole this month, Lolita was left on the desk. But now I could work a couple of months, pay off debts. Then be free. And this time: gather material for writing, don't be ashamed of it. If I try to go no-book, I won't be able to stomach it. But if I take a literary approach, I might. This will help him as well. After all, I can't play doctor.

This decided, I tried desperately to find a way out. I answered the want ads, made appointments. To hell with my back: I applied for a job at the university carrying cans of sludge to the laboratory. The card was returned: they hired someone better qualified. I tried to be a desk clerk at the Mission Inn: they found someone with a hotel-school diploma. Typist for a solar-energy concern? Nope, they never answered. O.K., my last seven bucks to a come-on: address envelopes in your own home. The rates were better than Lolita's. The reply came back: yes, you can address envelopes in your own home. All you have to do is contact businesses and advertise their products and send in their orders. Here's seven dollars worth of suggestions on how to get started.

Now flat broke, I receive thick pamphlets of instructions from the IRS. The government wants me to pay taxes, to contribute to the nuclear bombers from March AFB I see circling the mountains every day discharging funnel clouds of black smoke. I should pay for a puff. And here's a joke: it charges interest for late payment, but inflates money the year round. No, I won't be conned. I ask for an extension, and where it says amount owed — put in a neat zero. No interest, nothing.

An old woman who lived nearby asked me to type some things for her: she gave me some soup. The rent, implacable as the moon, was rolling around again. I phoned Carl long distance from an unattended business phone. He couldn't pay more. My only prospective employer went ahead and rented a pump-lift. No way out.

Hot bath, newspapers. Rosenzweig: still paralyzed, still dead. But just think of this guy's problems. It's not enough that he has lost the use of his limbs, can't do the things that everyone else takes for granted. Not enough that he must accept this, reorganize his life and decide every day to live. He must also learn how to attract an aide. That is, not plead. Put it forward as a regular job. Such and such work, such and such pay. But the work is not such and such: it's horrible. And the pay is not such and such: it's lousy. Not that it's his fault: the money comes from state funds. But he can't bandy excuses: here's the job, take it or leave it. And if you leave it, he can't move. In our phone conversations, Darwin remained positive. He needed someone, I needed rent. "Perhaps it will work out to our mutual benefit," he said more than once.

O.K., let's try the lift. A small shiny metal gallows with a piece like a solid clotheshanger at the tip of the neck. You slide one silken strap under the knees and attach the ring of each end to the hanger; the same with a second strap around the back and under the arms. Turn a little catch and pump with the lever on the back of the lift: the neck rises. At one point the body separates from the chair and rocks out toward the lift; then, as you pump, it is airborne, the back and rump drooping down. The whole lift then rolls away from the chair, and the horizontal legs slip under the bed. Turn the catch the other way: the body descends to the mattress. The trial was a success. Quite easy, slightly scary.

Rutger walked me out to my bike. He wanted out, because his grandmother had had a heart attack, but he couldn't leave because of Darwin. Generally speaking, he was tired, wanted to pull up his grades. I suspected bad feeling, but he assured me that Darwin was a great guy. "He'll bend over backwards to help you," he said with limpid eyes, not noticing the awkward expression. Something about his face, his big-boned hands, bothered me. Only a month later did I realize in a flash: he had yellow hair, blue eyes, a big straight nose and a trim yellow moustache, but his face was the spitting image of Hitler. A blond Hitler. I never mentioned it to him for fear of spoiling his life.

Decision time. I offered to work during the day, if Rutger would stay on at night. That way I could keep my apartment, my Wolf and part of my sleep. Rutger would have every day off. He'd get 100 bucks a month, I'd get 500. On Wednesday he'd show me the bowel care, then I'd be on my own.

Darwin, it seems, had things under control: bowel care on Wednesdays and Sundays, shower the same nights; laundry on the weekends. Meals were simple: carry his tray through the line. The cafeteria in the dorms provides the grub. I could bicycle over in the morning, get him up. Bicycle home and have breakfast. Bicycle back and take him to lunch. Bicycle home or wherever. Bicycle back for the 3 o'clock meeting — to empty the leg bag. Bicycle home or wherever. Bicycle back at 6 for supper. Bicycle home for the news. (My daughter Lara on a weekend visit had discovered a smashed TV in the dumpster; I fooled with it during the week and produced a green Cronkite.) Bicycle back at 11 or so for night duties and bed. Bicycle home (for green Carson or red Snyder). Then Rutger would turn him at 3 a.m. and answer any emergency calls: a cord led from the buzzer at Darwin's chin to the buzzer at Rutger's pillow. It ran out the door, up the wall and over the hall ceiling. People walked by and never noticed.

Hot water, my body half-floating. Enjoy it, Kern. Soon you'll be working, you'll be lucky to grab a fast shower. Jean'll be surprised. She keeps saying I can't get a job because I don't try. "You think you're better than we are," she insists. I don't know why she includes herself among the *we* who are somehow distinct from me, it seems to me a choice. Anyway, this will show her. I did get a job. Not that I'll be able to pay child support, but I will have to clean up shit. That should prove something. Actually, come to think of it, she's right: I am better than they are. Because we both can clean up shit, but I can write about it, and they can't. So why don't they just clean, and I'll do the writing? No, they won't see it that way. They'll let me do both: the cleaning and the writing. And maybe the reading as well. Water's cold, need more hot.

The next morning the blond Hitler showed me the routine. Taking down the sheet, unstrapping the legs, removing the styrofoam boots. Putting away the boots, the pillows, the buzzer. Putting on the leg bag, the pants, the socks and shoes. Unplugging the charger, rolling out the wheelchair, lifting Darwin to the chair — Rutger used the new apparatus, since his back had begun to hurt. Then spraying the deodorant, putting on the shirt, running the velcro straps through the slits under the arms of the shirt and securing the chest. Cleaning the glasses, putting them on, combing the hair. Fixing the electric toothbrush in his hand, catching the spit in a little tray; same with rinse and mouth wash. Getting out the electric razor, cleaning it after use, putting it away. Dumping the tray and night bucket in the toilet next door. Everything like clockwork, no pathos. No big deal.

However, a little deal. Before putting on the pants, Rutger had to treat the bed sore: a greyish, yellow pencil hole in the flesh of the left rump. It had once penetrated to the bone, they told me, but now was healing, filling in rapidly. It had to be swabbed with a saline solution and bandaged before Darwin could sit down. And then the toes: they crinkled, and dry skin formed on the ridge of the joints. The second toe of each foot had to be covered with a special little sock before Darwin could wear socks and shoes. And also the face, the scalp: psoriasis, a condition that can be treated, never cured. Some lotion had to be rubbed into the eyebrows, the hairline, behind the ears. Still, with all this, Darwin did get a break: his nose didn't itch all the time.

I forgot the pills. Four times a day: vitamin C, urocholine, mandelamine, lioresal (replaced by septra at night). For bladder control, other things.

I took over the job at lunchtime. It was a breeze. I even discovered a big salad bar in the center of the dining area, beyond the cashier and the cafeteria line, where I could load up on free food. Emptying the leg bag at 3 o'clock, handing out the medicine and even the bedtime routine posed no problems. No booze, no thundering hooves. My apprehension had been misplaced.

One last detail. Rutger showed me the next night. Darwin was put on his right side on the bed, his knees folded up to his stomach. Rutger, speaking somewhat medically and with forced nonchalance, placed some large cotton pads at the fold of the legs and put on disposable cellophane gloves. Applying a lubricant to the fingers of his right hand, he reported that Darwin had not been doing well of late, but recently had been eating crunchy cereal, so that tonight, "We expect good results."

He inserted his first two fingers, maybe his thumb.

"It's usually right here," he stated.

And, sure enough, he flipped a big brown clump onto the pad. I looked on with an impassive face. Darwin seemed to stare straight ahead. The clumps piled up on the pad.

"Good results," Rutger repeated with enthusiasm.

I nodded in approval and thought: this isn't good material for literature — it's just...

After some time, Rutger determined that everything was finished, wiped the behind with the edge of a pad, threw the whole mess with his gloves into a Hefty white petroleum bag and tied the neck in a knot. Then he gave the room a few shots from an aerosol can kept nearby and carried the bag into the hall, where it was dropped down the chute, another mystery story for the trash man.

Next time, my turn.

NINE

REALITY

Mahler is playing: the last movement of the Third Symphony. I usually save Mahler for a special occasion, but this time let it play. Otherwise I'd have to turn the radio back to Darwin's station — mindless mood music, or off. Better let him hear something good while I dress him.

I put on the toe covers, the socks, ask what color pants he wants. The violins play on, and I can feel the sorrow and love of all my life rising in my throat, my eyes. My movements are already automatic, unwilling. I pull the pants up both legs, turn Darwin on his side and slide the pants over his rump, then let him fall back and straighten them in front. The theme is repeated, quietly now, holding off the mighty conclusion. I am fairly choking, but in a controlled voice I tell Darwin about Mahler, try to interest him in each new invention. He nods his head, but really can't muster any enthusiasm. "Is that sock on straight?" he asks. I check the sock while the most glorious sound in the world fills my heart. I have to admit it: I care more for this music, and all that it means to me, than this crippled man flat on his back, dependent on my care. But the Mahler symphony, I thought, was about love — so how can this be? I put the straps around Darwin's back and knees, pump. His body lifts ponderously, like a sack of potatoes hoisted to a ship. I look at his face: it bears a distant, set expression. He's waiting for the next step, nothing more. There's a sadness here, but only if you think about it. In life, it's simply minute by minute. Specific suffering is boring, general sorrow is soul-stirring. I step back and turn down the radio: the monumental coda recedes into background music. This morning I can't afford ecstacy.

It's Sunday, when the cafeteria serves a late breakfast and no lunch. Darwin orders an omelette, polishes off waffles and ham while he waits. I cut his food, put the fork in his velcro hand band. Swipe some granola for myself at the end of the line, eat along with him. It's a nice arrangement: I help him out, get a free meal — a fringe benefit to compensate for low pay. Still, his hearty appetite bothers me: I know where the grub will end up. Maybe sewer men feel the same way when they drive past a supermarket.

After breakfast, the subject of Darwin's accident comes up. He was a boy, 15 years old, out swimming with two friends. They swam across a small, man-made lake, crawled out on shore and rested. Then they walked over a little ridge and dove back in. The first boy dove out far — he was not hurt. Darwin dove close in — hit bottom. The third boy saw Darwin's knees buckle, jumped in and saved his life. A vertebra in Darwin's neck had popped: he would never walk again. Later his parents tried to sue the owner of the lake, who charged admission, for not posting a warning about the concrete bottom at that spot. But he went b-k. Bankrupt. No compensation. This happened in Oklahoma, twenty-five years ago.

I was reminded of my accident at age 12. A bunch of us boys from the orphanage, crossing the street, suddenly started racing to the other side. I was ahead, then woke up on the ground with my head in my sister's lap. While the girls screamed at us from behind, we had all run into the grey chain cordoning off the monument grounds. I was hit above the eye, could have broken my neck; another broke his nose, another hurt his arm. It was all a matter of height, angle of inclination. I was no more observant than Darwin. Nor were the other boys.

I told him about it; he wasn't surprised. "There are all sorts of ways you can break your neck," he said and recounted other instances.

I told him about Greg; he commiserated. "It's tough in the beginning. You have to go step by step. He hasn't gone through the period of adjustment yet."

It occurred to me, in view of Greg's other troubles, that aides perhaps go through a period of adjustment as well. They must learn to accept reality, discount miraculous ideas.

Tonight I face reality. Put the trash can behind the folded legs, white petroleum bag in the can, open at the mouth. Pads on the bed, box of disposable gloves. TV left on, we can use the distraction. I sit down on the edge of the bed, place my left hand on his left hip. Now, here goes: insert the lubricated fingers. Fortunately, he feels nothing, which makes it easier

for me: less personal. There's results right there, as Rutger
would say. I scoop it out and throw it in the can: no clumps on
the bed for me. Again, another throw. Now I must dig deeper.
I push, but my fingers won't go that way — there's some sort of
tissue, sinews or something. The rectum doesn't go straight in,
it turns up and runs parallel to the spine. I can push only two
fingers up there. I can feel lumps of shit, but how can I grab
them without my thumb? I must try to hook into them, or
press the two fingers like scissors. Thus handicapped, I push
and curl and pull. The lumps begin to move. I scoop them out,
more come down. The rectum is stimulated: a slow bowel
movement is taking place. The lumps are hard, compacted
from many days: not too disgusting. But now I feel something
higher up, just at the tips of my fingers. I push, strain: it's
difficult.

Suddenly I know that I'm frowning. I look up and see
Darwin's face in the mirror straight ahead of him. He can see
me, I think. I look back, go on with my work. Now the stuff is
beginning to move, but this is softer, fresher. I try to help it
along with my two stretching fingers. It's messy, won't come
off the glove when I throw it in the can. I have to throw away
the glove, put on another. Again, the same thing. But now it
begins to move, and the soft excrement comes out by itself. I
catch it gladly, grateful that I won't have to scrape it out. After
two long columns, I figure it's over, clean up, dump.

Coming back to the room, I noticed the smell. Reached for
the air freshener: my forefinger wouldn't move. A muscular
cramp. So I had to do it with my relaxed thumb.

Now for the shower. I get the roller chair from the handicapped shower room. It has a toilet seat and a sponge cushion
with a big hole cut in it. Darwin is hoisted up nude and let
down in the chair. Then we put a robe on him backwards and
stack up the materials in his lap: towel, washcloth, special
shampoo for psoriasis, disposable catheter, liquid adhesive,
adhesive tape, scissors. I roll him to the shower room. Students
pass by in the hall, say hello. They walk. In the shower room
all the stuff is put on a shelf, and I spray him with a shower-
head attached to a coil. Of course, I have to take off my shoes
and roll up my pants, so as not to get too wet. But it's easy,
enjoyable. He can feel the warm water on his head, his neck
and right shoulder. I can soap him all over with the washcloth,
rinse him down. The hole in the seat provides for the nether

parts. We talk, take our time — as if we were taking a shower together.

After the drying, I must put on the catheter. This means painting the penis around the base with the white adhesive, running a strip of expandable foam — sticky on both sides — around the base, then unfolding the rubber over the penis and over the sticky strip, finally securing the outer rim of the rubber with a strip of adhesive tape. The aim is to make an airtight lock at the base, a threefold seal — paste, sticky strip, adhesive tape. This night Darwin did not urinate during the process, but if he should it must be begun again from the beginning. Should the catheter leak for any reason, it must be changed.

Back in the room, I blow-dry Darwin's hair, put him to bed and attach the open end of the rubber to a tube leading down to the night jug. The tube must be curled twice in a special way before being dropped from the bed. Darwin is put in his usual position: right side, knees bent toward stomach, feet strapped in styrofoam boots, bedsore swabbed, pillow placed between knees, pillow placed on top of left leg, bed strap pulled over top pillow and tied down, head pillow put under crown, left arm folded over stomach, right hand pushed up to chin, sheet pulled up over left shoulder, buzzer pinned to sheet. The wheelchair is rolled under the desk, the charger plugged into the wall and set. The leg bag that has been soaking is rinsed out and hung up to dry; the leg bag that was used is rinsed out and put to soak in the urine-cleaning solution. Darwin then drinks two glasses of water. I snap off the TV with the remote-control gun. We say goodnight. Lights out. Door closed. Bicycle home.

Reality.

TEN

UTOPIA

wish I could write: "And thus passed 8 weeks…" I know
the weeks will pass, and I will be able to look back on
them as a separate chunk, but right now each day must be
worked through, even if each is to be the same. The routine is
now well established: I may not be the most skilled aide in the
world, but I've already mastered the tasks and lost interest.
They've become something like my own semi-conscious activi-
ties of dressing, combing, brushing, except that some of these
things I don't do for myself.

And some things are painful, more painful with each day.
The bicycle ride, for example. I thought in the beginning that
the half-mile ride five times there and five times back each day
would provide good exercise, particularly since there is a double
hill in the middle; but as my sleep has been reduced and my
supper restricted to salads, the bicycling simply drains me. As
I push down with each foot, struggling to keep the bike upright
toward the top of each hill, I feel the wind pushing against me,
as if to say: "You measly little bastard, I'm going to make you
appreciate this: you must push, push, push." Attaining the
summit of the hill, when control and alertness must be at their
peak, since Wolf running beside me on his leash is likely to
lunge, the bicycle may topple or encounter someone coming
over the summit from the other side, and my depleted strength
must portion itself out for the acceleration downhill, — at
precisely this moment, more than once, sometimes two or three
times a day, an insect flies right up my nose, or in my eye, or
down my throat. There's a natural explanation: the insects are
swarming in the field above, at the top of the hill, and I
intersect them as I come up and shoot past. But again, I suspect
a personal affront. It goes without saying that the wind
reverses direction on the way back. I am the only cyclist in the

world who must pump downhill against the wind, pump uphill against the wind; turn around, and do the same.

Eight weeks to go: my hands are callused from gripping the grips, my fingertips split from chemicals and lotions, my fingernails ragged and torn from wool pants. Little dinky complaints, petty even to mention. Whom can I tell? To whom can I go? To no one: take it as literary material. But in literature you can write: "Thus passed 8 weeks."

On the other hand, some things are harder to describe than to do. The procedures of dressing, grooming. There's little point in detailing them, except as an exercise: how to convey actions by words, without gesticulation. Describe walking up a spiral staircase, knotting a tie, unbuttoning a shirt. Or, better still, the insertion of soft contact lenses.

Darwin's prescription was filled after I began work. The Sears optometrist, a waxen little man with fluffed hair, sun-tanned face, capped teeth, sports suit with flared bottoms and beautiful gold-rimmed glasses, who smelled pretty and chewed Dentine gum, showed me how to do it. You squeeze a few drops of cleaner fluid from a small vial in your left palm and drop the pliable little lens in the puddle; with the forefinger of your right hand you swish the lens around, turn it over and swish again until the fluid is almost dry. Then you hold the edge of the lens between your left forefinger and thumb while you squirt both sides with a rinse from a larger vial. When the drops have fallen on the rug, you place the center of the lens, with the rim curved inward, not outward, on the tip of your right finger, where it will adhere. Drawing back the wearer's upper eyelid with your left forefinger and his lower eyelid with your left thumb, you request that he look upward and then point the lens straight in his iris. Ideally, it will stick to the eye and leave your fingertip; the person closes his eye and you press and tap the upper lid to force out air bubbles and liquid. The lens adjusts itself over the iris, and the wearer can see. In less than ideal circumstances, which is to say, very often, the lens does not stick to the eye, or does not release its suction from the fingertip, so that it puckers and gets caught by the closing lids. In such a case, it must be rinsed again — as many times as you fail.

At the end of the day, each lens must be removed. You simply put the tips of your thumb and forefinger on it and lift it off the eye; it almost always comes off. You then wash it in your palm and rinse it, and place it in a little plastic contraption consisting of a round chamber with a mound in the center; the lens is put on the mound and held down by a swivel clamp; the chamber is filled with rinse and closed by a screw lid. Adjacent to this chamber is another, upside down, of exactly the same construction; the two are deposited in an indentation within a plastic box. The box is plugged in, its lid clicked shut, its button pressed, and the lenses are boiled, so they will be sterile in the morning. On the weekend, to counteract these chemicals, the lenses are soaked in capsules of water with an evil-smelling dissolvable pill; then washed, rinsed and put back in the eyes.

It is easier to do these tasks than to describe them — that is, describe them every time. But it is much easier to write this one description than to fiddle every day with those slippery slimy goddamned little slivers. Why in the hell couldn't he stick to his glasses? (He said the glasses slipped and chafed because his nose was irregular.) Each lens, by the way, was different: one for far-sightedness, the other for near-sightedness. If I accidentally switched them he saw things in reverse.

When I had become proficient in the handling of soft contact lenses, I found it easier to put them in Darwin's eyes while he lay on his back. (Rutger turns him at night from side to back.) In fact, I tried to do as many tasks as possible before hoisting him to the chair: lenses, pills, psoriasis lotion, bedsore treatment, toe covers, socks, pants, belt and shoes, fingernails and toenails if necessary. But there was one major problem remaining: the catheter.

The tube to the night jug is best left attached through all of these tasks, especially since the lifting of Darwin's legs to treat the bedsore presses on the bladder, as does the rolling around to pull up the pants. However, when he is hoisted up in the lift, it is awkward to keep the tube dangling through the fly of his pants to the jug and simultaneously roll the lift to the wheelchair; there is a good chance of the tube getting pinched. On the other hand, if the tube is disconnected and the catheter attached to the leg bag, the tube to the leg bag will be in upright position as Darwin swings over to the chair. In either case, the bladder is pressed by the folded legs and may release urine; should it do so before Darwin is seated and adjusted, the catheter will leak. Then he must be returned to bed, the catheter changed and the dressing repeated. If it leaks again, repeat again. We never really solved this problem: we would try one way, then the other. The best thing was to get to the chair as quickly as possible and get the catheter in order. Yet haste made waste.

Once Darwin was let down in the chair, he had to be pulled to the back. I would grab his pants by the belt and yank him back until his rear was flat against the back of the chair. Even so, he would unfailingly say: "Give it another try, Gary." This, just to make sure. Then the pants legs would have to be straightened – not an easy task while someone is sitting in them. My hangnails made it even more unpleasant, and again Darwin would say: "Give it another tug there, would you, Gary?" Always in a polite voice, never in a tone of discomfort or concern. Under such circumstances, it is impossible to object. So every morning I give the extra yank, the extra tug, if it makes him feel better. I lift his scrotum and double-check the catheter before zipping the fly.

After the shirt is put on and the straps fastened through the special slits under the arms, Darwin is pretty much in business. All that is needed is for me to release the break, and then he switches on the motor and does a little dance with his chair, steering it by means of an upright plastic prong beside the arm. I always suspected a certain glee at this moment, though Darwin would keep a serious mien, circling in a confined space as if to test the machine. After this, the combing, shaving and toothbrushing completed the morning chores. But, of course, there would usually be some little matter, and I noticed how sensitive I had become to detect it. I would reach out to turn down Darwin's collar before he would ask, clean the tidbit from his eyelash just as he opened his mouth. In a sense, I became a nervous system for him, responding to stimuli he could feel (about his head), but also to stimuli he could not feel (below his shoulders). On occasion Darwin would tell me he felt uneasy – an anticipation of sickness or fever; I would then search his body for the trouble spot – a wrinkle in his pants, a bulge of sock at his heal, anything that would make a sensate body uncomfortable.

Throughout such procedures, Darwin would endure quietly or give pointers in an encouraging voice, never with a sense of urgency. As if both he and I were meeting a problem, never as if he were causing it. When his legs would spring up from the bed and nearly strike me in the jaw, we would both laugh, and he'd say: "Whoa, there, come on, legs!" Or when his right foot would start shaking and jump out of its shoe, he'd say: "Where are you going, calm down there, now." As though the parts of his body were mischievous children, always up to pranks, and needed but a chiding, not a whipping. But there were also times when he seemed to forget, seemed to let his mind go somewhere else, while I attended to him: it was clear he had been waited on for years. When a serious problem did arise, one requiring urgent attention, his manner was still unrushed: don't panic, take the necessary steps. Everything will be all right.

As a rule, once personal matters were taken care of, Darwin would set to work. I would get out the books he needed and set them beside the typewriter. Then I would strap a splint onto the bottom edge of his right hand; it had a metal prong topped with an eraser, and with this he could poke out the letters, one by one. When he had nothing to type, I might attach the transparent plastic shield over the arms of his chair, so that he would be sitting at his own study desk. A vinyl mat (for sticking) and books would be laid out on top. Darwin had a great many papers to write for his courses in environmental control: demographics, statistics, economics. (I always wondered if his boyhood accident had determined the choice of his major, but never made bold to ask.) I would turn the radio station from the KPFK commentaries or classical music to his preferred soft music, put out a glass of fresh water with a straw and leave. Maybe a cup of crunchy cereal or trail mix too. Darwin could put in the typewriter paper by himself, adjust the volume on the radio. When I came back, there would often be papers and things on the floor, which he had dropped, and the trash can might have been knocked over by the chair, but otherwise things were in order. He studied for hours on end.

In the cafeteria, I at first noticed only the crowd of students, but once settled at the table with Darwin and able to observe at leisure, I was struck by the small number of white Americans. Riverside is rather far south, and its inhabitants are possibly a subspecies of the human race, but still it is nominally a part of the United States, and one would expect the university to reflect that allegiance. Yet here I saw a whole table — I mean a long dining-hall table — full of Japanese, another with Arabs or Iranians, and smaller tables with various Latins, assorted non-Japanese Orientals and a few Indians. American blacks were conspicuous, since they wore shirts with incomprehensible signs and messages, and periodically stood bolt upright at their table and bellowed in unison some sort of fraternity chant. (Some would dress in white and stand at attention through the hallways of the dormitory. They looked militant, but never effected a coup, so far as I know.) African blacks were more discreet, hence more discrete. The whites were dispersed throughout, perhaps were in the majority, yet seemed but a bland background. I made mention of this to Darwin, and he told me a little story.

A friend of his was filling out an application. Under the category of race he found Negro, American Indian, Chinese, Filipino, and so on, but not Caucasian. He asked the person in charge, who after some reflection advised him to check off Other. *Sic transit...*

There was another category, mostly white, yet indiscriminate as to race: handicapped. With good reason: UCR is ideally equipped to provide for the disabled. Every curb is sloped to accommodate wheelchairs (a bonus for the bicyclist); every building has a ramp, electric doors and an elevator; special bathrooms are found everywhere. There are reserved parking spots, special medical facilities, van service, wheelchair repair shop. My friend Edgar, a Harvard Ph.D. who can't get a teaching job, joked with me that the only way to save this university was to sweep out the mindless students and the dead-wood faculty, and make it a national school for the handicapped. Now, as I looked about me, this did not seem a remote possibility.

There sits a tiny girl, somehow deformed, with blond hair and bug eyes, propped up like a doll in her chair. There, near the aisle, sits a man, apparently unimpaired, dressed nattily in a suit, with a neat brown moustache and a studious expression, yet in a wheelchair with a transparent desk; he wears a hand splint and smokes constantly. There, just behind him, sits a handsome young man, robust in appearance, with silken black hair and blue eyes; his arms are as limp as rubber hoses. I suspect he had a football accident. And there, another, a black-haired Latin girl with a sweet face, a ready smile; her legs and spine are twisted. And there, the young man leaning back in his chair full of levers and cushions, as though it were a posh motorcycle; he can move only his chin. I hear the familiar whir of a motor; the studious man rolls past our table.

"Hi, Darwin."

"Hi, Tim, how are things going?"

"O.K."

Beside each invalid sits an attendant: the two can be considered a pair. Always together, like Siamese twins: the one needing attention, the other attending. Consequently, the first is outstanding, the second — near-invisible. You can see a person in a wheelchair a dozen times before you will notice the quiet shadow beside him, behind him. At the table the attendant could be anyone, while the invalid can be only one. But if you look closely, you will see the same person carrying the food, cutting it, spooning it up. In almost every case this person is calm, reserved, of the same sex. He or she does not talk much with the other students, does not talk much with the other invalids. He or she is simply there, feeling. The nervous system of the dominant twin. There is cause here for celebration: one fortunate person helping another less fortunate, and when combined — many people helping others. But also cause for dark reflection: healthy bodies subordinate to ruined ones.

One pair departs from the rule. The girl is bent slightly sideways and speaks with difficulty, slurring her words; yet she is remarkably vivacious, and this vivacity lights up her features, which are not in themselves very striking, with remarkable beauty. There is some sort of charm around her, some exceptional something, that draws your eyes to her and fills them with wonder, almost with joy. Her attendant is no hidden figure, but a tall young man with glasses and a blond beard who regularly appears in a white medic's garb. He evidently is pre-med, or maybe an intern. The two constantly play, talk loudly, engage the other students. Between forkfuls of food, it is not unusual for the two to smooch, sometimes at the front of the cafeteria. Horsing around, the medic may sit on her lap, half-fall on the floor. Then again, they may discuss more serious matters — at a distance: what salad to pick up, where to meet, what time, etc. I've heard that the young man plans to marry her, and his parents are upset. The student who told me was quite put-out at the parents. "Ann can have children, the same as anyone else," groused the student.

My thoughts were less certain. The girl is exceptional, no doubt of that — but can the young man really love her? As distinct from the role of the fine young man who loved the tragically crippled girl, the story of how the two overcame the tragedy with love? Perhaps others have no such suspicions; the young man is not capable of such a dissemblance. Only I am dark and twisted. It's a nice role, I must admit.

Most of the students, be it noted, cope very well with the cripples. They greet them with exaggerated bravado – a tone of forced cheerfulness, abnormal normality, the way people talk to children. "Hi, Darwin, getting ready for exams?" "Hey, Darwin, warm enough for you?" Darwin, for his part, responds in like fashion, and he remembers every name. He makes a point of saying the name even to the passerby who may never be seen again. He likes all the students, even indulges them, such as the buffoon Gustavo, who travels the world on his father's money, womanizes, drinks, hits the fire alarm bell with his key every time he comes down the hall and generally enjoys playing the wastrel with his broken English at UCR. Darwin lets him and others watch sports events on TV in his room, laughs politely at his infantile jokes. The students treat Darwin as a regular guy, pretend that nothing is wrong. When I show up to empty the leg bag, or simply begin to give him his pills, they have a habit of disappearing – more from uneasiness, I think, than discretion. Like students everywhere, they love to throw things, shout things, play bad music at maximum volume, eat like horses and assume that all this is amusing. Better for them to imagine that a handicapped person is one of the gang who happens not to be present on occasion. And, on a day-to-day basis, I cannot say this is such a bad tactic.

All in all, there is something utopian about the life of the students. Living in common in little identical rooms that line little identical halls, eating in common in the big cafeteria, and if not sleeping in common – at least commonly partaking of the rich sex life available in college dorms. There are many mock complaints about the cafeteria food, but actually the situation is ideal. You enter with your plastic card and order one of two or three entrees; desserts await you at the end of the line; machines in the alcove on the way to the dining room dispense drinks of a half-dozen sorts. The salad bar offers yogurt, cottage cheese, fruits, carrot sticks, bread, butter, tomatoes. Refills are unlimited until the end of the period; you may take your plate back for another entree. A huge ice-cream bar is rolled out on Wednesday nights; a frozen-custard machine is available at all other times behind the salad bar. In short, a perfect arrangement: from each the same payment, to each according to his appetite.

I think Thomas More would have approved, though he might have been dismayed by the superabundance and waste. For my part, I approved without reservation — as a criminal, a non-member of the commune, smuggled in under the cloak of an assistant. A starving spy, I felt something akin to panic. How to get as much as possible into the stomach before time to leave. How to stick fruit into Darwin's back satchel without catching the eye of "Colonel Sanders," the white-bearded old coot who patrolled the area. How to take advantage of this stroke of luck before some disaster — an earthquake, World War III, a change of cafeteria rules — should remove the food from my reach. I had Ik-fever: my gaze, my mind, my fingers were fixed upon food, and only after a week or so, when I felt certain the salad bar would reappear the next day, restocked, did I recover myself and the relaxed manner of one who is civilized. Yet I never forgot my former want, never became indifferent to the plenty. The students, naturally, took everything for granted. Accustomed to the privileged life, they complained about their veal parmesan, while I gobbled cottage cheese and millions of Ethiopians choked in the dust with starvation.

Sometimes I would notice a person looking at Darwin, a person new to the cafeteria. Darwin would be lifting the food to his mouth with his irregular movement, and the person's face would squinch, the eyes would narrow with secret interest. Then the conversation would draw the observer away, but later he or she would return. I would sit waiting for the next step: the discovery that there were two. One woman I recall with particular clarity, since her features were so easy to read. She was part of an adult lecture group that lunched for a week in the cafeteria. Her eyes were large, round, her nose square and her lips curvaceous within a fat face. She eyed Darwin carefully with unchecked revulsion, glancing at the wheelchair and inspecting the hand strap, then looking round quickly to make sure no one was watching. For two days she failed to see me, but on the third I could see the moment of thought, when she wondered how Darwin got his food, or how his plates had moved while she was not watching. Her big eyes rolled off Darwin, who was busy munching, and met mine. The spasm of revulsion nearly choked her, and she turned away. I continued looking at her calmly, but she controlled herself and never looked back.

One final category of person should be noted, again indiscriminate and unique. Young, healthy, big-bosomed, flamboyant, sloppy, neat, shy, seductive, tight-sweatered, tight-pantsed, round-bottomed, athletic, decadent, wide-eyed, sleepy-eyed, dyed, bleached, close-cut, long-haired, bare-footed, high-heeled, friendly, stand-offish, timid, loudmouthed, coarse, delicate, sweet, depraved — beautiful, beautiful, beautiful!

Darwin and I would watch them pass in parade. At first only a little word about this one or that, but very quickly we picked our favorites, and we observed them with rapt interest. We made up little stories about them — mostly, what they did with their boyfriends. We wondered what they studied, if anything. We sighed or suppressed a groan when one of the lovelies came near. And we knew, of course, that all the other guys were doing the same. This was not so much a cafeteria as a giant sexotorium, where the future of America (Japan, Honduras, etc.) selected food and drink and playmate. I suggested to Darwin that it would be interesting if a large screen could be put up at the front of the cafeteria, and at each meal the thoughts of one person be pictured thereon. He thought it a good idea.

From the sexotorium we would return to Darwin's room, and he would resume studying. I might have to put his typed papers in numerical order and clip them for presentation to his professor, or file away some class notes Xeroxed by a friend, or a magazine such as *Paraplegic News*. Darwin had plastic boxes for each kept on a high shelf. Personal correspondence was not filed, but deposited in the round file immediately after reading. No sentimentalist he. However, he often sent money home: I would press his check with a big rubber stamp bearing a huge squiggly signature. Business completed, pills taken, bag emptied, I was free.

There were three main places to go: University Village, UCR campus, KUCR. At the latter I could work on the Shostakovich tapes — reading the composer's acrid memoirs. Exchange drolleries with Clark, who protean-like, was always changing moods and attitudes. On campus I could browse in the library, though Wolf became impatient on the chain. Converse with Edgar, who had a carrel. He believed that in ten years the young Ph.D.'s (that is, he and I and other thousands no longer so young) would be needed again, when the fossils with tenure would be discarded. To this end, he pumped out paper after paper. If nothing happened, he said, he would go into his father's furniture business and forget about it. I decided to forget about it in advance.

Sometimes, in the evenings, just before dark, I would fold a Bambi pillowcase into my back pocket (it used to belong to the girls) and steal with Wolf into the orchard to pick oranges, lemons, grapefruit. I figured that if I got caught the university wouldn't prosecute a former professor, and if it did — it would make a great headline, if only on a back page. Again, I might take a hike with Wolf into the mountains beyond, where he would run at great distances and chase coyotes, and I would look down on the exanimate city, its little lights twinkling, and enjoy my superior position. Most often, I would simply go home, watch green Cronkite and plan to do something creative — perhaps add to my endless diatribe against the world.

And, of course, I would fall asleep in my beaten chair before alert Pushkin, ever-inspired. Cats would creep in through the flap in the screen left for Demon, my favorite. Wolf would not molest them: he had reasoned that the apartment was no-hunt; he wouldn't even investigate the gnawing under the sink, which began about 2 a.m. (Outdoors, he'd snap the spine of anything he could catch with one bite — even a gigantic opossum, to my chagrin.) The cats would creep in and scent the walls and chair, and Wolf would slink silently into the other room. I'd wake, curse the stench and pedal alone back to Darwin's — up, down, up, down — in time for nightly chores.

Now the morning procedure moved in reverse: lenses out, clothes off, transfer to bed with tube dangling. As noted, Wednesdays and Sundays were the big nights: I'd scoop out the poop while Carson cracked jokes or Rockford smart-talked a heavy. A perfect use for TV.

Past midnight I'd return home, take Wolf for his last walk, spread the sleeping bag out by the bookcases and bed down. Wolfgang curled himself on his own mat. In the dark I could hear him whimper as he raced through a recurrent dream. When I told people I was sleeping with a dog, I really meant it.

ELEVEN

A VISIT TO THE DOCTOR

Darwin feels sick. He's shaking, his face shows trouble. Like someone caught in a storm, or a leaking boat, he does not complain, but sets about seeking the remedy. I undress him, transfer him to the bed, examine his body from head to toe. The thought crosses my mind that I know his body better than my own: at least I have never seen my behind directly in front of my eyes. The bedsore looks strange — yellowish and spongy, and the hole is covered up by a flap of skin. But this might be an improvement; it might be filling in. The toenails look ingrown and have a lot of dried skin under them, but once cleaned out look healthy enough. His forearms are badly scraped and scabbed from banging into the arms of the chair, and the right one is covered with a grey metallic sheen — might bits of the metal have worked into his blood? Not likely, the arms are usually battered this way — some moisturizing cream heals them quickly.

Finally I examine the adhesive tape around the catheter, and there I discover a little abrasion along the edge of the tape. A pencil-point of skin has been rubbed away, and Darwin, unable to feel it, eventually must shake and experience chills until the spot is treated. I turn back the tape and swab the area with a maroon antiseptic, and swab the bedsore for good measure. Darwin is quickly put in position and covered with a blanket to his chin. Before leaving, I ask him how he feels and he says he'll be all right. The little spot could spell his doom, but he's taken the proper measures and refuses to worry.

But the next morning he still feels bad. The bedsore is the same, the abrasion improved, but only now do I notice that the right testicle is swollen. I touch it: hard as a rock. Darwin listens to my description and tells me this has happened before: the urine backs up and causes infections in the area. He will have to go to the doctor. It's a fairly serious condition, he told me matter-of-factly.

"I hope it doesn't have to be cut out."

"What do you mean, be cut out?" I asked.

"The testicle," he said with a soundless laugh.

He was concerned, I could see, but also willing to sacrifice a part for the survival of the whole. In that instant he had mentally accepted the excision: he was thinking ahead to recovery.

At the doctor's office a made-up secretary admitted us, speaking to Darwin as to a baby. But this was preferable to the cold knife-cuts they can dish out to male patients. In this case she didn't feel threatened, and I, of course, was invisible. Behind the glass a doctor was busy at the counter endorsing a stack of checks: he signed them one after the other, cutting down the skyscraper on his left and building it back up again — upside down — on his right. In the midst of his labors he tossed out instructions to another secretary, then swept the whole colossus into a bag and sent her to the bank. Out of curiosity, I checked my wallet and found therein six bucks worth of food stamps and three 25¢ coupons for dog food. Still, I'd rather have the Wolf waiting for me at home than a leper in the waiting room.

Naturally, we have to wait a half-hour. Our time is worthless, the physician's time is priceless. That's why he schedules six people at once. Darwin and I read magazines and both begin to snooze. We are awakened to go to the little examination room, where we can wait another quarter-hour. The urologist comes in — not Darwin's regular one, who is away on vacation, in Bermuda or Hawaii, but another. He has a boozy red face and fluffed-up moustaches; clap a monocle and pith helmet on him and he could go on safari: "What ho, chaps!" A young intern stands behind him, a novice with innocent eyes.

I have unzipped Darwin's pants and stripped off the catheter; a glass sample from the leg bag sits by the sink. The ruddy doctor sticks a tube none too gently straight up Darwin's penis and takes the urine in another glass. He leaves with this glass and his novice, who seems to have taken an interest in me, staring fixedly on his way out. What is it, am I some kind of novelty? Does he wonder about my medical expertise, as compared with his own?

I set about putting on a new catheter. It's impossible: Darwin's stomach bulges in seated position, and his penis, relieved of all pressure, contracts. I must pull it out, paint it with the white adhesive, get the sticky tape around it. My fingers are all cracked, the tape and glue have stuck to my nails, his zipper gets in the way. The only consolation is that we have no fear of his voiding in the process; on the other hand, when he does, the catheter will certainly leak and require changing.

Rah-Rah and the boy return. He says the sediment is not great and the infection is minor. Hands out some blue pills. Darwin and I glance at each other.

"Would you take a look, Doctor, to see if…" I ask.

The great man does not acknowledge that he has caught sound of my voice, but nevertheless steps forward and casts a cursory eye on the enormous red testicle.

"Doesn't look too bad," he declares and steps away.

"But, but…" Darwin and I sputter.

"It will go down," insists the busy man. He spies the glass by the sink, pours it down the drain. The door is open, the big shoe through it.

"Doctor," I say, "will this medicine go with the others he's taking? He takes mandelamine, urocholine…"

Tossing his moustaches, Rah-Rah waves me off, mumbles something. His white coat is gone; the novice sends me a pregnant look, as if I were a mystery he's like to probe, and follows. Darwin and I look at each other and break out laughing.

"He says it's all right, so it's all right."

"Must be," I agree.

"He knows his business."

"Doesn't even have to look."

"He's already seen everything," Darwin says drily.

"I hope the pills don't explode inside you."

"They won't, or if they do — it's not his fault."

And so we joked our way out of the office. Quads are processed like everybody else — no preferential treatment here. Outside, waiting for the UCR special-services van, we enjoyed the sunshine, the pre-summer breezes, and observed the people entering and leaving the building. Woeful sights — some with partial faces, one with a metal tube in his neck, another bent sideways, almost at right angles, helped along by a hideously ugly thin wife.

"Did you see that?" asked Darwin after they had passed. I was sitting on the edge of a bench, right beside him.

TWELVE

THE QUEEN OF THE BALL

There is only one thing I have refused to do. The bowel care, washing and dressing, even the contact lenses, must be considered necessary. Not so the aftershave lotion.

In the mornings, returning home, I would pour my cereal into the bowl, cover it with milk, lift the spoon to my mouth — and smell Mennen *Afta*. So strong and sweet that I gagged. Scrub my fingers, pour disinfectant over them, even crush leaves and burn paper under them — nothing would get rid of the smell. After a couple days of this, I remembered at the proper time and used not my right, but my left hand to pat the lotion on his cheeks, then washed my hands in the bathroom with the obnoxious dormitory liquid soap. Nonetheless, as I opened my mouth for *C.W. Post*, my breath was taken away by the fumes rising from the hand holding the bowl.

The day Rutger had shown me the routine, he had smeared the bluish paste on Darwin's face and remarked: "Darwin, you've been using this aftershave ever since I've been working for you."

"Stick with a winner" was Darwin's reply.

But I was stuck with it too, and it wouldn't come off any more than the piece of paper attached to W.C. Fields' hand. The cat scent could be left behind in my apartment; this scent came outdoors with me. I was afraid people would think that I used it, though they could think what they damned well pleased.

Finally one morning I asked: "Darwin, would you mind very much if we tried that other aftershave lotion you have up there?"

He was surprised.

"Why, don't you like *Afta*?"

"It's O.K.; it's just that it bothers me when I'm eating breakfast."

He consented at once to try the other, which smelled more steely – I liked it. Perhaps this hurt him, but I considered it a good lesson – show him that I'm willing to help, but have certain limits.

We have a visitor at mealtimes. An anemic student with a face so thin it has parallel lines down it; he has a shock of unruly black hair, wears glasses and smiles sweetly like a maiden. He came over one night and reminded me that we had met a year ago at a party.

Clark and I, I recalled, had spoiled a dinner party given by a Chinese disc-jockey from the station with the unlikely name of Franz. In the midst of sumptuous dishes prepared in the native way by Franz's mother, who retired out of sight, I assailed the idiocy of our nation, and in particular – Elvis Presley. This offended one girl who had enjoyed the thrill of once meeting the greatest entertainer of all time and who spoke in terms of "Elvis and me." Clark, playing devil's advocate, egged me on, telling me how great Elvis was, while I, stimulated by the mixed drinks and the presence of an audience, poured out the invective, listing all the mental diseases and natural disasters of the world into the bargain. At one point, while I was professing the worthlessness of anyone who could listen to the King for more than five seconds, my chopstick snapped and flew across the table into someone else's plate. This brought me up short and I could feel my face getting red, but later, drunker, I held forth on the decline of the West in the living room, while all stared at me in silence. The girl left after my declaration that American women weren't worth screwing, but the thin-faced young man asked a serious question and listened attentively to the hour-long answer, after which I had the decency to stagger home.

Now this same fellow was at our table, unwittingly reminding me what an ass I had been: I had relived the shame of the broken chopstick many times at two in the morning. But it seemed he wanted company. The people he usually sat with, he told us, always spoke of the same things. They were not interested in books or ideas. This naturally gave me the cue to be smart, which I took, begrudgingly.

"You could hardly expect them to be interested in books or ideas," I said. "They're students."

We somehow got into a discussion about noise. Joyce said he didn't mind noise, interruptions, the disruptive student life.

One shouldn't try to be an intellectual élite, he said, aiming the dig at me. If a thought is distracted, it will come back — if it is important. And if one has a private moment in the midst of interruptions, he will value it the more. Just live life, go along — the thinking will take care of itself. He sometimes goes places he doesn't want to go, does things he doesn't want to do — just to see how it will affect him. He regards himself as healthy, hardy, able to withstand the hard knocks.

I countered: What if the thought requires development, but is constantly distracted and replaced by other thoughts, for other thoughts will come. Does he expect the important thought to develop by itself, unconsciously, while his conscious mind is filled with thoughtless chatter? If a thought is important, why should it be treated so harshly, thrown outside to fend for itself, while banalities are given a mat by the hearth? And further, why should the conscious mind be treated as a garbage pail, a receptacle for other people's slop, while only the unconscious mind produces nourishment, repeatedly refused?

This and much more. I spoke pretty much half-heartedly, but oddly enough the distance and lack of concern strengthened my arguments. They flew out like birds of prey — swift and shrill. Darwin looked on with a bemused expression, like an owl that can see in the dark and fly on silent wings.

Joyce was taken aback, but didn't give up. He enjoyed the stimulation. This was what he had left his tablemates for, so in a sense I was doing his bidding. He said merely that one should mingle with ordinary people, not cut himself off and be a snob. This was the best way to learn about life. And there was no reason to get upset about noise and stupidity. After all, the normal state of most people is stupidity — it has been in the past and will be in the future, and there's nothing to be done about it. All the arguments of philosophers and the satires of clever wits won't change the matter one whit.

I: That's a wonderful apology for mediocrity, and a more cynical snobbery besides, for it considers people incorrigibly inferior — they can't be raised to thought. You place yourself in a superior position and then hobnob with the inferiors, praising yourself for not taking offense. You do nothing to help them, you don't criticize their mistakes, their ignorance, their adulation of false gods. You feel comfortable among them because you are not challenged, you laugh at their noise, let them entertain you.

Joyce: But it's the truth. Take linguistics. People learn their language when children, their minds are active, but at a certain point most of them stop. They're stuck with the language of an eight-year-old, and they never gain any insight into it. Others, only a few, continue to explore — they sense different meanings, nuances. They even begin to realize, on their own, the different origins of words — Latin, Greek, French roots. The others will never do this, even if you try to train them: the best they can do is memorize. This has been shown in linguistic tests.

Joyce, I am told, is a linguistics major. Like myself, he favors German, Greek and Russian — his strength is the first, mine the last. No one is strong in the middle. From his remarks on language I begin to take a more serious interest, though I still believe he's dead wrong.

I: People who never develop linguistic abilities may be stunted, but they are not necessarily stupid. They may have inherent intelligence. The important thing is not to pamper their stunted condition: tell them they're ignorant, tell them they sound stupid. An entirely different society is required, one that... And as I spoke I felt myself holding a position I did not want. People who do not feel language are stupid.

Joyce: It may sound harsh, but if something is broken it can't be fixed, or only a little bit can be fixed. People with stunted abilities will always be stunted, no matter how much you revile them.

I: Perhaps we differ on the amount that can be fixed.

The debate had taken an unwelcome turn. Darwin was listening, and I could imagine how he might apply it to himself. When Joyce used the word *broken*, I kept from wincing, but felt it very strongly, while he seemed not to feel it at all. Thus my final remark, stated quite truthfully, since Darwin had shown me that in his realm a great deal could be done, even if something broken never could be fixed. I got my dishes together, put them on Darwin's tray, and we prepared to leave. Darwin scooted backwards away from the table, while I turned toward the dishwashers. Joyce, picking up on what he had said, got in the last word.

"Not much can be fixed, but that little bit deserves praise."

Poor recovery, but he was stuck with it. To make sure we had heard, he repeated it.

Joyce is a sort I've met before — in the pages of Russian history. The tender intellectual who forces himself to be tough. The subjective thinker who subordinates himself to objective laws. The Nihilist, the New Man, the Trotskyite. But these are not rebellious times, and Joyce is not political, so there's no need to get excited. The next time we sit down at the table I hit him with a prepared argument: If chimpanzees can be taught sign language when removed from their cages and placed in a culturally enriched environment, then human beings, etc. The greatest impediment to a culturally enriched environment is precisely the intellectual who says take it easy, people have always been stupid. Joyce says he's tired, he has ideas but doesn't feel like expressing them. I remark that his ideas will have little effect if he doesn't have the energy to expound them. And we let it go at that. In future conversations we settled down to a friendly tone, relaxed a bit, flared up at times, but generally shared ideas and concerns.

When I mentioned this new acquaintance to Clark, recalling the Elvis party, he retorted: "Joyce? Don't you know? He's the queen of the ball."

I wasn't sure if Clark was putting me on, but later Joyce dropped the name of his best friend — Mona, a girl who worked at the station, whom I had once seen at a free concert with a leather-skinned dyke. Another time, he said he was going to a meeting and I would be shocked if I knew what it was about; from the posters plastered on campus I already knew it was gay night.

So there it was: I'm dining out with a quad and a queer. That makes me a what — a quirk? On the way back to the room, I broke the news to Darwin. "I wondered," he replied confidingly. We agreed that Joyce was a good guy, but we'd have to be careful about our remarks.

Often enough, Joyce didn't show up, since he slept at odd hours, and Darwin and I could give ourselves up to unmitigated girl-watching. Darwin seemed to enjoy my caustic comments — my bitterness about women in general amused him. Our views were remarkably similar on this score: women have tremendous power, they tease, they sleep with football teams... The viewpoint of a loser, I suppose. The pretty child I saw alone one day would turn up with a drooling bozo the next. Darwin had

a fondness for a very healthy-looking blond: she could have
passed for one of the Dallas Cheerleaders on his wall calendar,
save that she dressed more modestly, usually in skirt and
pullover sweater. I couldn't imagine what dreams Darwin might
have, let alone hopes, but he struck me as normal in all of his
attitudes, so this interest seemed normal too.

Then again, he told me a funny story about a man whom
he called Mr. Sex. This man he had met in the hospital during
his early rehabilitation. Without question, Mr. Sex had been a
lady killer, and now he found himself a quad. But even so,
Darwin insisted, he had a deadly effect. Nurses would come up
to him after hours and beg to massage him, make indecent
proposals. Darwin heard it all from his bed. One even tried to
crawl under the sheets, but Mr. Sex dissuaded her.

"What was his secret?" I asked in amazement.

"He had a little smile," Darwin answered, letting out that
typical shallow-breathed exhalation — the quad laugh. "A little
smile at the corner of his mouth."

"Anything else?" I followed eagerly, as if I could acquire
the technique.

"A little..." Darwin released another half-breath, "a little
twinkle in his eye."

"That's all? A little smile at the corner of his mouth and
a little twinkle in his eye?"

"That's all. He'd look up at the nurse and just kinda smile,
and then there'd be a little twinkle in his eye. You could see
her hands start shaking, and the next minute she'd be rubbing
his neck and his shoulders and asking him how he felt."

Clark, to whom I mentioned this as well, discounted the
story. "He probably made it up," he said, dropping a long strand
of hair, which he had just plucked from his head, from between
his forefinger and thumb. He has a morbid fear of going bald,
which will surely become a self-fulfilling prophecy. "More
likely," he continued, picking another strand from the shoulder
of his shirt with a look of fatality, "he saw *Coming Home*."

In addition to everything else — playing the piano, composing things on the synthesizer, collecting foreign cars, making
films, taking photos, writing horror stories, running a radio
station, Clark goes to the movies. He's a media man.

And he's right: Darwin mentioned the Jane Fonda film,
which I had not seen, not wanting to pay for her ego-trip. No

doubt this story — a beautiful woman's true love for a cripple — had given him, and many men like him, such hopes.

We saw another Hanoi Jane film together, *They Shoot Horses, Don't They?* It was shown free in the sexotorium one Sunday night. Darwin and I sat to one side, but the sound came from the speaker on the other side. We moved to the other side while the second reel was being put on, and then the sound came from the side we had just left. On the third reel we stayed put, and it came out right. We liked the film, and Darwin would repeat "yassuh, yassuh" in Gig Young fashion for some days afterwards, without apparently reflecting on a story in which a pack of sick, starving, straining people race round and round in a circle for a prize that will be absorbed by the expenses of the race. He preferred the humorous touches to the film.

All in all, it was easy to forget that Darwin was paralyzed. His reactions were normal, he got around well on his own. In fact, I believe that he himself sometimes forgot his condition, as for example one night while I held his resisting legs up on my left shoulder and swabbed his bedsore with antiseptic. Carson at that moment cracked one of his proctologist jokes, and Darwin let out a soft chuckle. There I was, laboring on his behind, heavy and forever immobile, pierced with a pencil of death, and he was so insensitive as to chuckle at a quip about "the power of positive shrinking."

"What's he laughing about?" I asked myself.

THIRTEEN

DREAMS

few mornings Darwin told me his dreams.

> *He's taking a test. Other students are sitting around in the large room. The test is handed to him and he sees only a few words with a lot of blank spaces. This puzzles him. He looks around. One student explains to another: you must fill in your own information. He looks back at the test and realizes it is a will: I, ________, being of sound mind and body, hereby ________ .*

This is all he remembered. When he told me the dream he stumbled over the word *body*. I, naturally, could not interpret the dream, though the fear of death seemed clear enough. Darwin proposed a likely pretext. He had talked with a student the day before the dream who was carrying Elisabeth Kübler-Ross's book, *On Death and Dying.* This, plus the worry of his Master's exams, he thought, was sufficient to precipitate the dream.

I could supply the pretext for the next dream he told me. We had a gala Filipino supper in the cafeteria — colored streamers, posters, costumes, spiced chicken, peculiar vegetables. Darwin let me get him a refill and dump it into my salad plate. In Southern California there is a plethora of organized jollity, perhaps inspired by Disneyland. Restaurants have themes, supermarket cashiers wear clown outfits, schools make little shows for parents on PTA days — all done in an empty-eyed android fashion, without a quiver of life. Anyway, that night Darwin had a dream.

> *He enters a large room. Perhaps the cafeteria. Some student cries out that a great entertainment is going on*

over at the other side. All the students get excited. Laughing and playing among themselves, they bustle to the other side. They are out of sight. Darwin sits alone in the large room. He hears outbursts of laughter, but never knows what the entertainment is.

The last dream he told me was the most curious. Unlike the others the meaning was not clear. It had to do with me, which I took as a bad sign: I'd rather not be in people's dreams. But here it is.

I'm changing his leg bag. Now it's not me, but an old man. The old man tells him that he regularly takes all sorts of drugs. All sorts, any combination. Cocaine, marijuana... He rattles off a combination that Darwin knows is fatal. But the old man replies: "I'm still here, aren't I?" Then the old man tells Darwin he smokes Brillo.

Naturally I was intrigued by the dream and assumed that the key to its interpretation lay in the word *Brillo.* There must be some association, probably a verbal one. I decided to test Darwin later, when he was thinking about something else. After a few days, finding a completely different context, I asked Darwin to submit to a short word-association test. He was amused and answered readily the first word that came into his head. The results:

green — *grass,* blue — *sky,* classroom — *professor,* coke — *drink,* pizza — *Shakey's,* Brillo — *wash dishes,* fun — *Disneyland,* students — *rowdy,* test — *stress,* old man — *grandfather.*

These answers seemed so normal to me that I gave up and told him my purpose. He had forgotten the Brillo in the dream and laughed at my recalling it. He could not attribute any special meaning to it. Could it be simply what he thought — washing and cleaning? I wash and clean, but also take dope? And what do I have to do with an old man — his grandfather? I suppose there's something interesting here, but it would take more dreams, more questions, more analysis, and I decided not to probe. Besides, Darwin told me no more dreams.

FOURTEEN

QUAD THREE, QUAD FOUR, QUAD FIVE...

'm getting to know the quads.

The one with the complex wheelchair and the use of his chin is named Drew. He's very bright. Grade-point average of 3.8. Accepted to law school at UCLA, Harvard and somewhere else. He decided on Harvard — the second quad in the school's history. Darwin told me that he had first studied at Berkeley, then moved to UCR when he discovered the available services. It's the best campus in the country for the disabled. Drew strikes me as a bit curt, possibly resentful. I exchange a hello when we pass in the hallway, Darwin usually stops and has a pow-wow. Once, as I was about to go through the doors to the outside, I caught sight of Drew rolling toward me. I went through, then thought he might want me to hold the door for him and heard him say, "No thanks." I turned back and said "O.K.," but he had already sped into a side hall. Then I realized that I had not spoken first.

The Latin girl, I believe, is named Dolores. She loves Wolf, always stops beside him when he's chained outside and enjoys his sniffing and licking over the arm of her chair. She asks if it's all right to feed him, brings him slices of roast beef, milk and other good things. Wolf gobbles it up, sticks his big moist black nose up for more while she laughs. He doesn't distinguish between the abled and the disabled, which must please her. Darwin informs me that Dolores has a bad case of arthritis: she's not exactly a quadriplegic, but is confined to a wheelchair. Darwin himself, it seems to me, would better be classified a paraplegic, since he makes valiant use of his hands, but he always refers to himself as a quad. "We little quads need all the help we can get," he says when a new ramp is installed.

The studious fellow is named Tim. He works in the Administration Building, which accounts for his daily suit, though the spiffiness is surely a personal touch. Right after graduation, he saw the job advertised, applied and got it. Started at $18,000, now makes about $22,000. When Darwin told me this, I confess I felt offense. Damn, quads don't have it so bad after all. Then Darwin estimated his expenses. Attendant — at least $600 a month, taxes — about the same amount (a whole stream of jet smoke), rent — $250 or more, medical expenses, pills, food, etc. He just about breaks even. So the handicapped person is hit financially if he tries to make it on his own, since he must cover expenses not known to the non-handicapped. Obviously it's easier not to work and to accept checks from the state government, but for some there's the matter of pride.

And then there are Garry, Larry and a very little man with a rough black beard and swirled brown eyes. Ann has cerebral palsy. On the back of her wheelchair the book bag is embroidered: "I may not be perfect, but some parts of me are excellent." She's the supervisor for her hall in the dorm, an active and exceptional student. The special brightness about her continued to impress me, and I would force myself to look away. Just imagine if I were attracted, and the medic and I had to compete for her affection. That would make an interesting story too, and people would wonder. But, failed as I am with women, I don't feel the need for this type of relationship. The little scenes: "Yes, I love you, I don't pity you." Or: "I love you for yourself, not because you're crippled." Or: "No, I'm not trying to prove what a wonderful man I am." And so on — day-dreaming.

Even away from the dorms I run into quads. The last few Thursdays I've been attending a class in American Sign Language (Ameslan). Not from a desire to help the deaf, but because I was intrigued by the tiny woman in the corner of my defective TV, gesturing frantically. I got some library books, began to recognize some signs. The program itself was utterly boring, something about problems in L.A., but the possibility of communicating without speech fascinated me. An experimental (*i.e.,* free) course opened up on campus, I enrolled. The other enrollers, for the most part, were caretakers of one sort or another. Some worked with the deaf, some with disturbed children, one planned to teach a chimpanzee — the plain students quickly dropped out. One evening we signed to each other, indicating our jobs, and the woman across from me signed that her husband was HC — *i.e.,* handicapped. Another quad.

His story, as she told me by speech afterwards, was gripping. He was riding his bicycle, and the traffic light at an intersection malfunctioned. It signalled green to him, but immediately signalled green to a truck at right angles. Trucks, as we know, are bigger than bikes. I thought with a shudder of an accident I had avoided at an intersection only the day before. Guessing that the car would not stop at the stop sign, I held back while the driver ran it, never noticing me. But let her continue. Ron, her husband, refused to accept himself as a cripple. Forbade the physicians to bind his hands and curl them, rejected most of their advice. He came back to the house hell bent on recovery, which the physicians assured him was impossible. His wife had to do everything at first, but bit by bit he improved. He could move his wheelchair farther and farther, a powered vehicle having been refused. He hired a therapist to work with him three hours every night. And, while the doctors were busy writing him off, he was studying books on rehabilitation and trying to interest them in his progress. Now he rolls himself around the city, uphill as well as down. He can take care of his needs. He expects to stand on crutches in six months. All by dint of willpower, hard effort and disbelief in doctors.

I came back to Darwin brimming with the story. It was Thursday night, shower night. (We were having problems; evidently I was not getting all the soft stuff out the night before.) I rolled him to the room, doused him with warm water and began scrubbing. Then I related the inspiring story of Ron — not so he would follow, but rather be encouraged. Darwin, however, knew Ron. The chief thing, he informed me, is which vertebra of the neck is broken. The higher to the brain, the less you can do. The lower, the more. Quads refer to their type by the C number — cervical vertebra. Now Drew, he was C2 — the only one Darwin knew who had lived. He had been injured in an auto accident 7 years ago. His wheelchair was equipped with highly refined devices: the antenna on each side of the head raised or lowered the back of the chair at a touch, the cup at his chin steered the chair forward or backward or around. He also had a special device that enabled him to type with his mouth. But no amount of willpower would give him the ability to lift his arms — the nerves were severed. Darwin himself was C5 — some movement of arms. Tim was also C5 — he wore the hand splint at all times, could write and feed himself. Ron, though, was C7 — and those two vertebrae made a world of difference. He could use the muscles of his arms, move his fingers. He might get up on crutches, he might do wonderful things. But there's a fixed limit, and nothing can remove it.

So then, I thought, lathering his back. Anyone can be a quad. A fouled light, a car not driven by you. A moment's slip, a snap. But there are quads, and there are quads. Some get a bad roll of the dice: snake eyes. Others are lucky: 7. But who's rolling? And should I feel blessed, terrified, or outraged? Am I swabbing this back because it might be mine, against the future possibility that it might be mine? Like Gerasim in *The Death of Ivan Ilyich*: "I do it, master, because someday I may need care in turn." Or is it simply an unfair set-up: some get broken, others don't. No rhyme or reason, and no compensation.

Darwin was cleaned, catheter taped on. I put the robe over him backwards, piled the things in his lap and pushed him to the door. He looked fairly pathetic, with his wet hair, unshaven face, but this was what he was used to. His accepted life style.

The chair was hard to get out the door: a bump at the threshold, faulty supermarket-style wheels. We see Darwin's girl leaning toward the wall, her arm outstretched on the shoulders of her boyfriend. They're kissing: again and again. I trundle Darwin out into the hall.

She looks up enthusiastically: "Hi!"

Darwin responds politely, though I know his heart is pounding.

The boy looks up sleepily: "Hi."

He has the face of an ad for a deodorant: fluffed yellow hair, black moustache, rugged sports look. I push my cart down the hall away from them. We can hear her whispering and giggling.

"Well, Gary," Darwin tosses back over his shoulder, "it looks like we just don't have good luck with women."

We go in his room, leaving the hall to young lovers.

FIFTEEN

LOVE STORY

She smiled at me.

Petite, self-possessed. She walks with short steps, a straight back, upheld head. Long black hair, excellent demure figure. Jeans, a shirt. I ran into her repeatedly by the salad bar: fate threw us together, but I paid little attention. She was only 20, 21, whereas I... Besides, she would have her admirers: some guys would go crazy over a girl like that, I would not join their demented number. But just now, sitting at the table with Darwin, I watched as she returned from the soda fountain, our eyes met. I would not be outstared, nor would she. My look became brazen, hers – impertinent. She glided by, her head revolving as her eyes stayed fixed on mine. A saucy smile.

Turmoil. Darwin laughed: "Well, Gary, what do you say about that?"

I tried to brush it off: just an incident. But it's been such a long time. Maybe she had noticed me at the salad bar, she planned to... Now she was glad I had stared... No, no, nonsense! How many times have you fantasized yourself into a nightmare? It was just a little tease. Just let it go. Leaving Darwin's room, I saw her in the hall. She started to pass, up the stairs. I stepped in front.

"What's your name?"

"Eileen," she said, "what's yours?"

I told her.

"Hello, Gary."

And up the stairs.

Wow! She likes me. I'm going to... I mean I'll... Well, I could... That is, I... What in the hell could I do? No car, no cash, no credit. But I'm on campus, same as my competitors. We could... walk to a free concert? Maybe see a cheap film? Sit down on the quad – the grass in front of the library, I mean.

There are lots of things. Better not imagine. Invent no scenes, no dialogue. Everything will happen by itself. I'm not going to set up a contest between dream and reality. I'm not even going to get up my hopes. I'm a grown man and... And thus passed the day.

And the next. I caught glimpses of her in the halls, tried to determine if she avoided me or not. When she turned off once, I thought it was because she disliked me. When she passed me another time, I thought it was because she was indifferent. But this was a losing proposition: she could only turn off or pass by. Perhaps the first meant that she was too nervous, the second — that she couldn't resist. Idiocy. Resolve on a tactic, either make an advance or steer clear. Or bide your time, take up some work, find something to do.

The Shostakovich tapes were in progress. Not exactly creation, but close. While Clark rattled papers, leaned back in a squeaky swivel chair and missed my cues for music, I tried to voice the bitter memories of the composer with fine changes of pitch, intonation. Whenever I flubbed a word or two, had to cough or something, Clark would stop the tape, move it back and crack jokes, mostly disrespectful squibs about Dmitry. Yet on occasion, during a break, he would say: "That was intensely moving, Gary." His mind clicks on and off, like a synthesizer. My mind, on the contrary, is a single current, and clicks only stall it, never switch it. After tape 10, I threw a temper tantrum, ejected the offending chair and demanded unrelieved seriousness. Thus we finished the fifteen half-hour readings. On the days following, I spent every spare moment splicing out flubs, swallows and sniffs. I wanted the tapes pristine, the thought flowing. Reading, after all, should be better than life.

Here was something to impress Eileen, if she had ever heard of Shostakovich, Russia or music. No, hold back a little: let the tapes play, the perfected self sound. By chance she might pick it up. This would make much more of an impression than if I begged her to lend an ear. To increase the chance of a spontaneous hearing, I made a promo cart to be played on dumb rock shows. And, of course, I gave everyone else advance notice.

The first broadcast went well, right up to the end, when the student running the tape lopped off the final words and broke in with a blaring rock PSA. At home I was so infuriated I couldn't move, my muscles rigid, thinking how much I wanted to beat the brainless jerk into a jelly. The second broadcast, following my reminders about the final words (the "outro"), ran without a hitch. I was happy, but on the night of the third broadcast, just in case, I phoned and politely asked the engineer to let the tape play out. The tape came on 25 minutes late, and indeed the outro was permitted to play, but also 30 seconds of dead air besides, after which the blockhead mumbled complaints that nothing more was on the tape. "The guy who made the tape," he blabbed on the air, "can get mad at me, but I let it play and there's nothing else here." I left a message with Clark to cancel the series, but the next morning he fired the twit for screwing up a news program with off-the-cuff commentary. And so the show goes on.

Wednesday night. Program №4. The last words, music, flawless. Perhaps the Little One was listening, and now she's thinking... A knock on the door. I grab Wolf's collar as the door opens. It's Jean. She's had it with Riverside. The blank eyes, the lifeless monotones. Working like a dog all day, not breaking even. She's gone as far as you can at the Court without a degree. Now she ought to get one. So she's decided: Off to San Diego, where a friend will help her get settled. There she will work for a two-year degree in the Criminology School. I'm a deadbeat, will never provide child support, but if I agree to move back in the house with the kids, I could do my bit that way. She breaks into tears: she really needs this opportunity, I shouldn't hold her back, etc. I agree.

"But I don't know how I'll pay the rent."

"Get a job."

"I can't."

"With a degree from Princeton? I don't believe you, you're just not trying. You think you're better than we are."

"That degree is an albatross around my neck. They won't even let me haul sludge. I'm telling you, they take a look at my application and..."

"Then how come I was able to get a job? I'll tell you: I went out and looked for it. I begged: my children have to eat, I'll work hard."

"You're just lucky there are more crooks than people who want to study Russian."

Our positions stated, she turns to her personal life. This man, that man... I provide psychological commentary. She evidently wants me to know how well she's doing without me. Guess I deserve it, the way I behaved.

"Really terrific!" she says about some guy.

"Good for you," I remark, thinking to myself: "So Jocko had to prove he was a man, and she had to pass on the proof to me. What are they doing — straining their guts out for my benefit?"

She goes on talking, but by habit I turn off: it's hard for an introvert to listen. I only hope she is doing well, not acting within the confines of my vanished world view.

She left, grateful. I fell into a blue funk. A house, furniture — responsibility. But also the reality of a broken family, disrupted lives caused by my failures — these things weigh on me. To return to the scene of my expulsion, not as conqueror, but as a concessive half-parent. The kids doubting my authority. And what about Eileen — the infatuation looks silly now. The sort of thing I did in the past, which got me where I am today. Besides, aren't I handicapped in any courtship attempt? She would learn, and have to accept:

> my age
> my knowledge
> my thoughts
> my wife, my divorce, my past
> my children
> my lack of car
> my lack of cash
> my lack of credit
> my work
> my quad.

Try the proven method: accept the obstacles, take the necessary steps. But there's a difference here: she's not a condition, she can speak. And what she might say could hurt, since her smile thrilled me. And where would the steps lead — to impossibility? The truth is, I don't belong here among students. Nor with Darwin. Only with the Wolf, on top of a hill, away from all people. Or in the wreck of my chair, with the gesticulating dwarf in the corner of the screen, the gnawing under the sink past 3 a.m., while I gaze at the caped man, striding into everlastingness. Or perhaps in the dark of a library, interred in a book that I myself have written, closed, on a shelf.

The next day, after morning chores, I collapsed in the lounge. A student was supposed to meet me for tutoring in Russian. He had missed the first two meetings, made the third, and this was the fourth. I didn't expect him, didn't want him. He had fluffed orange hair and wore a piece of blue silk in the collar of his white shirt. Someone like that would never make it past the present tense. But I started skimming Herzen, just in case.

The door opened, Eileen walked in. She sat down on the couch opposite me, smiled and opened a book. I closed my book and stared. She looked up, smiled.

"What are you reading?"

I started talking, and the words, experiences, reflections on quadriplegics, thoughts on suicide, references to unknown Russian writers, Greek etymologies, even the goddamned degree came tumbling out, together with opinions on every subject, criticisms of every show.

Eileen said: "So you're into criticism?"

But she put up with it, no doubt because there were many unconcealed flatteries to herself. We left the lounge, stopped by her room as she picked up her books for class. She showed me her art work — six copies of a city scene. I was asked my opinion about the various prints, tried to find something in favor of the least mediocre. It felt like visiting a nursery.

Walking across campus, I caught sight of the wheelchair. Darwin, in the company of environmentalists, rolled toward us. I knew it would be hard for him to suppress a smile, or even a laugh, but he pulled it off famously. Pretending not to see us until the last moment, he looked up and said with surprise: "Why, hello, Gary!" And was past. I burst out laughing, and then had to explain to Eileen. She was left at the door to her art class, bearing a heavy load of psychological materials. They could be sifted, or dropped. I ran in the opposite direction, back toward Darwin's room. It was time for the 3 o'clock bag-emptying. My right knee jammed, the back started to go. Arriving with a bad limp, I told Darwin the whole story.

So then, obstacles can be surmounted. Just take it easy, let life come to you. Still limping, I went with Wolf up in the orchard. A fox crossed our path. Beautifully grey, with a black moustache-line and a reddish brown patch on his back leading into a fiery red tail. I had seen it once before in the area, but hardly so close: it stopped only three avocado trees away.

Then, as I marvelled, it bobbed its head and crept two paces toward us. Wolf, though he saw it, behaved strangely and jerked his head to the other side. I tried to hold him steady, for the fox seemed to have taken an interest in him. Another step, another. What was happening I couldn't imagine, until Wolf tugged on the leash. A cub jumped out of the weeds behind us and ran down the hill, toward the place where I had first seen the fox. Now I understood: we had come between mother and cub, and the mother was keeping an eye on Wolf. Once the baby was safe, she skipped through the avocadoes and into the brush. But now I knew her lair.

Well, it's not the usual sort of proposal, but why be usual? The sight was rare, exciting. Who else could offer it to her? I caught sight of her walking from the dorms with her room-mate. Catching up on my bike, I initiated a conversation. The two girls kept on walking, the roommate closest to me, between bike and the object of my affection. She presented a stiff smile when introduced, baring a row of lower teeth, then pretended to be absent while I rode alongside and chattered. Eileen peeked out from the other side of her friend and followed my words, apparently with interest. They were headed to an event on campus, kept a fast pace. The roommate peered straight ahead: her neck was fixed, the bones fused together. I mentioned the fox. Eileen thought it nice, but not overly thrilling. I made my proposal. She had to study.

Great. More glances in the sexotorium, passings in the hallways. Sometimes she walked beside a male friend, but not the same one each time, so it was nothing serious. I still had my chances, but where was the opportunity that life should provide? Talking to Clark on the telephone, available without charge to students in the front hall, I heard the magic words.

"Ted Kennedy is coming to the station tomorrow."

"The Ted Kennedy?"

"That's right, we're going to interview him."

"No kidding!"

"No, I'm not kidding. The secret service men will come first, with trained dogs, to search for bombs. There will probably be a lot of reporters from the newspapers, and then the whole Kennedy entourage, his staff, the people following his campaign. It's big, Kern."

"Say, Clark, do you suppose I could bring someone to see him? I mean, I don't care about him, but there's a girl…"

"Don't tell me you're getting action."

"No, Clark, just tell me. Could I bring the girl to see Kennedy? She's young, she might be impressed. I'll tell you about her later."

"All right, but you'd better show up early — around 10:30. He's due at 11. And tell her not to tell anyone, we don't want a big crowd."

"Thanks, Clark."

I hurried from the phone, looking for Eileen. There she was, in the lounge. The approach, ahem. The look up, yes? How are you doing, etc. Chat-chat. Start to leave. Oh, by the way, would you be interested in seeing Ted Kennedy? The Ted Kennedy? Yes, he's coming tomorrow, you know. It's a big deal, hush-hush. Police dogs, bombs. We don't want a crowd. But I work at the station, I can get you in. You might see him up close, exchange a few words.

Her face changed expression. The practiced *savoir-faire* vanished: she was impressed. Like a little girl offered a big cookie. Well, uh, tomorrow? Her lower lip pouted. I think it even trembled slightly. I felt sorry for her, lost interest entirely. The arrangements were made. It was simply a matter of finding the right fox to snare the juiciest grape.

In the morning it was drizzling. An excellent opportunity to wear a turtleneck sweater: all my other shirts have holes or buttons missing. Wolf was rushed through a short walk — he'd have to stay home today. I got Darwin up, performed my chores expertly, entertaining my boss with the story of my conquest. Then I arrived only a minute or two late for the rendezvous. Eileen was waiting, in a big fluffy blue and white sweater. Sorry, she had a paper to do. I looked at her: she had reconsidered, regretted her childish impressionability. O.K., I didn't care anyway.

At the station no one was stirring. I asked Teri, the secretary: "Aren't you excited about Kennedy coming here?" She wasn't, walked off to the head in big sloppy jeans. A station regular, wearing his usual garbage, hadn't even heard. He looked like he had slept in a dumpster. A third in attendance, who always wore a suit, piped up:

"It's not Ted Kennedy, it's his son."

I objected: Clark himself had told me. But something started sinking inside me. Where was Clark? Six minutes to eleven. Clark runs in the front door, goes straight to his office, refusing to speak to anyone. We hear him typing.

"Clark," I bang on the door. "Is it *the* Ted Kennedy, or Ted Kennedy Jr.?"

"Don't bother me," he shouts with a give-away laugh, "I've got to type these questions."

Two minutes to go, and he's typing the questions? Teri opens his door and tosses a book at him. He throws papers back at her; they start a playful wrestle. A small group of people is sighted outside of the window. The entourage: a woman in black, a light-skinned Negro with a camera, a curly-headed kid limping in baggy drawers. Clark bumps Teri out of the office, types some more while the front door is opened and the crew comes in. I'm the first person they see, and the curlyhead extends me a hand.

"Hi, I'm Ted Kennedy Jr."

Clark comes out, grabs me by the arm.

"C'mon, Gary, I know you're dying to do this."

We go back into the studio.

After the interview, I draw Clark aside.

"Clark, why in the world did you tell me? Don't you realize I invited a girl to come here? I'm just lucky she turned me down. God, suppose she had come and seen this kid instead of Ted Kennedy. I would have looked like a flaming..."

"Don't tell anyone," confided the station manager, "but up until the last moment, I thought it would be Ted Kennedy."

When I got back to my apartment, Wolfgang was waiting at the door to go out. He'd crapped and vomited on the floor. He's been feeling bad lately.

SIXTEEN

THE OLD WOMAN

olf bolted the moment I unleashed him, as though he had already been running. I screamed, clapped my hands and hobbled after him through the cacti and weeds up to the orchard. There it was peaceful: sun shining, birds twittering, hawk circling overhead. I would have liked to spend an hour walking around, but a man was lying in bed waiting. Wolf could be heard digging furiously under some dry leaves. I approached, and he looked up at me as though I were a stranger. He wanted to run, but the urge was too great: he returned to his digging. I clipped on the leash, he left unwillingly. I knew what he was thinking: I haven't run for a long time, I'm always chained up, stuck in the apartment. Things aren't the way they used to be, let me go, let me go! Or, more likely, since he's a dog, only the last words: let me go! Or, since he has no words, only a dumb urge.

I got back to my bike. We were late, no time to stop by this or that bush. Down the hill — not too fast, students were coming up the walkway. Naturally, they cannot master the logistics of man on bike with dog alongside: they consistently take the wrong tack, persistently aim between the bike and dog. Then they stop and look dumbfounded when the possibility occurs to them that they might not be able to pass through the chain. I roll the leash in my hand, draw Wolf right beside the bike and veer around them, while they ponder. But once I am behind them, the problem is removed, and they can proceed on their enlightened way. I, of course, must now pump with my full weight uphill, since I was not permitted to gain momentum downhill. Reaching the top, drawing deep breaths, I am delighted by the bug darting up the nostril and the midges diving in the water of my eyes as I swish down the slope toward the dorms. It means that things are in order.

Darwin has not been doing too well these days. The coordination between tasks, plans and bodily functions has become strained, like an old car beginning to give out at weak points. I examine the catheter: the adhesive tape is frayed, it will leak. I hear myself say the necessary words, against my wishes: "Looks like it'll have to be changed."

Antiseptic, white rubber glue, sticky strip – the legs spring up, the knees konk me on the side of the head.

"Whoa, there! Sorry, Gary."

"That's O.K."

I peel off the sticky strip, pull out the hairs stuck in the glue – it would make a feeling man howl. But this body has its own system – the knees spring up again, the feet dance madly in the air. I grab the legs with my right arm, press them down and, still restraining them, tend the penis with my left hand.

"Gary!" he warns.

The penis begins to urinate: I grab the night bucket – no, it's already full; there's an empty one – too late. Urine in the sheets, the legs spring up – I wrestle them down, hold the bucket in place. Now I must get tough: climbing up on the bed, I hold the knees down with my right knee, use both hands to tend the penis. The catheter is finally put on, the tube attached to the night jug, the scrotum and perineum washed with a warm cloth, the pants rolled up to the hips in a relatively dry spot of the bed. We rush to get the body to the chair. Swinging him over, I hear the hateful words: "I've got to go." (He can feel it a few moments in advance.) Quickly down in the chair, the tube – it's twisted, the catheter's swollen up like a balloon, urine's seeping out in his crotch. Back to the bed, legs kicking.

I hate this body. It's an ill-behaved bastard that opposes Darwin's attempts to live a decent life and my attempts to help him. Unthinking, inherently evil, it will permit him no certainty, embarrass him, try to rob him of dignity. Because of its insensitivity, he must enlist the aid of another, constantly testing his patience, spoiling his good will, wearing him down with every aggravation. But he can do nothing about it. Like the parent of an idiot child grown into a monster, he is forever chained to his mistake, which he cannot hide in a faraway room of an estate, but must take out with him everywhere and put on display – here, here is my horrible deformity! Look how it moves, look how it refuses to obey, look how it mocks all human life! And look, there behind it — the fool chained to it by necessity!

Pumping back — up, down, up, down. Wolf comes to a dead halt. I straddle my bike while he squeezes out a watery crap. Mail — bill from IBM, reminder from Princeton about $300 outstanding on the ten-year loan, junk. Coming in the door, I'm ravenous. No time for eggs, I spoon up the cereal: one bowl, two bowls, three bowls. These are the hands that splashed out the urine, held the retracting penis, cleaned up the bed. No matter, I'm hungry. I eat, poop too — it's life, human life. But, God, I'm sick of it. I wish there were something better.

Return trip: Wolf snapping at skittering lizards, students stymied, breath lost, bugs up the nose. Into Darwin's room, no time to spare: "Gary, could you check the catheter? I think it's leaking." No, it's all right — it must be all right. But the lenses are in the wrong eyes.

On the way to the cafeteria, we see an ad posted. Drew is looking for a summer attendant, free trip to N.Y. At the front desk, we notice a new display in the case opposite. Gay day. A bunch of posters, photographs of smiling ugly girls in sweat shirts, literature.

Darwin scoffs: "Say, fellow! You want to stop and look at all the nice things?"

I reply in kind: "Love to, but only after lunch."

Darwin executes a speedy right-angle turn and shoots through the automatic door, I limp along after. At lunch he eats heartily, I sip a coke. Later, when free, I return to the case. Everything's nice and neat: colorful headings, tasteful arrangement. As though it were about a group of artists, or a section of town, and not about guys who do certain things with each other. To my horror, I see that handicapped gay is represented: A red-purple poster of a man in a wheelchair from the neck down, with a memorable subscript in small white lettering: "It was harder for me to come out of the closet. I had to kick the door open to make room for the fuckin' wheelchair."

Now there's a touching sentiment: he's a normal homosexual who happens to be handicapped (*i.e.*, no different from you and me, 'cept that he's in a wheelchair), and he and his buddy (and the wheelchair) do the usual sort of thing in the closet, but because of unthinking discrimination against the disadvantaged he found it more difficult to make a public assertion of his legitimate sexual preference. Quads have a right to be gay too.

I stood wondering at the poster, which showed a muscular arm, tattooed as I recall, Levi's and cowboy boots. Macho cripple. He'd be a tough one to work for.

At supper Joyce greeted us with a sweet smile, the parallel lines of his face bending into deep dimples. He was happy, work was going well on his universal system of knowledge. This consisted, evidently, of word categories determined by linguistic-psychological criteria. I didn't expect much from it, but applauded the effort. Joyce is an original thinker, and the project, while ultimately worthless to mankind, or destined to be dropped after Joyce does more reading, will certainly develop his own thought. I mentioned Kant, of whom he was aware, and particularly W.T. Stace's book on Hegel, which includes a fold-out diagram of the entire system. It's an awesome experience, holding the origin and history of the universe in front of you, then folding it back up into the book. I don't recall that Hegel accounted for mistakes, or quads, but they could hardly upset the system. Joyce was delighted, promised to scout up the book. I figured it would ruin his endeavor.

The Little One promenaded by, on her way to the salad bar. She's divine, but likes to eat too. I look aside, but she draws my glance and gives me a warm, friendly smile. Well, I'll be damned, she does like me, after all. I get up and hurry up behind her.

"Say, Eileen, I wanted to tell you..."

She goes about her business, not turning her head. Cottage cheese, lettuce, a few carrot sticks. "About the other day, Eileen..."

She steadfastly ignores me. "It wasn't Ted Kennedy." She looks up sideways with a bored expression. "It was his son, Ted Kennedy Junior. You see..."

She walks off, back toward me. "That's nice," she says in a monotone.

Back at the table, I was furious. How could I have been such a fool? Why did I run up behind her? Why did I open myself to her adolescent *sang-froid?* I voiced these complaints to my comrades, and Joyce, discovering the nature of the problem, burst out: "Eileen? Is she the one you've been talking about? Don't you know about her? She's a bitch. She keeps five guys on the line at one time. One night she goes to one guy's room, another night to another's. She smiles at a guy, lays him and then, for no reason at all, stops smiling and stops laying. I've heard all about it from friends of mine."

"I only got the smile," I lament.

"Consider yourself lucky. If you'd been to bed with her, she could've hurt you more."

"Reminds me of someone I knew once, whom I also didn't lay. She'd make Eileen look like a tottler."

"Why does she do it?" Darwin asked.

"I think she has psychological problems. She's afraid to admit her latent Lesbianism. She really wants another woman, but she forces herself to have sex with men, then she's revulsed and seeks escape."

And with evident self-satisfaction he expounded this view to his captive audience. The Little One passed by once more and made her way out of the sexotorium, through the side door. I studiously avoided eye contact, and did so for the remainder of my term at the dorms. I can't say that she appeared deeply troubled.

Before parting with Joyce, I happened to mention Drew's ad. Joyce, who imagines himself a financial wizard and has many debts, was immediately interested: he'd love to spend the summer in New York and make money besides. He'd check to-morrow, he had a certain meeting tonight. To plan hall displays, no doubt.

My activity for the evening was also planned. The Shakespeare Plays, produced by the BBC with the money of Time-Life, would conclude the season with a performance of *The Tempest.* I had watched the preceding four plays on KCET and become intoxicated with Shakespeare's music. At the start of each it was hard to become attuned to the language, but after a while I would find my mind singing Elizabethan phrases, with long periods, balanced metaphors and jaunty turns. Perhaps my singing was all drunken blather, and on the following day my words, if I could have recalled them, would have sounded like the heroic drivel of Hercules films, with English dubbed over Serbo-Croatian, but while my critical faculty was drugged I heard glorious music.

Returning home, I fed Demon, took Wolf for a final walk in the fields, where he sniffed out weeds, ate them and vomited, then settled down to an evening of high imagination before the nighttime duty of reality. Both sets were plugged in – the defective and the dumpster – and the wires wound round the antennae outlets and run out the window: either set would give a clear picture or clear sound, not both together, so I resolved to watch Shakespeare on the defective and listen to him on the dumpster. With meticulous adjustment of knobs, wires and spark-producing things in the back — the cases of both sets were detached — I got a decent picture and clear sound. Next, I fixed myself a cup of tea, lit up a cigarette purchased with change from food stamps, stretched out my legs and anticipated joy. The familiar music came on, pseudo-renaissance by Sir William Walton, and I heard a scrape at the door. Nay, I must dispatch the unworthy intruder, the sober face at my poetic revel. I opened the door, and my heart sank. It was the old woman.

She lived nearby in the same apartment complex. Old, wrinkled face, big veiny hands, glazed eyes.

"Gary," her voice shook, "I was wondering if you have the paper I showed you."

"What paper?"

Some sounds were passing at the edge of my consciousness: *"Heigh, my hearts! Cheerly, cheerly, my hearts! Yare, yare!"*

"The one I showed you… you know."

"You mean the one I typed for you?"

"Yes, yes, that's the one," she hastened.

"Nay, good, be patient."

"I gave that back to you, remember?"

"When the sea is. Hence! What cares these roarers for the name of king? To cabin. Silence! Trouble us not."

"No," she fumbled, "I can't remember them."

"Remember them?"

"Find them, I mean."

She wanted company. Poor old thing, I had been neglecting her since starting work for Darwin. We used to stop and talk about the cats — Demon and the three left by a young couple who used to emit animal cries in the bathroom behind me; the old woman now fed them (the three cats). And, above all, I used to listen to her epic about lost millions and offer *ad hoc* legal advice. But now she had nothing but the cats, and they dumped all over her furniture. I stepped aside, and the old woman shuffled in, sat down at my desk.

"I have great comfort from this fellow: methinks he hath no drowning mark upon him; his complexion is perfect gallows. Stand fast, good Fate, to his hanging: make the rope of his destiny

our cable, for our own doth little advantage. If he be not born to be hanged, our case is miserable."

"What is this you're watching?"

"It's Shakespeare."

"Oh, I love *("Yare! Lower, lower!")* Shakespeare. I used to know all his plays *("A plague upon this howling!")* by heart. I mean, not really by heart *("Shall we give o'er and drown? Have you a mind to sink?"),* but Laurence, he was such a learned man, you know, and we loved Shakespeare *("Hang, cur! Hang, you whoreson, insolent noisemaker!"),* we lo-o-o-ved Shakespeare, both Laurence and I *("as leaky as an unstanched wench")."*

"Just a minute, I'm trying to hear."

"And we used to read Shakespeare, all the good things. Laurence, he was such a man, you couldn't find such a man today, you know."

I glared at her as she rattled on, but she was unaffected. She simply looked back with an innocent smile.

"Uh-huh," I forgave her.

"O-o-oh my, I should tell you, when I was a young girl, I loved Shakespeare, I knew all of his plays, well maybe not all."

I watched, gritting my teeth.

"Now I would give a thousand furlongs of sea for an acre of barren ground, long heath, brown furze, anything. The wills above be done! But I would fain die a dry death."

She dropped her keys. A big ring of keys to her apartment, her chest of drawers, her suitcases, her storage bins in Palm Springs, her dying white Cadillac parked in the back. She leaned over *("Oh, I have suffered"),* picked them up, but her fingers couldn't grasp them properly, and they fell with a crash again *("Dashed all to pieces").* She leaned over *("O, the cry"),* picked them up *("very heart"),* dropped them *("any god"),* leaned over *("sunk the sea"),* picked them up *("good ship"),* rattled them while trying to get a better grip on them *("fraughting souls"),* dropped them *("O, woe the day!"),* leaned over, picked them up.

I sat in bafflement. Alack for which the grasp of keys doth meddle with my thoughts.

She smiled blissfully, dropped the keys.

There was only one remedy.

"Sorry," I said, "I have to take Wolf out for a walk."

She stood up as I attached the leash (on Wolf), followed after me as I went through the door, which I closed on the uneven twins — the defective and dumpster TV's.

"'Tis far off and rather like a dream..."

Wolf crapped a bit more while I kept the old woman in my sights. She wandered around, looking for her apartment. Then stopped, looking for me. Finally, by hit and miss, she found her door and went in. I returned to my chair and watched with throbbing head. *Sans* music, *sans* bliss, *sans* sense.

Darwin dozed off during the bowel treatment. This offended me, though practically speaking there was no reason for him to stay awake. But on this night I had to turn him at 5 a.m., since Rutger had gone to visit his girlfriend's sick grandmother. (The second sick grandmother of late.) It was going on 1 a.m., I would get less than four hours sleep, so I thought Darwin should stay awake, like a passenger in a car when you are driving late at night. It's not fair for him to snooze.

On the way back, the streets were deserted. The lawns were all wet from the automatic sprinklers, the air fresh and thrilling. I pedalled up the sidewalk and saw the fox run out from the trees. She stopped in the street while I passed, not more than twenty yards distant, watched me. We considered one another. Then she slipped behind a bush and headed up to the orchard. A hard life, but free.

SEVENTEEN

THE MOST UNFORTUNATE PERSON ON EARTH

It was time to look to the end. Darwin received notification from the State government, which I fetched from his combination-lock mailbox, informing him that as a result of his interview some weeks previous he stood 13th in line for a position in environmental control. Not a bad ranking, but indefinite in respect to time. I dialed the number for him, and he tried to pin the bureaucrats down. They would not be pinned: he could expect a job in a week or a decade, after the preceding 12 slots had been filled. Whether each slot was filled by one man or twenty was not stated. So Darwin was left in a quandary: to move directly to Sacramento, there to set up an apartment and await further notice, or to make temporary home here in Riverside until the happy day. Brock, the burly fellow with the frontal ridge, had agreed to move with him to Sacramento, since he had a girlfriend up there. But should Darwin decide to stay here, he would need a new set-up, since all students had to leave the dorms at the end of June, or (with an extension) the end of July.

The thought occurred to me that he could move into the house, pay part of the rent and all of my salary. I would not have to pedal to his place five times a day, take him through the cafeteria line or put up with students. Get him up, make breakfast — the day should go easily. He would be right on hand should any problem arise, yet I could get away from him by setting up an office in the garage. Wolf could join the other dogs in the backyard, the girls could stay in the house and go to the same schools, I would not have to pound the pavement looking for work. In only a few months I could pay off my bills, while secretly, in the garage, I could type up my notes on quads into a publishable book. A book about no-book, something like that. The situation seemed ready-made: it even had the look of a literary conclusion. The only thing needed to make it work was a positive attitude, and Darwin had that. Should I sail the highs and lows of manic-depression, I could count on Darwin, the daily routine, to steady me.

And yet there was a grotesque twist to this finale. The home would be recovered, but without wife. In her place would be a man – the most reasonable, considerate man you could ever find, yet with certain needs, problems, a quad. My children and I rejoined at the kitchen table, and this man – polite, good-natured, a quad. It might be instructive, inspiring even, for them to see him overcome his handicap, but what would they think of their father – his healthy Siamese twin? And where would he sleep – in Kira's bed, or the forsaken connubial waterbed? Changing the catheter in a waterbed? Fighting spasticity? Better not think about it, as about other things. But when you pour poisons from your conscious mind, they pool in the unconscious.

After much hesitation, I mentioned the possibility to Darwin. He was excited, but by habit responded in a low key. "That would be a good arrangement. We could help each other out that way. I haven't lived in a house for a long time."

The final remark wrenched my heart, I wanted to set up a home for him. But I said: "It's not definite yet, my wife... well, there are problems."

Poor Jean, taking the blame. We left it at that. Darwin, with customary self-control, asked no more questions, save one: "What do your children think about it?"

I had asked them, and both thought it would be better than moving out – they didn't mind. But children say they understand when parents ask their forgiveness, then they live with the misunderstanding until it surfaces in later years. I told him they thought it was fine.

These days the routine was disrupted: Darwin had meetings with other grad students; they were preparing for the general exams. And there were special events. A luncheon was held in the faculty club for the university's handicapped students. Darwin went ahead while I had breakfast, so I entered the faculty club alone. The place was packed: professors in suits and lounging jackets busy piling plates on their trays, sitting down at tables, smoking pipes. I saw one of my former colleagues accepting a plate of meat with tomato sauce from a hand, another lifting a thick slab of chocolate cake.

They were at home, unashamed. Was I ever one of them? I looked at my shirt — two buttons missing. My stomach — no flab. No, never was. But once I was less fierce.

I joined Darwin in a side room. Wheelchairs were parked around a long rectangular table, with just enough room between them for the attendants. There were some familiar cases: Drew, Dolores, Tim, the tiny man with the swirled brown eyes, the big deaf woman from the cafeteria with a signing attendant, and also some new HC's. The trays of food were put in place and attacked in individual ways: by straw, by one's own fork, by another's.

The guest speaker arrived at the front of the table with the former university chancellor. She was a little woman, slightly deformed, wearing an expensive dress-suit and permanent curls. Her face was rouged, her lips sticked, her eyelashes mascared, possibly falsified. The former chancellor looked his usual self, only the grin was more ingratiating. He introduced the woman with unrelieved affability, as though addressing a kindergarten. The woman, we understood, had become a big-time lawyer, but before speaking she wanted those present to introduce themselves.

From her right, around the table, HC and aide pronounced their names with greater or lesser precision and identified the subject of their study. All these words, of course, served primarily to improve the mood, since they were instantly forgotten. When it came my turn, I said: "Gary Kern, defunct professor, no study." The chancellor knitted his brows: here obviously was a problem. But Darwin, and another, and another spoke with propriety, and the affability returned.

Now the little woman began to list her accomplishments: college, law school, law firm, appointments, etc. Lots of names, places, terminology — an impressive list. After the list, she stopped. Any questions?

The audience was enthusiastic. (Later, when I mentioned to Drew that she never really gave a speech, only a list of accomplishments, he replied: "That was all that was needed.") They asked her about discrimination. She said she had encountered more trouble as a woman than as a handicapped person: The men thought women were too emotional to become tough lawyers, but she showed them. They asked her about college. She told them about the difficulties of reading, typing. They asked about her private life. Not so private: she was presently getting divorced, had custody of her 13-month-old child; another man, she intimated, was waiting in the wings. They asked about her income. No exact figures, but big. And so it went: they did not hesitate to ask anything about her, and she did not hesitate to answer. It should have been uplifting, but I was thinking: A tiny little cripple, and she has a career, an income, a sex life and marital problems. Someone asked her how she took care of the child. She answered: live-in attendant. So someone takes care of her and babysits besides. All kinds of poop. What a life.

But there are worser fates. In sign-language class a discussion arose on the theme: Which would you rather be, blind or deaf? The teacher, Kathy, is sister to a deaf boy — hence her lifelong interest in Ameslan. She has a bizarre personality, with her enormous eyes and disjointed speech, as though she were handicapped, although she can hear perfectly. She has, moreover, that exaggerated facial expressiveness of mutes, which I find so affecting — we speaking, hearing clods have put on plaster casts. Kathy explained that most people would choose to be deaf, not because it is the lesser misfortune, but because its miseries are less apparent. The person deaf from birth will have trouble learning words, and without words thought is minimal. There are peculiar difficulties of perception, such as making the connection between moving the lips and affecting someone who is out of sight. And, as always, there is the problem of dealing with the non-handicapped: even when well-meaning they make wrong assumptions, do things that irritate, isolate you. Deafness, she repeated, is the invisible handicap. Still, some were not persuaded, preferred to see — friends, movies, sunsets. I couldn't make up my mind. Above all, I would not like to give up music. Not to hear Beethoven — who could stand that?

The discussion continued, we weren't doing much signing. Only at the beginning of each statement, then voice was needed. Kathy decided to finish off the session with a proof that "there is always someone more unfortunate than myself."

She said she remembered a certain case and always recalled it when feeling in the dumps. A woman she knew had a husband who fell while trying to fix the roof — he broke his back, a quad. The woman gave birth to a normal baby — whether conceived before or after the accident I didn't hear. The baby developed a tiny hole in its heart. The necessary

operation was not the most difficult, but it was botched —
certain machines were turned off too early. The baby wound up
deaf and blind. Kathy exclaimed, her big eyes widened, her
fingers turned out: Think of that poor woman with her poor
husband and poor child. She is the most unfortunate person on
earth. At first I was surprised — we should pity the man, who
was helpless, or the baby. But, no, Kathy was right — it's the
healthy wife who must bear it all, the other two in a sense are
exempt. And now, I imagine, she is no longer healthy.

Still, all is not misery. There are bright moments. The
forgetfulness of college, the cheery communal life. On my way
to Darwin's in the evenings I must pedal through the brigades
of merrymakers ranging over the hills, sweeping down on the
other team and pummelling it with water-filled balloons, carried
in satchels at the side. Sometimes they even hurl them down
from the top of Lothian Hall, the dormitory on the first hill,
ahead of Averdeen and Inverness, where Darwin resides. The
students also pull pranks, filling unlocked cars with trash or
millions of white styrofoam balls or furniture stuffing. Windows are soaped, shoestrings tied together. Rutger was busy in
the hallway, lugging away some guy's disassembled bed to hide.
All this hilarity belongs to Scot's Week, a year-end tradition at
UCR. The place, you will notice, is loaded with Scottish names,
no one knows why. It has nothing to do with reality.

EIGHTEEN

HE NEVER SAID A WORD

The crisis has passed. As Rah-Rah had predicted, the testicle slowly softened and subsided, though it remains rather red and larger than the other. The spongy material in the bedsore was a favorable sign: the sore is filling in and will someday be gone. The psoriasis has been driven back beyond the hairline, though it crops up of a morning in the eyebrows like small flying things that got caught. They are dispatched, but others will return. The scabs on the arm have healed, and the skin has been smoothed with emollients, but on occasion Darwin returns from the library with banged arms, rivulets of blood. The eyes are fine, the teeth. The abrasion above the penis has closed over, though the catheter still gives us trouble. Really, if it were not for the bowels and the bladder, there would be little trouble at all.

Rutger owed me a favor, and I had occasion to ask it immediately, since Priscilla was coming to L.A. and wanted me to see her. She had written weeks ago, and I had not seriously considered it, but a reminder came at a welcome moment. It might be relaxing to drive to L.A., to talk with someone in the Russian field. Her lecture would be missed, since I did not want to meet other professors, but I could see her afterwards and renew the old friendship. A somewhat peculiar friendship, since it thrives on short lively letters and feels threatened by rare, awkward meetings. We know each other well on paper, poorly in person. But, what the hell, I needed a break. Rutger agreed to do the afternoon chores, I borrowed the car, promised to pay for the gas and took off.

Naturally, I got lost in L.A., drove through Chinatown or Koreatown: everyone I asked for directions was a different Oriental nationality. But eventually I made it, met Priscilla at the home of her friend Selim, talked, ate, reminisced, listened to her complaints about the profession, shared some experiences

and impressions of recent weeks and, in general, had a good
time. I remember that on leaving I congratulated myself: yes,
this time I had not overtalked, I had listened, been moderate.
Driving back late at night, barely avoiding a fatal collision, I
returned in time for the Wednesday-night routine. The bowel
treatment was particularly difficult, since Darwin had not been
eating grainy things. Most of the feces were soft, hard to get
out, but when I figured there had been enough, I stopped.

The next day I paid for my slackness. Darwin informed
me, as I appeared for the lunch hour, that he thought he had
had an accident. No need to look: the smell confirmed it. But
the sight was distressing: yellowish brown fluid had drained
out of his seat and down on the top of the battery case. He
advised me to get him some lunch on a tray, since he was quite
hungry, and he could eat after the cleaning. I set the tray of
hamburger, fries, coke and chocolate frozen custard to the side,
on the boxes of catheter supplies, and considered logistics. The
best way, I told him, would be to get him out of the wheelchair
and straight into the shower chair, then go to the shower room,
where the pants could be removed and hosed, and he could be
given a bath. While I was washing him, the washing machines
in the cellar could be doing the week's load, including the pants.
Then he could return to the room, get dressed and have lunch,
while I cleaned the soiled rubber seat and straightened up the
shower room. The clothes could be dried, folded and put away
afterwards. That way he would have his Thursday-night
shower in advance (the shower had been moved back a night
since bowel treatment took so long), I would complete the
weekend wash in advance, and the chair and rubber seat would
receive a useful scrubbing. Not exactly a stroke of good luck,
but a minor triumph over adversity. He agreed.

There are certain aspects of that afternoon that I would
rather not relate. My approach in writing this account has been
to conceal nothing, reasoning that these are areas of human
concern that are indistinct, twilight, truthful. But the feel of
reality cannot always be transmitted in words, and some things
are so unsavory in human experience that they had best be
flushed down the omnivorous toilet of time.

I will describe only, as indicative of my side of the experience, the cleaning of the rubber cushion. This is an inflatable
contraption, made of durable black rubber; one side is flat like
a mat, the other composed of eight rows, if memory serves

correctly, of twelve bulbs each, standing up like elongated eggs. When placed on the seat of the wheelchair, the cushion juts up the rows of bulbs firmly, yet gives way at individual points to body pressure. It is most comfortable to sit upon, as I learned one morning when I tried it, but when removed flaps open in rows like underwater polyps, anemones or sponges, and when you hold one spot it flip-flops every which way. Now picture to yourself such a device covered with brown fluid: yes, you carry it as best you can, hose it off, but you must clean between the rows, around each bulb, and the ninety-six or so bulbs are waving and rolling, and you're in a hurry. I won't elaborate: imagine not me, with my hands, but you, with yours.

Darwin's side was hardly more enviable. He felt embarrassed, though it was surely not his fault; he could even have blamed me for insufficient diligence the night before. But human relations do not work that way, and he apologized more than once. I told him: "Don't worry about it, it could happen to anyone. Everyone, at some time or another, drops a load in his pants." He wasn't cheered, but withstood all the indignities and in time found himself cleaned and dressed. At this point he asked, to my surprise, that I put on his plastic desk, which I did. He grabbed a couple mouthfuls of hamburger, drained the coke, swivelled around and took off.

"Where are you going?" I hastened to ask.

"I've got a final exam."

"Really? When does it start?"

"About a half-hour ago."

"Why didn't you tell me? I would have…" Though to tell the truth, I could not have moved any quicker.

"That's all right."

And he sped away — the outside door was propped open. I stood in his room in amazement. Just think, he never said a word. He patiently endured every minute of hoisting, washing, drying, dressing — the entire encyclopedia of procedures, knowing that the exam was beginning and he would be late. Hunger was tormenting him, since he doesn't eat breakfast, and yet he showed no concern. He would be at a disadvantage if given the exam a half-hour in advance, but now he would have to start forty-five minutes after everyone else. But not a word crossed his lips: he knew I was doing my best. I picked up the carton of melted custard, sipped it. He's quite a guy.

That night, in the final sign-language class, Kathy signed a song in time to a record. John Denver singing "Sunshine Always Makes Me High." I don't like Denver, consider the song mawkish, yet the great expressiveness of sign language and the big strange eyes of the teacher held me transfixed. For some reason she kept her eyes on me a long time, and I was sorely disturbed and wanted to cry. Fortunately, the music stopped, and with it the signing: I reverted to protective cynicism.

During the final parting, Marcia asked me if I would be working the summer. Her husband, Ron, might be needing a morning attendant — $150 per month. The girl who was working for them was "beginning to burn out." Evidently this happens to attendants, they have to be rotated.

I said I didn't know, took down the address. Of course, I recognized the literary potential. I could move to another quad, one with superhuman determination, become involved in his program, listen to his theories, share his contempt for the medical profession. But, on second thought, why get mixed up with quads at all?

At bedtime, while tending Darwin, I must have said something about rehabilitation, and he recalled a detail from his own story. When he first lay paralyzed in the hospital, he did not understand the extent of his injury. He asked the doctor if he would be well enough in a couple of months to go out for the football team. The doctor wisely told him they would have to wait and see. After two years, he knew he was not leaving the chair. Then another doctor told him.

"You've got as much mobility as you'll ever have for the rest of your life," the doctor stated, "now let's see what ways we can use that mobility to best advantage."

Darwin was grateful to both doctors: the first because he did not want to shock the hopeful young boy, the second because he took a positive approach. Other doctors, he knew, were less feeling. They told the injured person right off: "You'll never walk again. Face it."

There's a photo of Darwin in his top desk drawer, which I've come across several times while getting typing supplies. It's in color, slightly blurred. A wasted, sickly looking boy sits in a wheelchair, hunched forward, wearing green jeans — the kind with straps over the shoulders. His eyes are closed; he blinked when the camera clicked. He's smiling.

NINETEEN

THE NEW QUAD

On a bright. sunny afternoon, as though life were placid and without cares, Darwin came to see the house. Jean was at work, the girls at school. The back door had been left unlocked for me. I tilted back the chair and, with the help of Suzanne, the student van driver from Special Services, heaved it through the front door. The three of us roamed the house, they like visitors, I like a foreigner. Darwin liked the place. Kira's room was large; we could get most of his things into it. The shower was equipped with a detachable sprinkler; we could both fit into the stall. The halls were narrow, but he could manage them with deft turns. The garage was encumbered with boxes of Russian books, but there was still ample room for his spare wheelchair, half-sized refrigerator and supplies, not to mention my desk. Only a short ramp would have to be built at the front door, and perhaps another one over the step of the shower stall. I plunked the baby grand piano for the two, a gift from the grandparents for Kira. In this new room he would be able to hear her practice Beethoven; she might even play for him sometimes.

That is, if he moved in. At the freezer I stopped and joked: "You see, I used to own things like this. I was once a man too."

Darwin rejoined, not missing a beat: "Aren't you a man now?"

We laughed. But I had to be careful not to show my indecision. I didn't want to set him up for a letdown. Besides, it was still quite possible we would continue together. There was no time to look for another job; both Darwin and I had to move out of our apartments on the same day. He — because of university policy, I — to escape another month's rent. Also the dog fee, which I had never quite paid. I'd have to slip out at night. To complicate matters, Jean kept delaying the date of her moving: she had a special date in mind. Nevertheless, things would be simpler if I moved into the house with Darwin, reaping all the financial, occupational and psychological security he would bring.

But emotionally I was a fast burner. The signs appeared before my eyes as though produced by somebody else. I would see myself grab his legs and force them down in the bed, actually fight with them. I would throw swabs, soiled catheter across the room at the trash can, pick them up off the floor later. Giving him the pills, I would pronounce not their names, but the initials. Once I spelled S (septra), C (vitamin C), U (urocholine), M (mandelamine). We thought it funny, but I was becoming tactless. There were audible signs as well. I would hear myself curse at the spilled night jug, the twisted pant leg, if not yet at a part of the body. Perhaps in the house, with more sleep, more control of the situation, I would relax, and my nervous spasms would cease like scratched itches. But then there were deeper spasms I couldn't quite scratch: my dreams.

They didn't shock me awake like bloodcurdling nightmares, merely left me uneasy, as if I had misplaced something sickening. When this sensation became conscious, usually late in the morning, bits and pieces of images would surface — the flotsam of a dream, which I would try to fit together. The first reconstruction struck me as amusing.

> *Some sort of race is going on. A wheelchair sits empty to the side. I must drag myself on the ground: my legs are broken. I curl my fingers into the grass, pull my body forward: it's too slow. Other bodies are moving past me, dressed in track uniforms. Shiny cars swish past me on both sides, professors behind the steering wheels. The race is proceeding around the world. The first cross-continental race for cripples.*

Well, my unconscious mind was a plagiarist. I think I even saw Gig Young in the dream running up and down by a rope on the sidelines, exhorting the struggling cripples. And it was a cute touch to put the professors in their cars: they would never get out and crawl.

The next dream, though grisly, was still not alarming. I dreamed I was going bald.

Now why should I dream this? Was Clark involved — his
mania about baldness, our jokes? No, this was more serious — an
acceptance. The next dream gave away the secret: there was
no way to put a funny face on it. The pieces came back to me
in the evening as I splashed my burning eyes in the bathroom
and looked into the mirror.

Crippled legs, thinning hair, facial bedsores: I was turning
into Darwin. I was becoming a quad.

TWENTY

A REAL LETTER

$\mathcal{A}$mong the bills and junk mail I discovered a real letter — from Priscilla. This would be a treat: she would recall our meeting and relate her further adventures in California and her trip east. I finished breakfast, fixed myself a cup of strong coffee, got comfortable in my armchair, lit up a cigarette and opened the envelope. I read:

Dear Gary,

I am very glad I saw you last week. And I must tell you that you frightened me. You are leading a terribly strenuous life, both physically and emotionally. Somehow it wasn't possible to say this to you when I saw you, I was too busy listening and trying to understand what is going on with you. Afterwards I talked with Selim a bit about my impressions and he confirmed them, and so I make so bold as to convey them to you. I hope you know that what I am going to say comes from affection and concern for you.

You seem to be so strained by all the hard things you've been through that your sense of reality (whatever that is) is shaky. If you want what I took as evidence, I can cite first that living alone so much has made you come in and talk for almost 5 hours straight with little interaction with us. That's understandable and possibly within the realm of "healthy" or whatever, but your story about the old lady in itself seemed as strangely out of touch as the old lady herself. And your relationship to the quadriplegic(s) too is disturbing, and I don't mean your idea that they're better off dead, but your in tense, ambivalent involvement (revulsion, sympathy, dependence, fear, I don't know, all mixed up).

No doubt you have reasons for each individual remark. Nonetheless the total impression remains, and it's not just mine.

Therefore I am seriously alarmed by what you are proposing to take on: moving in with two children and one quad is making a large responsibility rest on your shoulders all alone. It will take most of your time, you will not be able to do your own work, you will not have enough money, you will wear yourself out physically and emotionally. I think you are headed for a breakdown...

Naturally, I laughed through all this. Priscilla was reacting all at once to a situation to which I had become accustomed stage by stage. Her remark about my verborrhea — this was particularly funny; she had forgotten that once I warm up to an idea there's no stopping me. As for reality, her advice was far off the mark:

Rest. And then start looking for academic jobs in the east. If you need money for transportation, I'll loan you some... Talk about it with Jean, get her view of it. Or even with Selim if that appeals to you. But get some help from somewhere — you've been going it alone too long.

Didn't she know there were no jobs? The door had closed on Russian literature a long time ago. American literature too, for that matter. And did she have any conception of the cost of moving? The problems of storage, transportation, Wolfgang? I read over her letter, chuckling to myself. It was sweet of her, but she was simply out of it. One of the professors — better than most, but sequestered from bitter reality.

There was one item, though. How could I have left that impression and not known it? I distinctly recall thinking I had been reserved. Could it be I was so wrapped up in my thoughts that I failed to detect the reactions of others? I was talking, talking, and they were wondering about me, perhaps exchanging glances, and I didn't see a thing. Was I blind? Stupid? Nuts?

The answer must wait: time to go.

TWENTY-ONE

TO EACH HIS OWN

've got to get out. There are too many quads, too many people tending quads, too many coincidences involving quads.

One girl in the cafeteria, whose face is twisted by scar tissue, while visiting Darwin, repeatedly calls me Drew. I correct her, and she replies: "I don't know why, I keep thinking your name is Drew." What am I to say, how can I object? The link is made in her mind, so it will do no good to skip and jump and say, "Look, look, I'm not a quad!"

I talk to another girl, someone I just met, mention my job, and she says: "My boyfriend worked for a quad. It was terrible. He got high on LSD and left her out in the sun. She burned up." I don't even ask for the details: Did the woman get sunburn or were ashes found in the chair?

Mona tells me: "I worked for a paraplegic. But only a short time. I couldn't stand him giving me orders."

Everyone has worked for a quad, known a quad, known someone who worked for a quad. I phone a friend from Princeton: he's not teaching, but doing well, selling stocks and bonds; he has an 800 number. A business voice answers and tells me Lew has had a heart attack, he's lying paralyzed in bed. Another friend writes: Bell's palsy, one side of the face won't move. My own brother in D.C. must take time off: his bad back has incapacitated him, he's wearing a brace. Everyone's a quad, going to be a quad, quaddity is sweeping the nation.

I need advice, talk to my few friends, to acquaintances. Give them the pros and cons.

The pros: Darwin will pay rent, provide a job, instruct the girls in a unique way. Yes, that's true, my advisor agrees. I will be able to type, translate, even write. Yes, that's true. I will have the satisfaction of making a home for Darwin, enriching his life, while helping him with the necessities. Yes, indeed, that's true.

But the cons: I may get stuck in the job — for many years, for a lifetime. You can't find a new attendant quickly, especially outside the university. I would never return to the profession, I would never lead a normal life. Yes, that's true. Any my children — they may like him, but emotionally they may not understand. Why should they require this lesson in courage, why must they see their father in this role? And what about new sicknesses, new physical problems? I like the guy. Could I watch him deteriorate, undergo operations? That's true, it's tough.

So what do you think? Should I go ahead with my plans and be glad I can pay the rent? Or make the break now while I can and give myself up to uncertainty? Gee, I don't know. What do you think?

Advisors are no good — Sartre was right about that. You can lead them wherever you want. Because ultimately they do not give advice, only words. They believe it is wrong to state an opinion and stand behind it; you yourself must decide. This is called responsibility, actually it's non-involvement. Yet Priscilla...

No, I must decide, weigh the pros and cons, balance the present against the future pain. I agonize over it, but not too long — there isn't enough time. I balance, balance, throw over the scales. To hell with the horoscope, my Libra sign. The only question is this: Would I feel relief if Darwin didn't come, would there be hope? The answer is yes. And would I feel a burden if he did come, would hope be removed to the future? The answer is yes. Therefore: away with all quads, away with sympathy! Quaddity is none of my business!

But how can I tell Darwin? He thinks he's coming. His mind has been relieved, he's finished his final exams without worry. I have a few days before the cut-off date we set, but entering his room I hear him on the phone. He's talking to Brock, and Brock is apparently saying that he will not go to Sacramento. Darwin happily releases him; I put the receiver on the hook.

What's up, I ask. Darwin replies that Brock has applied to work for Tim. Another quad on the scene, I should have known. Brock expects a call from Tim tomorrow, and if asked will accept the job.

"But Darwin," I say, "we agreed to decide at the end of the week."

He cocks up his eyebrows like a wise old bird: "Oh," he almost laughs, "is there a problem?"

C'mon, Jean, help me out one last time. "Well, Darwin, I'm sorry, but..." I hold off the irrevocable no, but things are turned around.

The next day Brock is left a message: Darwin may want him after all. Tim has not yet phoned. At lunch I tell Darwin that I am forced to think long-term for my daughters: he may move in, and then be called to Sacramento; I would have to help him move, get set up there, meanwhile leaving the girls and paying rent in Riverside. And it happens there are two positions opening up at the library that require a knowledge of foreign languages, including a little Russian. It's a terrible choice to make, but since Brock is available now... Darwin listens reasonably, agrees. He will extend his stay in the dorms and ask Brock to work for him. If at the end of that time I have not found a job, we may go ahead with our plan. I think this is an excellent solution: I will get a rest in any event, and with a healthier attitude I may welcome him into the house.

At supper Darwin gives me the news: he reached Brock and hired him. Tim never phoned, and he might be mad when he finds out, but that's his tough luck. He dawdled, Darwin seized the day. We explain it all to Joyce, who is sitting with us, dabbing at a meringue pie. And what about his application to Drew, how did it go? Joyce smiles dimples and says Drew prefers female attendants.

"Why?" I ask.

"He just does."

"So what are you going to do?"

"I've got another job. I'm going to work as an attendant for Garry."

By sound, I am unable to distinguish: Is this the quad Gary, or the quad Garry? Joyce informs me it is the second, the one with two r's.

"Then you mean Gar-r-r-ry," I say. "You must pronounce the difference between one *r* and two."

"Gar-r-r-ry," he repeats. As a linguist he thinks this is proper. On the way back to his room, Darwin remarks: "I wonder if Garry knows about Joyce."

"I guess not," I say. "I doubt Joyce would mention it."

"Well, I suppose it doesn't make any difference, but it would give me a creepy feeling."

"I suppose so. But you're not going to tell Garry, are you?"

"No, I wouldn't do that. It's his business."

"And what about Drew, preferring female attendants. Why do you think?"

"I don't know, some quads do."

"And you?"

"It would feel funny."

To each his own.

TWENTY-TWO

FINALES

Graduation day. Darwin gets dressed in a new blue suit, sent from Oklahoma. A crisp white shirt (with slits sewn under the arms by his mother), creased slacks, a grey vest, a jacket, matching blue socks. Rutger is summoned to put the knot in the tie, since I never wear one. We go down the hall for brunch (it's Sunday), the students all remark: "Looking sharp, Darwin!" "Congratulations, Darwin!"

Some of the environmentalists confer on the order of ceremony: "Which number are we?" They muse over the professor's final ploy: After the final exams, when grades were in, graduation numbers assigned, the good professor was assailed by doubt. He called in each student for a one-hour oral exam, just to make sure. Probably he was having a minor breakdown; I've had little collapses at year's end, when students leave and you feel four years older. We enjoy a huge brunch: granola, raisin toast, apple strudel, orange juice, a chili omelette for Darwin. The Little One is nowhere to be seen. So who's looking?

There will be no accident today: Darwin's safe. As for the leg bag, he's had a new gadget installed. The tube beneath the bag is now squeezed off, not by a plastic clamp, which I must attend, but by an automatic clamp below the foot rest. Darwin can stop by the shrubbery, the tended flower beds, flick a little switch at the front of his arm rest, and water the university soil. He's delighted with this: one more piece of independence, pride. Making the most of the mobility he has. I am no longer needed for the 3 o'clock check. If only he had gotten it sooner!

It's a terrifically hot day. The temperature will exceed 100 degrees, but fortunately the smog has not blown in from L.A. On some days you can see it from the mountains: a blue-grey shroud rolling into the valley, covering the houses, closing off the background, then the foreground. Darwin cannot sweat, he suffers badly from the heat, but today is a special day, and he plans to do it proud. Rutger and I drape the philosophical gown over him, tucking it into the sides of the chair and hooking it at the back. And over this — some sort of ceremonial hood, an odd-shaped thing with blue velvet and gold silk. We set on the black rectangular cap, toss the tassel to the side. There he sits, a scholar. He's done it all — taken the classes, the books, the tests. Mastered them all. A Master of Science. A Master of Self.

"Did you wear the cap and gown at your graduation?"

"No," I answer, "I called in sick."

"Didn't like the ceremony, eh?"

"Hated it."

Darwin wants some pictures for his relatives. We get out the Polaroid One-Step, load it up. Outside the dorms, in the blazing sun, we take pictures, one after another. Darwin alone, coming out the door. Darwin alone, in front of the concrete bench (where lovers sit at night). Darwin with Larry, who helped him through exams: a sincere, studious guy with glasses and a black handlebar moustache; old jeans and crusty boots stick out under the gown. He is one of the few who talk to Darwin without a special tone. Darwin and I, taken by Rutger: I look skinny, ragged, heavy shadows in my cheeks. My unaccustomed white shirt hangs limply. Darwin and Rutger, taken by me. The photos lie across the other concrete bench, dry in the sun.

The day moves swiftly, we proceed to the campus. Darwin in chair, I on bike. People milling around with hotdogs in their chops, papers in their hands. Tables with letters written on paper squares, stuck up high on a pole. Lines of students, wearing one-time finery or the usual rags. Like a medieval pageant, or a Bulgarian bazaar. Despite centuries, the university can find no better way to do things. Darwin asks this person, that. Stops by friends in wheelchairs. Introduces me to his advisor: "Dean So and So, this is Dr. Gary Kern."

The dean winces as though receiving a low-voltage shock.

"Why did you do that?" I ask afterwards.

"I couldn't resist," Darwin explains. "The dean has only an M.A."

I see professors, former colleagues, students I have known, pretty girls I have admired, guys from the radio station. They're all here: the fuddy-duddy parents, the fidgety younger brothers and sisters, the squawking babies, even a few loose dogs running around and pissing on the pillars. God, I hate society!

The sweat is pouring off me, Darwin is probably expiring, but he finds his place in line, and the line inches forward. I go off to the side, Polaroid in hand. My assignment: get some good shots. I station myself outside of the ropes; inside, the throngs of spectators fill up the folding chairs. *Pomp and Circumstance.* Edward Elgar was a consummate musician, no question, but so British you could die from *rigor mortis.* Whoever decreed that we must suffer him periodically throughout our lives? Why not some outrageous tune by Charles Ives — or electronic music, or the theme from *Star Wars,* Kiss, disco, since that's what the students prefer? Why not the Coca-Cola song, *Reach Out and Touch Someone,* the music for hemorrhoidal suppositories? But no, it's *Pomp and Circumstance* — again and again, as the young seekers after truth file in.

There's Darwin. *Snap.* Move over here. *Snap.*
"Hey, you can't come inside the ropes!"
"Just a minute." *Snap.*
"I said..."
Brainless jerk. *Snap.*
"If you do it, everyone will want to do it."
"Yeah, sure, and if you eat shit, everyone will want to do that too. We'll have no more pollution."
I duck behind the ropes. Four shots, two may be good. Now some stuffed shirt blows into the mike. The hardcore boredom commences.

After a few speeches, I can stand no more. I've got to get out. Where's Rutger? Like a death ray, with an unerring sensor, I hone in on Rutger. Through the lines of rickety chairs, the fat ladies, the fancied-up hicks, the big-time bankers, the honorable Japanese, Arabs and Jews with prurient teenyboppers displaying pubescent wares, I spy the face of Adolf Hitler, accidentally blond. Here, here, Rutger, I've got to go, could you take the rest of the shots? Sure, Gary, no problem. He's really a good guy, he doesn't look anything like Adolf Hitler. It's just me. God, let me out! Everyone here is insane! There's the bike, away, away! The quad full of celebrant noisemakers pushes farther and farther behind me.

I stop at the station, do some splices on my tapes. The broadcasts have been spoiled a couple more times by dumb engineers, I don't even listen anymore. But I've got to do something to settle my nerves. It's an uneasy feeling: everything is ending. I want it to end, but while it's present it's solid. I turn out the overhead light, sit in the cubbyhole with only the light from the Revox, start a tape.

Shostakovich recalls the painter Kustodiev — he had sarcoma of the spine; a growth was removed on the fourth operation, but only after the local anesthetic had worn off. Kustodiev maneuvered his wheelchair with ease; he used a special device to tilt the canvas so he could reach it with his brush. Sometimes Kustodiev gritted his teeth from the pain, and his face divided sharply in two: red and white. It's no surprise I hear about Kustodiev; if I picked up a book of physics the pages would fall open to Steinmetz. Even so, the sound of my own voice, rubbed over by buffers, soothes me. It assures me that someone exists who is I, someone who will go on.

In the evening, a free concert. Bach's *St. Matthew Passion* concludes the academic year. I can attend since Rutger will take Darwin to the *Bull and Mouth* (no cafeteria service tonight). Jean drops off the girls, we walk to the auditorium. The choir fills in the stands from both sides of the stage, back rows to front. They remain standing in their blue robes while, from the left side, two wheelchairs roll in: two handicapped women, also in blue robes. One of them I recognize: It's Dolores, who loves Wolf. Professor Reynolds enters to warm applause, raises his hands.

The music begins: the orchestral prelude. As usual, the university strings sound a bit thin, even though beefed up with older musicians hired from outside. Now the chorus enters, the long lilting lines of male and female voices intermingling. "Come, ye daughters, share my wailing…" The hall is filled with rich human voices, all are singing, singing, the organ joins in. The girls sit up and take notice. The faces of the students lose their daily appearance, take on an expression of time; each individual face acquires a general significance, becomes a representative of all mankind. The rows sway with each new wave of sound. And to the side, I see them: the two figures in wheelchairs, lifting up their voices, joining in the praise of the Lord. How wrong I am, how wicked! Now I can see, now I can hear. All are the same, all belong to each other, united in harmony and love.

But later, I have my duty: to show Brock the technique, as Rutger once showed me. I go about it matter-of-factly; Darwin endures in silence. Brock, though, is not a model of tact, he asks: "Can't you feel that?" Darwin shakes his head no. I continue the process, which goes fairly well. Brock seems impatient, watches the TV. Rockford is sassing a bully.

Finally, when I'm finished, Brock comments: "Well, I guess, it's not so bad, if you have the TV on." Delicacy, perhaps, stands in inverse proportion to one's frontal ridge. Next week, though, I plan to watch Rockford in luxury. I'll buy an imported beer, light a cigarette and lean back in my leather recliner. The dud and dumpster sets will be ditched in the garage; I'll be watching the sharp-focus trinitron purchased in my former life. And the rest of the world can go by.

TWENTY-THREE

NOTHING EVER DIES

Out, out – out of the apartment! Chairs, trash cans, light bulbs, stolen spoons, broken TV's, repaired typewriter, cinder blocks, boards, books, books, books! All of them – out through the door, into the car, away through the night and into the garage. After Jean moves out, I'll straighten things up. Trip after trip – even the great slab of office desk is shoved into the hatchback and hauled away. The battered old chair – one more night, then off to the dumpster. Heartless I am: I sit in it for months, take the best support of its life, save it for one last night, then chuck it away. But don't blame me – blame the cats who have loved it. Somewhere out in the junk-pile it will find new friends – bugs, rats, termites. Birds will take bits of fluff for nests, spiders will build webs between the springs – nothing ever dies, it just gets rearranged. And for the landlord, who raised the rent, never heated the pool and left big lumps of dog poop – not Wolf's! – on the walkway in front of my door – an empty apartment with balls of hair, ten thousand cockroaches and newspapers scrunched up in the bathroom. Go rip a dog fee off some other sucker. *Quid pro quo*, fink!

The next morning – farewell to the chair. I go out on my bike, call Demon in the fields. He comes skipping down over the weeds. Nuzzles up to Wolfgang. I take the pillowcase out of the basket, stoop down to pick him up. No, he's alert to the situation, skits away. I call him back coaxingly, plunge him headfirst into the pillowcase. He comes out the other end, claws slicing through the cloth like the proverbial knife through butter. He's wild, he wants to stay. The fields are home, the scraps are supper, the fleas and Nathaniel are life's impediments. I understand the feeling, let him go. Pedal back to the house, Wolfgang trotting at my side.

Jean has finished packing. Time to say farewell. Jean and Lara get in the car: Lara will spend the summer in San Diego, then return before the start of school. Did I get the divorce papers, inquires Jean. Yes, they arrived. Now she becomes emotional, as befits the moment before a new beginning. She thinks she's doing the right thing. And I should find a job — a real job, do my little bit to make the world a better place. And to help my self-esteem. I've got loads of that, I tell her, and to hell with the world. She thanks me anyway for going along with her plans. Perhaps she realizes these months have cost me something, though she doesn't suspect the act of penance. The Pinto rolls down the driveway, we wave. Kira and I go in the house, fix a big breakfast. Now what? Unpacking, lifting boxes, arranging books. Putting up Pushkin, still striding. Busy work.

A day or so passes. I give Darwin a call. No answer. Well, that's all right. After supper I call again. Still no answer. Better check on Demon, I should each day. I pedal over to the old place, leaving Wolf in the yard. The old woman's lights are not on. I knock. No answer. Knock again. A muffled sound. I try the door, it's open. I walk in. The old woman is sitting in her chair, the TV is playing a program in Japanese. I change the channel for her, ask her how she's doing. She can't move. She's starving, but too weak to go to the fridge. I look in the fridge: bottles of vitamins, soya powder, oysters. Nothing to eat. The cats are running over the floor, over the satin couch. New piles of poop, still wet.

"Oh, I'd love some ice cream!" the old woman says. "If only I could have some ice cream!"

I ask her when she last ate. She can't remember. Would she like anything else?

"Yes, a hamburger, a hamburger!"

I check my wallet: three bucks. O.K. I ride over to the new restaurant, just across from the phones. Gala opening: two or three people sitting in the booths. The waitresses swish down on me: Can I take your order? They're hungrier than the old woman. I look at the menu: no wonder. Sky-high prices. A hamburger — $1.75, a donut — 40¢, a glass of milk — 70¢. I can't afford the ice cream.

I transport the neat white paper bag to the old woman's apartment, fold it out on the table beside her. She's delighted: her wrinkled old mouth wraps around the food, moves it around in circles, a big lump goes down her throat. She sips the milk:

it drains like water into sand. I check her phone: dead. Better go over. The old lady is left munching.

Up, down, up, down — this must be the last time. The dorm is locked. I don't have the key anymore. It's starting to rain. I take my bike around to Darwin's window. All the other windows are black: Darwin's alone is lit. I see Darwin in the chair, Brock standing behind, leaning his rump against the desk. They're watching TV. I rap on the window, catching the streams of water from the roof. (Someday drainpipes will come to California, probably as a fad.) Brock cranks open the window: he will let me in.

The halls are deserted: all the students are gone. The floors are filled with rubbish from Scot's Week, parties.

Darwin is glad to see me. We exchange some jokes. I tell him about the phone.

"They've all been disconnected," he informs me. "I spoke to the telephone company, and they said my phone would be live. But I guess they couldn't manage it."

"What's the matter?" asks Brock, none too gently. "Did you think I'd left Darwin?"

"No," I invent, "I thought you might have gone out for hamburgers, and your car might have broken down."

"It was nice of you to come by," says Darwin.

We chat a bit. Brock, it turns out, got secretly married. The girl from Sacramento will be coming down to Riverside, they will live in the next room. Brock told the father over the phone: that's the way it is, take it or leave it. Later in the summer, man, wife and quad will move into an apartment.

Well, it's getting late, almost time for bed. I feel like reaching for the medicines, but restrain the impulse. With a farewell glance at Darwin, a nod, I leave. Pedal through the rain.

Back home, I reflect. The job was probably a stroke of good luck for Brock. He won't be pestered by sensitive feelings. He won't have bad dreams, or if he does he'll lose them. He's the better man for the job. I did what I was hired to do: to get Darwin through finals. Beyond that, I have other plans. Darwin will have to take care of himself, and there's a good chance he'll succeed. Good luck, Darwin.

Out of curiosity, I pick up the newspaper. I don't intend to go job-hunting right away, but for old time's sake I look through the ads. Accountant, administrator — the same old business.

But suddenly I stop: it can't be! I check the date of the paper,
picked up at the station. Yes, yesterday's. But there it is, the
same as before:

AIDE WANTED

For Quadriplegic. Experience
preferred. Must be reliable.
Good pay.   Must be able to
drive.   Call 735...

The ad has been running daily, no doubt.

TWENTY-FOUR

SISYPHUS

A few people to whom I have mentioned my experience have been reminded of Sisyphus. Indeed, the labors are similar. The quad must get up every morning, heave the stone of his body, only not with his hands – with his mind. True, he has helpers, but they must be manipulated, only not with the fingers – with words. The body, heavy as a boulder, constantly slips downward, opposing the straps, the pumps, the salves, the pills, the crunchy cereals, the booties, the tubes, the glues, the rubbers, the scratchings, the scrubbings, the specially made clothes. It slips downward and, unlike the boulder, opposes not only the mover but sometimes the force of gravity as well. Sudden twitchings, tremblings, leapings, flailings change the course of direction, overturn the mind's understanding.

Still, the quad has something not permitted to Sisyphus: mechanical contrivances. Strapped in the chair, empowered with a motor and steering device, the quad would seem to have conquered the stone: he can rest and propel it through automatic doors. But the burden remains: the body may be straining the heart, the lungs, absorbing heat, mixing poisons, while the intelligence above it loses the struggle without even knowing. Sisyphus, as Camus reminds us, was punished for his flippancy toward the gods, tattling on Zeus and putting Death in chains. He mocked the metaphysical set-up, and when finally laid low he tricked Pluto into letting him return to the earth, from which Hermes retrieved him and led him back down below, where his special torture awaited. So too the quad, upon breaking his neck, contrives to escape Pluto's clutches and live above earth, because he still loves life. And above earth he lives, only with the same punishment: to push the boulder: the dead, resistent weight of his own declining body.

Actually, the quad's punishment is more severe. Sisyphus, being the craftiest of men, the father of Odysseus by some accounts, can easily find loopholes in the system. Odysseus sees him in Hades shoving the rock to the top of the hill, straining to push it over the summit and standing by helpless as it tumbles back down to the bottom, then returning to the damned thing and getting it moving again. But after Odysseus has left perhaps he has a breather: he can let the thing slip away from him half-way up the hill, walk back down at his own pace, sometimes quickly, sometimes slowly. He can measure his steps, count them, keep time, tease the summit. It's all mad, of course, but he has certain freedoms. At least, as Camus boldly declares, he has the freedom of contempt: "There is no fate that cannot be surmounted by scorn."

But the quad? He has no breather — his lungs do not generate sufficient air. There is no respite for him, no moment's reprieve from the body: he's stuck with it, the boulder is he, and even in his sleep (in Darwin's case, at least) he cannot measure his steps. There is no summit for him to attain, no tantalizing chance to throw off the load. The hillside is perpendicular, and it's infinite. Darwin can cut jokes about medicines, scold his disobedient legs; but he does not win pride by scorning his condition, rather by accepting it, making the most of the mobility he has. Does this surmount his fate?

And if his fate is worse than that of Sisyphus, what of our measly misfortunes? Do we, the non-quads, push pebbles — and even so, with the aid of cars and elevators, and not only uphill, but on flat land and down? Is our heroism reduced to naught by the handicapped, or put in another arena? I must state frankly that when I get up in the morning I do not want to get up, and a large part of the day is spent in seducing me to hope; by nightfall I am beginning to forget my incompatibility with what passes for society, to associate with the shades of the past, to pretend that my thoughts have meaning. Early the next morning I am enraptured, striding with Pushkin, trying to read everything and write down everything and despairing that I must break off my joy and go to sleep. After a frenzy of insomnia, I fall into a deep sleep and wake later in the morning with the implacable belief: it would be better not to get up. How can I compare this to Sisyphus — or, more to the point, to Darwin? My hill is much smaller, a hillock to Sisyphus and Darwin, yet still they might not like it. Does this mean everyone has his own hill, and all climbings are equal?

I don't think so. The quad gets up every morning, putting his mind to the task. Someone else supplies the muscle, putting his mind to the task. This someone else — he pushes not only his own troublesome pebble but the quad's relentless rock. As my experience taught me, the aide, the healthy twin, must re-live the quad's tragedy — in less time. He must learn to accept the limitations, the endless, hopeless struggle; he must bend his back to help a bent back. He must halve his life to help a half-life. He must, psychologically speaking, become another quad. Unless, of course, he is not conscious of these things; then he is as free as the brutes. In any event, he can walk away.

But why this effort? Who needs a quad? There are too many people — women take pills, men get vasectomies, fetuses are thrown in the slop buckets. Human life is cheap, an impediment to the living, and still we pretend each individual is precious. The handicapped can still lead "productive lives," though if you figure it out they have to produce for two; and then, no matter what, some will not produce. Are we to measure them on this scale: The aide should be inferior to the quad, otherwise production is wasted? If the aide has superior work to do, he should stop being an aide? And let the quad lie? And how do we measure the productive life — by the pound, the dollar, the wit? Why, in fact, should life be productive? Wouldn't it be better, as Schopenhauer advises, to squeeze off the human race and leave production to nature? If not, then why is life precious, if not by production? By what slogan do we practice feticide, while extending the days of spastic blind babies and moaning old men and women? All life is precious, except the unborn? So we hold onto it, whatever the effort?

The answer is simple: cowardice makes heroes of us all. When the life is present, we dread to lose it, to end it, to take it away from another. With heroic efforts we preserve it, prolong it, hold it away from death. But when we have a chance to deny it, to hold back the unreached hopes, the pointless labors, the mangled human relations and grinding loneliness to seeds, to blobs, to squinching babies beginning to kick in rosy women's bellies, then we show our true colors — we dash them out, destroy them, spare them the agonies of life! Only when forgetful, distracted by happiness, or deluded by the hope of happiness, do we welcome new life, new friends, love. We shall soon enough be reminded.

As for the quads, they should never have survived. Darwin should not have been pulled from the water. Drew should have gone down with the wreck. The truck should have run over Ron. Ann should have died in her boyfriend's arms. But since they didn't die, among us cowards they afford examples of limitless courage. Of course, God should have arranged things otherwise, then we wouldn't have to go through all this, because it's true, as Schopenhauer said: God created not only existence, but also possibility. I don't accept the bunk about suffering, fortitude and a special purpose for us all: it's all bugs up the nose. God could have done a better job, or does He require our help?

I thought about Greg's ad appearing daily, finally decided to give him a call. I thought I might persuade him to consider the university, with all of its many services and its better opportunities for attracting an aide. The incentive of a university degree might work wonders. Greg himself answered, using the phone box. I introduced myself, he needed reminding. I touched on the long night of the thundering hooves, using different terms. He couldn't place it: it had merged with all the succeeding nights. My one-night stand, which I could describe in rich detail, was forgotten, only an occasional thing. All the same, I told him about the university, suggesting its possibilities. His resistance could be sensed over the phone. Darwin's innovations didn't interest him. After a few moments, he broke me off: he had something to do. I was tossed out in the street, an unwelcome visitor from the past. The mind, not the body.

New days began, but the story of the quads had not ended. I ran into Marcia near the station. It turns out she works in the next building. We chatted, and after sign language was exhausted we turned to the other thing we had in common: quads. She was leaving Ron: it was she, in fact, who had burned out. Five years, she said, five years of living that life! She felt guilty, but had left the children with him, so he wouldn't be without family. I reassured her, relating my conclusions; she agreed right down the line. You can't let yourself become a quad. Then she bucked up and told me, quite openly, that she had taken a young lover. I looked at her in surprise. She wasn't pretty — sad as sad can be, and what must she think when...

But she smiled a rosy smile: "I had forgotten what it felt like — to be this much alive!"

I thought of the man at home — exercising, exercising, cursing the doctors, looking to the day when he would grab those crutches and hoist himself out of the chair. He had already foreseen the loss of wife, of course, loss of children, friends, attendants, pets — but, damn it, he would walk, he would show them all.

Late one night in Alpha Beta I came upon Joyce in an empty aisle. His hair was fluffed up, he looked jovial. Shopping for Garry, he hadn't much time, but the job was no trouble, he assured me. I asked if he had passed through the stages — no, it wasn't difficult, everything was fine. Besides, he said, he had only 37 days left to go.

At summer's end Clark informed me of Joyce's new job: male prostitute in L.A.

"How can he do that?" I asked.

"He'll do anything for money," Clark replied. "His complexion was healthy," he went on, complaining. "Maybe spunk does that to you."

Finally, approaching the end of these pages, I was told by an acquaintance that a man in a wheelchair the previous morning had been aiming himself at passing cars. The police had been summoned and wheeled him away. The incident took place near Darwin's new address. I didn't think Darwin capable of such despair, but it had been a while since I had spoken to him, and Brock was a bit of an unknown.

I phoned, Darwin answered. He was in good humor, laughed at the story, then sympathized with the distraught man. We talked a little. I told him the library had not hired me, but I was receiving welfare, and there might be a CETA job at the station.

"Anyway," I concluded, "I didn't think it was you. But don't do that."

TWENTY-FIVE

BÜCHLEIN

Well, I wrote something after all. No-book didn't work for me. I followed my notes, typed up the pages, let them rest. I didn't feel guilty for exploiting the experience, because without this purpose I would not have been able to help. Others may be interested in what I have written, or may not. But now I've gone through the experience twice: a quick revision, then I'm free to do other things. No-quad.

I let the typed pages rest. I myself was made restless. I re-sorted my books, put them on different shelves according to new categories. The death mask of Rosenzweig appeared: I still hadn't finished his book. The title in English as translated by Nahum Glatzer, is *Understanding the Sick and the Healthy* (New York: Noonday Press, 1953), but in the original German it is "Little Book": *Büchlein vom gesunden und kranken Menschenverstand.* After Rosenzweig finished writing it, paralysis began: for the next six years he was unable to speak and to move his limbs. Yet a special typewriter was constructed, and the quad who had wanted to go out into life continued his literary production. He translated the poetry of Judah ha-Levi and, with Martin Buber, the entire Bible. He wrote essays; his correspondence was voluminous.

I picked up where I had left off. Rosenzweig, giving good commonsense advice about God, world and man, helps the philosophical paralytic through the stages of convalescence. Lifted up from his bed, rid of logistics, the reader is able to go back to work, meeting life with a bold, simple and healthy attitude. But Rosenzweig does not end here. If he did, his Büchlein would get a sentimental taint: life is sweet because we write it that way. No, Rosenzweig was not on that level. Unexpectedly, the mood changes:

We have wrestled with the fear to live, with the desire to step outside of the current; now we may discover that reason's illness was merely an attempt to elude death. Man, chilled in the full current of life, sees, like that famous Indian prince, death waiting for him. So he steps outside of life. If living means dying, he prefers not to live. He chooses death in life. He escapes from the inevitability of death into the paralysis of artificial death. We have released him from his paralysis, but we are unable to prevent his death; no physician can do that. By teaching him to live again, we have taught him to move toward death; we have taught him to live, though each step he takes brings him closer to death...

He must direct his life to no other goal but death. Only then does life become simple, inasmuch as it no longer seeks to elude death, being willing to chant the dirge at any moment, while advancing in the face of death. He must know that at the end of the path of graves, a grave is already being prepared for him.

There is no remedy for death; not even health. A healthy man, however, has the strength to continue toward the grave. The sick man invokes death and lets himself be carried away in mortal fear. In health, even death comes at the "proper" time. Health is on good terms with Death. It knows that when the Grim Reaper comes he will remove his stone mask and catch the flickering torch from the anxious and weary and disappointed hands of Brother Life; it knows that he will dash it on the ground and extinguish it, but it also knows that only then the full brilliance of the nocturnal sky will brightly glow. It knows that it will be accepted into the open arms of Death. Life's eloquent lips are put to silence and the eternally Taciturn One will speak: "Do you finally recognize me? I am your brother."

I closed the book.

OLD WOMAN

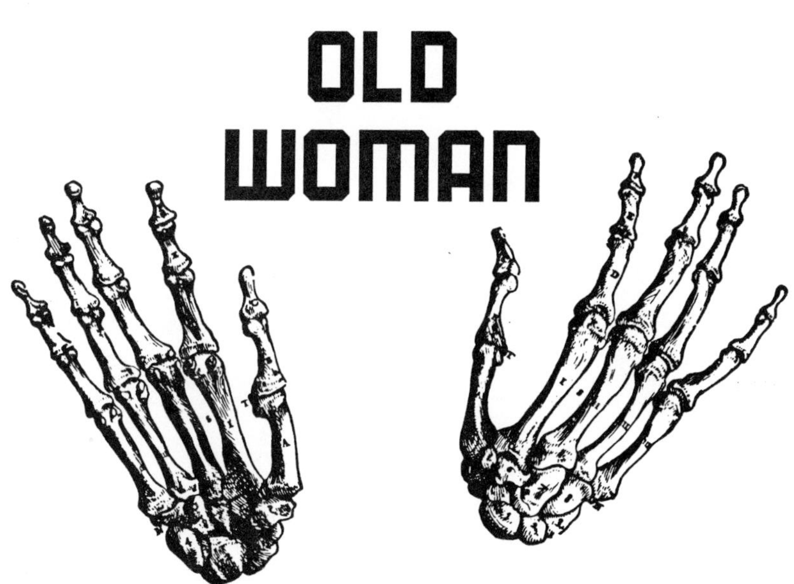

PROLOGUE

MY IBM Selectric snapped a wire last night, so I am forced to pound a manual Olivetti if I want to write this story. But this turn of events is appropriate, because I acquired the Olivetti from the old woman. On this very machine she banged out her innumerable pleas, explanations and chronologies, so quite properly it should receive the honor of summing up her life. Perhaps the resistance it offers my light touch, accustomed to the highly responsive IBM, will impart a slower pace to my account, befitting the old woman's movements. The flaws in the machine — the way it fails to hold the tabs, for example — also strike me as meaningful. All in all, the use of her typewriter is auspicious, and the fact that I must resort to it on the day I had planned to start writing gives me a creepy feeling, as if not I were telling her story, but some superior storyteller.

Anyone who has attempted to write has surely been impressed by the esthetic shape of reality. Once, at the start of a trip, I decided to record everything that happened while it was happening. The artistic structures that arose before my eyes surprised me, but I kept on scribbling. The beginning and ending of my travelogue had the same setting, the same sort of people (the bus station); the route to my destination was reversed on the return trip; the events in the center (the new city) were themselves centered by the conference that I attended. And there were many other correspondences — so many that I feared my factual account would look fictitious, even falsified. And so with other events: everyday life, when recorded, takes on a contrived appearance, and its proximity to fictional form becomes intriguing. Because, after all, there are departures: sticky little details that gum up the form, either by failing to fulfil it or by fulfilling it so completely that the work seems standardized, copied. In such cases the writer must agonize: to make a good story or to tell the truth. Or a third thing: to attempt both.

My intention is to attempt both. I will tell the story as it happened. I will not change anything around, but the volume of details will have to be reduced. The old woman brought me her story ready-made, fully provided with introduction, exposition, rising action and climax; I witnessed the falling action and catastrophe. In this respect, the reality I seek to record differs from everyday life: its scope is broader, it presents a whole story. Usually, in our day-to-day affairs, we get only an incident, an anecdote, a turning point in a person's fate. We have to rely on art to provide the pretext, the complications, the deathbed scene. Or on hearsay. But it was my fortune to come in at the end: another's fate was revealed to me. And now, with the aid of her typewriter, I will reveal it to you.

ONE

CATS

THERE WAS no first meeting in particular, rather a series of them. The old woman would be standing outside, usually admiring the cats, and I would pass by and say hello. She presented a vigorous appearance: her white hair was swept up and knotted, her cheeks were rosy and her blue-grey eyes were large and alert. She had rather fat lips, which added to the hale exterior, and her large yellowish teeth looked like her own, which was fairly remarkable for a creature her age. From her wrinkled neck and hands, still fleshy, it was clear she was well in her sixties or seventies. She dressed comfortably, usually showing herself in slacks, a white button-up knit sweater and soft blue-grey zip-up shoes. The latter particularly conveyed a feeling of relaxation, and overall the old woman seemed at ease with herself, retired and enjoying the crisp spring weather. It was pleasant to stop and chat with her about the cats, even when I had something else to do, so as to share in the spirit of old age content with itself.

I will not say that her conversation was scintillating. For all her hardiness, she was old and limited. Besides this, there was a peculiar naivete in her voice, as if she were newly arrived in the world and utterly unacquainted with the manners of cats. I might observe to her that one cat was chasing another, or one cat running from another, and she would declare "Oh-h-h!" with a rising intonation of disbelief, or perhaps delight. "Well," she would decide, "he's quite a guy!" And then she would tell me about the exploits of her favorite cat.

There were plenty of cats to talk about. Probably the main reason I had moved into University Village was its admittance of pets. The necessity of leaving wife and daughters was hard enough, but to be deprived even of dog seemed a gratuitous punishment. (It was Wolfgang, now that I think of it, who had brought the old woman and me together, for she was naturally impressed by a Siberian husky and asked me questions about him.) So, despite the rent inflated by a location near the university, Wolf and I moved in. The very first day we were visited by a woebegone cat: black and white, ragged, ensnarled with weeds and brambles, disfigured by a stiffened, shrunken ear and protruding ribs. He whined, but shied away from petting, permitting himself to drink milk only at a distance. It took a few days to win his confidence and the right to scratch behind his ears and lift him for a moment, but not to examine him closely. When turned on his back in my arms, like a baby, he revealed a very pink nose and a very distant cast to his eyes, but the next moment these same yellow eyes would glint and he would leap away, clawing. Once I succeeded in fastening a cloth flea-collar around his neck; the next day I found its clawed shards outside my door. For such behavior I named him Demon. Unlike other cats, Demon took an immediate liking to Wolfgang and rubbed up against his legs, under the sniffing, inquiring snout that could have crushed his spine. As for Demon's ear, I suspected mites and was resolving to do something about them when a curious incident took place.

One morning I caught sight of Demon under a car with a rag of some sort over his head. Coming closer, I was horrified: his ears, it looked, had been cut off and adhesive tape wrapped around his neck. He slunk back under the car and fled, keeping low to the ground. At length he let me approach him, but the sight so revolted me I didn't know what to do: cartilage and bone were sticking out of the ear holes, blood and orange mucus seeping out into the fur. I considered he needed expert attention, but even so doubted he could be saved. The Humane Society, of course, would automatically put him to sleep, as it had almost done Wolf. Unable to decide on a course of action, I left the matter till evening, hoping his owner, if he had one, would take care of him.

When nothing was done, I caught him and took him into my bathroom. As I cut the tape with scissors and pulled it as gently as possible from his fur, the ears popped out: they had been folded back and turned inside out, forcing the cartilage outward; the bad ear was stitched and coated with medicine — the supposed orange mucus. Evidently I had foiled a veterinarian's work. (In my defense I must say that no vet should wind adhesive tape tightly around an animal's neck directly on the fur; furthermore, this tape was wet and apparently constricting. Also the owner should not have the cat run around looking like the victim of psychopaths.)

Demon was obviously relieved by the removal of the tape, but to prevent injury I kept him for two days in the bathroom, together with box, food and drink. Late in the night of the second day I decided to take him for a walk with Wolf's chain. He walked a few paces in the ivy and was fine, then started jumping and turning somersaults, hissing and rowring. The young couple who lived in the apartment behind me came running out, and the girl snapped: "That's my cat!"

Everything was explained; the couple had plunked down 80 bucks for the operation. When I excused myself by asking why Demon had no collar, the scruffy lad answered: "Well, uh, he's kinda wild."

So Demon returned to his claimants, but crept around to me for a steady diet. Very soon his coat became silky, tufts sprouted from his cheeks and he assumed a more weighty, regal appearance.

"You're not her favorite person," the old woman told me, indicating the mistress of Demon. "She considers you her enemy."

We laughed over the incident and agreed that the couple took rotten care of their cats. They had expected to pay the vet $5, the old woman informed me, and were flabbergasted when presented with the bill. They didn't know the vet, notorious to local pet owners for his extortion.

Besides Demon, the couple had four more cats about their place, all babies; a pure black skinny thing, which looked

Egyptian; a thin, but perfect Russian Blue; a lush, fluffy Himalayan; and a diminutive white cat with one blue eye and one yellow eye. The couple had incredibly stupid names for these cubs, for instance they called the Himalayan "Bullwinkle." The old woman invented her own names for them; she considered both the white cats female, though they were male. And I had my own names too, so it was good they could not understand English.

The couple, incidentally, were extremely slovenly in appearance: the male never shaved, wore smudged jeans and spent a lot of time tinkering with his motorcycle; the female was fairly shapely and had a salacious face, pock-marked or pimply. She appeared most often in a ragged nightgown, carrying out the trash or transporting clothes to the laundry room. Early one morning, when out walking Wolf, I noticed her entering her apartment in a white uniform; she probably changed bedpans to support her sweet mate.

Above all, the twosome were heard, not seen. Their bathroom adjoined mine, and through the wall came sounds of a shower, giggling, screwing and crude exclamations. The radio would be playing (it was kept in the bathroom), and the young groom would let out whoops and yelps of pleasure. Animal cries would pierce the air, as far as my living room: monkeys and tropical birds, bleating elephants and enraged tigers. Their bathroom was a menagerie, a pleasure dome and also a sanctuary from which the young anchorite would call for the toilet paper. But I digress. The two had loads of cats, which ran loose, and the old lady and I often fed them.

My situation at that time was almost ideal. I had found living alone not so bad, preferable in fact, so long as Jean brought the girls over on weekends. I could do my work during the week without neglecting anyone, then make big breakfasts and play games on Saturday and Sunday.

The real work had already been completed, a gruelling, mind-boggling translation; it had been sent to the publisher and a check had come back. Now I could write whatever came to mind. Placing a completed play on my right and filling in scenes and reflections between the lines of dialogue on a fresh copy to the left, I fabricated a novel. Success would be easy: I had, so to speak, inserted my foot in the door of the publishing house with my Augean labors on the translation; now I had merely to slide the rest of my body past the editor. With this work I would fulfil my life plan — namely, to acquire a name as a translator, so that, as I had imagined 20 years earlier, my unwelcome fictional creations would be granted access to the light. With this fond hope, I refashioned <u>The Mad Kokoschka</u>.

The old woman, cats, ululating neighbors — these were diversions from my daily routine. As soon as Kokoschka was completed, posted, I started work on a Beethoven scenario, making use of another unperformed play. Hollywood was not far away, and who had ever seen a film about Beethoven? The money would last, though I was living rather high. A steak sandwich almost every night, a Bass pale ale. Going to and from the supermarket, I would occasionally see the old lady, who lived beside the back lot, catty-corner to the young couple. I'd wave from my bike, she'd call out hello. The acquaintance took a turn one morning when I stopped beside her car. She was just about to go on a milk errand for the kitties. I looked over the white Cadillac, with its massive chrome bumpers, armored doors and sweeping sailfish tail-fins (vintage 1959, my friend Clark tells me), and felt entitled by our friendly relations to speak candidly.

"Why don't you get rid of that monstrosity and buy yourself an economical little car?"

"Oh, no-o-o-o, I couldn't possibly do that," she laughed, plopping down in the seat. "I've had this car for years. It's so solid and comfortable."

The question was ruled out, I went my way. But I don't give up easily, and on another occasion repeated the question. And on another, pressing my case with a list of the benefits — saved money, manageability, parking space. It really seemed to me the old woman would be happier with a VW, putting around town like a hot mama. Besides, it was a new subject.

But she countered: "Oh, no, I don't have to worry about money. You see, my husband left me millions. Only I can't touch them now." She smiled inanely.

"Why not?" I bit.

"His sister has the money all tied up. She's a nun — the most vicious people, you know. She's grasping, she really is. She wants it all for the church."

"But how can she get it? The wife is the natural heiress, isn't she?"

"Oh, you don't know how tricky they can be! She got a crooked lawyer — the crookedest man in the world. He just lo-o-oves to strangle old women, he lo-o-oves to take every last penny away from them. He lo-o-oves," and for the third time she extended the word, "to suck the blood out of old women, to drain them dry."

"But you have a legitimate claim, you're the wife."

"Shocker!" she exclaimed.

"Yes, I suppose so."

"Shocker, he told me: 'I just lo-o-ove to twist those old women. And if you tell anybody I said so, they'll never believe you.' But he said it, he said it bold as day."

The old woman had become agitated, but the fire of determination could be seen in her eyes. She squeezed her fist when she spoke of Shocker, snapped her horse teeth open as she spat out his name.

"So you're doing something about it?"

"Oh, yes! You bet I am. I've got it all written up. I'm typing every day. When I get a new lawyer we'll take care of those hoodlums — that nun and that crook... Shocker!"

At this point we were distracted by the cats. Demon shot out from the bushes and slipped under her car; from the same spot a head poked out, a fiendish-looking head. It was mostly white and tan, but the dark brown and black flecks over the nose made the cat look cross-eyed (which he was not) or demonically possessed (which he may have been). The head was followed by a heavy, tough calico body. This was Nathaniel (my name), the top cat in the project. He was owned by no one, but well-fed. All the other cats ran when Nathaniel showed up; Demon's ear was credited to him. Because he was The Boss (the old woman's name), he felt within rights to spray his scent everywhere — over your door, your windows, and — if he could get inside — your walls. You could scrub and scrub, but the penetrating pissy odor never went away. Nathaniel might let you feed him, but never touch him. Catching sight of us, he tripped back into the bushes. Demon, living up to his name, crept after him.

The conversation about millions was thus broken; the old woman drove away in her tank. I was left to reflect: this old woman is perfect bait for a hustler. Someone who could get into her good graces, help her with little tasks and then collect when the millions roll in. I imagined the kept man, living in luxury, admitting a young woman into a spacious living room while the old biddy was out, or casting a conniving glance past the prattling old thing to his paramour along the railings of a yacht. The mention of millions does that to you: you start dreaming. It seems the millionaire has only to reach into his pocket — or her purse — to solve all your problems.

But I had no reason to feel anxious, my problems were still distant — just peeking over the horizon. The rent had been raised, I had no income. <u>The Mad Kokoschka</u> was sitting on the editor's desk, and even if she liked it, months might pass before I would receive filthy lucre. The Beethoven was a shot in the dark: I knew no one in Hollywood, my style was unconventional. But I had money in the bank, hopes in the heart. In reality, my wealth, my comfort, was a spell of good weather, iced on both sides by the frost. And unlike the ant I was not a good storeman.

Late summer. The old woman left her door open and could be heard typing inside. I went on working, though Kokoschka stalled and Beethoven fell through. I'm not a member of the Screen Writer's Guild — that's one thing. Another is that to become a member you must have an accepted film script to your credit. New talent, therefore, can only come through the back door.

As my finances became more precarious, I felt more the need to settle spiritual accounts. (An economics not analyzed by

Marx.) Next project: Lev Lunts. He had died in 1921, but had carried me through graduate school. I figured I should produce a volume of his works in English, lest I die with the debt unpaid.

Still alive at the end of the year, I put together a collection of articles on Evgeny Zamyatin for money. A friend of mine, who is a publisher of Russian literature, sent me $250 advance. But things were really getting tight. No more steak sandwiches, no more pale ale. Fried rice and Coors. Food stamps came to my rescue — but not Wolfgang's, since for some reason they do not count him as human. You have to buy something for a quarter, get the change from the $1 food stamp, walk out of the store and then walk back in for the dog food, beer or cigarettes.

At this crucial juncture, my typewriter broke. I was thrown in despair, deprived of a livelihood, such as it was, for I could hardly submit handwritten manuscripts. Besides this, the Russian publisher had sent me relief work that required precision typing — both in English and Russian — precisely on an IBM. To crown my misery, <u>The Mad Kokoschka</u> was tossed out on the street, along with my life plan. The rains came, cold weather — I had no thought for the old woman. Yet I did see her in passing.

"How're you doing?" I asked, not stopping my bike.

"All right," she called out, "but I've got to finish in three days."

"Why?"

"The lawyer, the lawyer."

Three days went by, and still she was typing. I minded my own business, but another week went by, and still she was typing. My machine was making trips to the company: I would carry it down on the bus, walk three blocks with it on my hip, pick it up several days later, take it home and discover a defect. Clark, the radio-station manager, drove me down once or twice. And meantime she was typing past her deadline, and I was feeding Wolf bowls of fried rice.

Finally, on one of our chats, I asked her: "Would you like me to type a cover letter? Something to sum up the case to the lawyer?"

She was thrilled: "Oh, would you? I was hoping you'd ask."

The typewriter was just now serviceable, though requiring adjustment, so I suggested we do it the next day.

"But I want an agreement at the outset," I told her. "Yes," she said, completely at my mercy.

"I'll type the letter and you'll pay me in cat food. Just so it will be square and proper."

"All right, but I can give you more."

"No, the cat food will do it."

I figured this way: I didn't want to take advantage of an old woman, and while I was on the scene I might prevent someone else from doing so. If she didn't get her millions, I would have received fair recompense; if she did get some dough, I could request dog food; and if she did get her millions she might want to reward me more generously. (I sometimes carried her trash to the dumpster.) But I was not going to con her, nor strive for the role of gigolo. After all, I have to live with myself (and Wolf) — millions or no.

I went back to my apartment. Things were running downhill: I had stopped cleaning after Beethoven, littered the bathroom with want-ads after Kokoschka. Demon and Nathaniel had waged a war of scents in the front room, taking advantage of a slit in the screen. Wolf preferred the back room, consisting of rug and books. I leaned back in my battered armchair (my new leather recliner remained at the house). So then, I would do a spot of work for an old woman. Not the most prestigious work, but honorable. There shouldn't be too much trouble. I'd help her get started, then the lawyer would take over.

But to tell the truth, and I am not making it up, I sensed that there would be some trouble. I had just stuck my foot in a very slow quicksand.

TWO

WHITE PIGEONS

MY MEMORY of that day can fix the old woman, but not the surrounding circumstances. There was some difficulty, some rush. I was busy past noon, then Jean wanted me to sit that evening with the girls, or take the car to the gas station, or something. Anyway, the important thing is that I called on the old woman at about 2 o'clock and had only until 5 or so to help her.

I entered her apartment authoritatively, attempting to quicken her actions, for I perceived confusion and disorder at the outset. Her apartment was not merely cluttered; it was blockaded. Big, expensive furniture congested the living space: a huge couch by the wall, square armchairs at right angles and an office desk opposite, composing a square room within the room, the center of which was filled by a thick coffee table. The dining area was taken by a wooden table and boxes; the small kitchen was dwarfed by an enormous refrigerator; large metal pans overlapped the burners on the stove. On the table I noticed the typewriter (that is, the Olivetti Studio 45 — I am reading the plate in front of me); over all the other furniture I saw papers, mostly legal size, and folders. Decorated bowls sat on the kitchen floor, half-filled with bits of liver and cream: the spoiled cats scampered throughout the premises, confident the food would be there always.

I gathered up papers and folders, holding up a parcel at a time and demanding: "Is this important?" The old woman, however, would not be rushed; her answers never stated plain yes or no, but embarked on long-winded explanations. Cutting her short, I grabbed everything that looked important and encouraged her to come to my apartment. There I sat her in my armchair (the footrest recently acquired from the dumpster would not support her), placed myself at my desk and, papers before me, tried to put things in order. Whatever was dated was properly filed, the other items were held up to the old woman for identification. Her mind, I discovered, was quite sharp on certain details: she could identify and explain each item precisely. She was unable, however, to mark off borders: each item opened the door on a disorganized world of experiences, people and words, every one of them equally relevant. Jean, I recall, stopped by my apartment while the work was in progress and must have wondered at the presence of a crone. But she said nothing.

The facts, as I determined, were these. Violet V., at about age 21, began work as a secretary for one Laurence W., an architect, in 1932. An office romance developed, but Laurence did not divorce his wife and marry Violet until 1947. During these years business was booming: after the San Francisco earthquake Laurence received many commissions and made a bundle of money. One of the legal-size sheets of paper, reproduced in various forms on other legal-size sheets of paper, totalled up a net worth of 7 million dollars for 1949. But all was not bliss: Laurence was an alcoholic and his sister Mildred a nun. The sister objected vehemently to his second marriage and strove relentlessly to make him godfearing. Fortunately for Violet, Mildred lived far away, in Fresno, while she and Laurence settled down in Palm Springs. Fine clothes, fine food and pet dogs — these were what occupied Violet. As for Laurence, whom she characterized as a marvelous man, educated, capable and brilliant, he hit the bottle. The pet dogs were particularly close to her heart, and she frequently lapsed into accounts of their behavior and the tragic sickness of the mother, which got cancer and had to be put to sleep. Violet had written up a little story about the dogs some years ago that she thought was quite touching and wanted me to read.

Anyway, she lived happily enough as the ominous forces gathered. First, for unknown reasons, Laurence signed over a piece of property in Los Angeles to his first wife. Violet, consulting a lawyer, determined this to be illegal. Acting entirely on her own, she recovered the property for her husband. Her adversary in this instance — that is, the first wife's lawyer — was Victor E. Shocker. Second, Laurence went into the hospital for drying out, and Violet attempted to secure a conservatorship. She failed. Mildred hired Mr. Shocker, and the two of them, as Violet told me in virulent detail, poured liquor down Laurence's throat — whether before or after the hospital I could not quite make clear. After Laurence's recovery, which somehow was effected by Violet spooning him soup, a court hearing established that he had never drunk. Shocker suborned relatives to testify that they had never seen Laurence raise a glass to his lips, although the hospital records confirmed his alcoholism.

Now matters worsened: Mildred persuaded Laurence to move out of his home and into her house in Fresno, which he, by the way, had given her. Once separated from Violet, he was prompted by his sister and lawyer to file for divorce. Violet, understanding nothing, was called to a hearing and informed of the decision. She was not permitted to contest it, nor were statements of communal possessions, recovery of property or continued secretarial work admitted. The court awarded her the house in Palm Springs, with its furniture, and a cash settlement of $21,000, which she insisted she had never received. The matter was settled in 1967, some 20 years after the marriage.

The next year Laurence died. Violet was not informed and learned of the event only by chance. The property, the millions earned by her husband — with her secretarial assistance, re-member — and everything else passed to the nun, the sons of his first marriage and Victor H. Shocker. Naturally, Violet protested: she initiated a series of appeals — the files and folders that littered her apartment. But Shocker told her in private: "I lo-o-ove to twist old women, I lo-o-ove to squeeze every last drop of blood out of them, and you can't do anything about it."

It was Shocker, in fact, who was responsible for Laurence's death: he had started him drinking again; he paid a doctor to administer the juice. Or was this in the hospital? Whatever, Violet's finances collapsed: she was forced to mortgage her house to pay legal fees, but Shocker, keeping tabs on her, bought off each and every lawyer. At length she suffered foreclosure, but this did not stay her. Leaving most of her possessions in storage in Palm Springs, she moved with Cadillac and furniture to Riverside, closer to San Bernardino, where the final appeal was scheduled. In her blockaded apartment, she tried every day to make sense of the past, adding page after page of explanations, commentaries and financial statements, until I and the Wolf appeared.

Such was the approximate course of events. Another writer, I suspect, would take these materials and compose a splendid dreary picture of the old woman's travails, transforming her disconnected, or over-connected, reveries into a freely flowing narrative and filling in the white spaces with reconstructed conversations, descriptions, etc. Laurence, I imagine, would be rather thin and not too tall; he would wear a suit with baggy pants, circa 1930-cut. Mildred would be wispy, with a sharp nose and piercing eyes. Shocker would look nondescript: a puffy, out-of-shape, ordinary man with the smell of cigar or damp socks. Only in private, behind the closed doors of his office, or perhaps in the courtroom when he had pinned his opponent, would his grey eyes shed their scales and glare with malicious triumph, and his dull voice sharpen and stab.

But these are imaginary images stirred by Violet's carbon copies and obsessively repeated claims. I never saw the real-life figures. What I did see was a photo album containing many boring pictures of a younger Violet holding up clothes, talking to unknown friends and generally looking rich. I also saw letters between herself and her husband, where she had underlined in red Laurence's question: "Why are you seeking a divorce? I don't understand." And also two wills handwritten by Laurence, naming Violet sole heir. Not much, but still many rich hues for an artistic portrait. However, I entered the case not as a painter, but as a quasi-legal aide, to be paid in cat food, and I tried to prepare these things for a lawyer, using my best pseudo-legal vocabulary. Now that I have occasion to write an account, I find that I cannot transform the material: it entered my mind in this form, and to correct it would seem a transgression.

The reader, no doubt, has already wondered: Why did the author let himself get sucked into the old woman's delirium? It's obvious to me, if not to him, that her case is a nightmare. Who can tell what is fact and fiction? Shocker may be a respectable and highly ethical lawyer. Mildred — well, it's not unnatural for a nun to oppose a second marriage. The divorce and disposition of the estate may have been aboveboard and legal. The old woman probably couldn't accept the turn in her life and took it as part of an evil design. Perhaps she was motivated only by avarice and a desire for revenge...

Indeed, these are plausible views. But there was one sticky fact that gummed them all up and weighed the scales in the old woman's favor — raised her delirium, if you will. The lawyer <u>against</u> Laurence in his dealings with his first wife, and <u>for</u> Laurence in his dealings with his second wife, was one and the same, Victor E. Shocker. I suppose it's not impermissible to represent a man you once opposed, but when that man has millions and a debilitating habit something smells fishy — could it be caviar? Violet, besides, produced a copy of a declaration of censure against Shocker by the California Bar, albeit for an unrelated case. However unbridled her memory and exaggerated her complaints, the old girl mustered an impressive attack. I could not resist the image of an innocent wife, typing business letters and tending the roses, muscled aside by grasping in-laws and a shifty lawyer while an alcoholic husband lay idle by. Yet looking at her now, at her wrinkled face and lively eyes, I mentally compared her with her album photographs to the latter's discredit: she looked more interesting now. I told her so, and she was pleased, but not to the point of relenting her pursuit of a happier self.

After the IBM messed up a couple of sheets, I succeeding in typing the cover letter. First I emphasized the salient objective points, suppressing Violet's vituperation of lawyers and the entire legal spawn. I presented her as a victim of circumstances, which included a malevolent sister-in-law and a skilled lawyer, who, incidentally, had once been censured. Violet's inability to cope with legal intricacies was cited, and an appeal to the lawyer's wisdom made. Then I made a list of the documents to be enclosed, together with a brief statement of their relevance. For example: "Indio Nº12976, the divorce hearing. Note that communal property not mentioned." These documents, of course, I did not peruse, but only skimmed and put in order, arranging them under three headings: <u>property</u> (that recovered by Violet), <u>divorce</u> (which she now contested) and <u>husband's death</u> (without benefit to her). Into these categories went hospital records, death certificate, photocopies of handwritten wills (which we would have to make), financial records, deeds to property, and so on.

Among Violet's papers there were also some chronologies entitled "History of My Marriage," or "Events 1932 to 1949," and so on, occurring in various versions, retyped over the years, so that page 1 may have originated in one year, page 2 in another, page 3 exist in 4 copies of different redactions, page 5 not exist, and so on, much like an epic receiving fresh layers and emendations over the centuries, save that these versions were shuffled. I quickly established a canonical text, leaving the variorum edition for future historiographers, and put it at the front.

Then I completed the letter with an assurance of gratitude and ample reward upon the successful outcome of the case. Violet signed the letter, and the whole load was stuffed into a huge manila envelope with the lawyer's address, prepared in advance by the indefatigable ex-wife. Having demonstrated my priceless talents, I advised her not to touch the envelope, but only to read the cover letter for approval. The next day I would go with her to make photocopies and mail out the package. Parting at her doorway, she agreed that I had earned my fee.

Actually, it was just before parting, on the way to her apartment, that I picked up one of the choicest tidbits of her story. The influence of the sister over Laurence had bothered me. Why hadn't he told her to cram it? After all, he was a grown man, a master builder, even if a boozer; he didn't need a younger sister to teach him how to tie his shoes. Violet informed me that a mysterious incident had occurred in his childhood. She herself was not certain what had happened, but somehow Mildred had been hurt and Laurence made responsible. It may be, she whispered, swearing me to secrecy, that Mildred had attempted suicide. I asked why she thought that, but she became very upset and tried to squirm out of an answer. Whatever did in fact go down, the little girl became the darling of the family, the delicate child. The parents died not long after this, leaving Laurence the role of father. And so, to the end of his life, he tried to make it up to his sister: she entered the convent on account of the incident, while he studied for a time in the seminary. Likely she wrecked the first marriage; she riddled the second with demands for donations to the church of time, work and money. Laurence never opposed her, save that he did leave the seminary and did get married, twice. But we can imagine how he overruled his wives' tentative complaints, and how smoothly the Scotch must have slipped down his gullet. The whole thing is a cliché, a predictable play in the worst melodramatic style, only the players were real people, and their roles took every minute of their lives. Since Violet was assigned the most tragic part, I feel justified in breaking her confidence — exposing the secret of the plot, so to speak.

The next day I went round to her place. It took some knocking to rouse her; she complained of absolute exhaustion. As she spoke, I noticed for the first time that her drawn-out words, her expressions of absolute this and utterly that were not signs of a childlike nature, but rather the rodomontade of the ultra rich, now softened by age. Or could it be that she was childish in nature, and afterwards rich? She admitted me into the apartment, served the cats their breakfast on fine china. It irritated me slightly to see the pampered things lap up the thick cream, which I would not have refused. Especially the odd-eyed one, which Violet called "she" and "Angel": he was diminutive and especially smart-alecky; he pranced and stalled before taking his sip.

Turning to the desk in the stuffed living room, I discovered with dismay that the manila envelope had been opened and some papers removed. While the old woman busied herself at the sink, I rearranged the disturbed documents and reinserted them in the package, but could not find the cover letter.

"Didn't I leave it at your place?" the old lady answered my demand.

One sheet, fortunately, was found beside her bed in the next room; the other two sheets were lost amid the stacks of discarded papers. Back at my apartment, I was able to reconstruct them from the spoiled sheets in my trash can, incorporating a few refinements suggested by Violet. At length, we set out in the Cadillac, myself behind the wheel, and made our way to the photocopy shop, then the post office. The package was sealed, stamped and safely entrusted to our dependable civil servants.

Violet felt like celebrating. We stopped at the supermarket across from the post office and parted with separate carts. For me this was a luxury — to have a car, not a bike, for my groceries. I checked my food stamps and headed for the half-price bread. Violet showed up at the cashier with luxury items — Manischewitz gefilte fish, gherkins, calf's liver, oysters and other oddities, plus milk, cream and a big bag of Purina Cat Chow. This, for me.

Outside, she tried to persuade me to go to a specialty fish shop. The smoked sturgeon, she assured me, was es-peth-ally delicious. I tried to explain that with food stamps you tend to cut down on your quota of sturgeon, but she failed to understand. I let her drop me off at home, then the tank went a-hunting for delicacies. I hoped the matter had ended, but later Violet showed up beaming at my door, proffering a portion of fish and a wrapped bantam hen. I let myself be persuaded and paid for the goods by listening to Violet's rambling for an hour or more. Declining her offer of dinner, I repaired to my repast, dropping a chunk of the fluffy white meat for the excited Wolf. As usual, he swallowed the morsel without so much as one chew — from floor to stomach in less than a second — and looked up expectantly for ten pounds more. But he did not get it: I savored each flake with regret that it would have to be swallowed, and I would be brought that much closer to my nightly rice. Demon also came to the feast: he treated his morsel more appropriately, tearing at it and chewing it with a thrashing head. Then he was rewarded with a crumbling mound of chow. We had a happy night, despite the IBM bill, the defective typewriter and the hyena laughter behind the wall.

For the next several days, Violet was in a fine fiddle. She dressed in varicolored slacks and blouse and open-toed golden sandals. I noted with surprise the painted toenails; the finger-nails, alas, were forgotten. Necklaces of wooden beads and green-glass lumps were worn together, and flying-bird earrings adorned her lobes. She invited me in for supper, and when I declined suggested we go to a restaurant. I begged her indul-gence, citing a previous engagement (Wolf had to run in the hills). In return for a half of cooked chicken, I provided lemons and oranges from the orchard. She figured right off that I had nipped them, and this seemed to add to her contentment. Though rich in the past, she had had occasion to develop a resentment of wealth and power, here symbolized by the university, owner of the orchard.

I tried, in our conversations, to compare my own misfortune (non-renewal at the university) with hers (deprivation of millions) — not very convincingly, I fear. But it seemed to me necessary to prepare her for failure: the odds, after all, were against her. I mentioned that I had spent 13 years in school and 7 years in teaching, so that my loss of 20 years was equal to her own. Further, it pained me to think of the fat salaries paid to dead-beats, petrified professors who had drawn on someone else's idea for so long that it had crumbled to dust, while I was bubbling with spring-fresh conceptions. Fifteen minutes with me was worth a year or more with those desiccated fossils, but... And so on. Yet it would do me no good to be eaten up with envy, to protest to the university, to waste my time seeking restitution. And so with her: she had a good life right here, soaking in the sunshine and spoiling the cats, munching on mozza balls and gossiping with the neighbors.

But she cut me off, sweeping her hand back into the apart-ment: "Why, this is hell! This is absolute hell!"

What could I say? Violet never cursed and once rebuked me when I had released a few mild imprecations: "That's not nice." So if she said hell, she damn-well meant fire and perdition.

I argued that this would be Shocker's final victory: to make her waste her life in a fruitless tangle.

She replied that he would like to do this, but she was going to win. "I can't let them get away with it!" She shook her fist and sputtered with a babyish or affluent lisp. "I just can't! He can't strangle old women forever! I'll get him — that Shocker!" Her glass jewelry rattled.

Sooner than expected, the lawyer's reply came back. It was hardly encouraging; in fact, it said nothing. He began with a disclaimer: "As I told you over the phone, I would probably not be able to..." He proceeded to offer his services in the capacity of advisor and recommended that the old woman get in touch with the legal clinic of Riverside. Then he signed off, returning all her materials. No word about the merits of her case, her best course of action, her prospects. No indication that he had even read one page of the hundreds she had sent him. It was, all in all, like a standard rejection notice from a publishing house, save that it was individually typed and didn't take 8 months.

To my astonishment, Violet was not disgruntled. She simply snorted about the legal clinic, "It's worthless," and tossed the package in a heavy armchair, terrifying Rocky, the Russian Blue.

"The legal clinic won't do any work on speculation. He knew that before we started."

"Then why did he recommend it?"

"Shocker," she said, "he got to him."

"Now wait a minute," I demanded, "Shocker doesn't know anything about the letter you sent or to whom you sent it."

"Oh, you don't know these lawyers. They lo-o-ove to find rich old women, they squeeze the blood right out..."

"But Shocker doesn't know where you are..."

"Oh, yes he does."

"You're dreaming, Violet."

"Am I? You think the lawyer didn't get on the phone? They're thick. He probably said, 'Now, Mr. Shocker, I have an old woman here who has a bad opinion of you.' And Shocker told him, he told him, all right."

The old bird had me: it was quite possible. Attorneys know each other from L.A. to Palm Springs, and probably far out into the desert. One calls another, and whom does he believe — an irate old lady or an associate of the profession for the last 25 years, who suffered a little vote of censure a few years back? Even if Violet had an airtight case, she would have trouble convincing a law man, let's face it.

"No, Violet, he just figured it was too much trouble. He saw all these lawyers' names, all these briefs and dockets, or whatever they are, and he decided he wanted money up front, that's all."

"Yes, you're right," she conceded, forgetting her wrath of a moment's passing.

"So what are you going to do?"

"Find another lawyer. I'll phone, I'll get advice. They can't stop me."

"O.K. Save the file and the cover letter. You can use it for the next lawyer."

"Yes, I will."

It was at about this time that I raised the question of using the newspaper. I happened to know the woman in charge of "Sidelight," the human-interest page, and I thought a feature on Violet might elicit a response from knowledgeable people, perhaps even an offer of free legal service. There are a lot of rugged feminists out there, whom I would not like to meet in a courtroom or back alley, but they might be a welcome sight to an embattled old crone. We could call the "Sidelight" people and... But at once Violet was frightened: Shocker might see the article. We went over the same ground. Finally, it was resolved that if a lawyer could not be found in due time, we would summon the forces of the American free press.

I was going to her place quite often now. Taking out her trash, which she deposited in a small, but exceptionally heavy wooden basket, finding documents that she had laid aside, performing odd chores. For example, Violet bought a swinging bar — that is, a metal bar that fits into the door jamb and may be used for exercising. I tightened it in the doorway between her living and bed room and watched with approval as she hung like a heavy ourang-utan and let her old bones and tendons stretch. She was a bit of a health-nut, receiving packages of vitamins from Lindberg Nutrition. She knew Carlton Fredericks when I mentioned him. I had other things to do, of course, but since I had become involved, I decided to see the matter through to the end. For this end was not far distant: somewhere in the middle of a tirade or other, she remarked that the cut-off date was in April. Only now did I understand: she had one month left out of 10 years, or was it 12 or 15, in which to make her final appeal. Beyond that date the matter (divorce, probate or whatever else) would be settled for all eternity. I had no legal knack and a dreamy disposition, but no one else was rushing to help her, so I would have to do. She, comforted by my assistance, gave me cat food and cans of soup, dressed up like an old movie star and swung on the bar.

Her habits, as mentioned, were expensive, but her finances, I was beginning to realize, were not unsinkable. I saw her whip out her checkbook, and I saw the slavering alacrity of clerks, but I could not fail to notice that margarine had taken the place of butter, and plain chicken was nudging out squib. She was glad to get the stolen fruit from the orchard, not from the store. She even asked for vegetables; she had kept such a nice garden in Palm Springs. Her phone bill, of course, was titanic: she had phoned lawyers over vast distances. Her income, she divulged to me when singing her woes, was a paltry social security account left by Laurence. As for his other provisions, I contacted an insurance company to check the numbers on one of Violet's sheets, and the company phoned back from Newport Beach with the information that both policies had been small and cashed in by Laurence before his death. To get to the bottom line, the old woman was practically broke.

Meanwhile the cats were living in splendor. The old woman fried them cuts of chicken, liver and other meats, which they gobbled up or eschewed. They had free run of the apartment and were none too civil, for yellowish brown puddles were beginning to appear along the floorboard and under the furniture. The old woman covered them with carpet cleaner or disinfectant, which added a foamy white layer over the dried humps. When I came to visit, I made it a practice of flinging the cats outside, but they rushed back in when I opened the door to leave. Angel even slept with the old woman — "she" would have to be removed from "her" nest in the woolen red blanket. (His opposite eyes peek in the window as I type. I call him Two Face now.) In short, the old woman became their doting mama, they — her naughty children. It seemed they had no other home, and indeed they hadn't.

Suddenly it struck me: the wall was silent. No cockatoos, no whinnying rhinos. The loving twosome had flown the coop. I went round to the old lady's and learned that the scruffy lad had told her they were going on a trip to Hawaii and would appreciate her taking care of the cats. He would pay her upon his return, he said, and then laughed in a funny way, as she told me. She willingly accepted custody of the little monsters.

The Himalayan (which she called Fluffy) was shaking his head: his ears were loaded with mites. It was necessary to take him to the vet, and for me to go along, so the cat would not run wild in the car and the vet would not rip Violet off. We arrived without incident, but when the vet started digging Q-tips down Fluffy's ears like a construction worker drilling a sidewalk, Fluffy made the intelligent response: he sprayed shit out the other end. We cleaned him up, wrapped him in his blanket and put him back in the wicker basket, where he completed the voiding of his bowels on the return trip. Holding him inside, I spied from my passenger's seat a familiar figure walking down the sidewalk: the bedpan cleanerette of recent memory. She turned the corner with a swish of her tail and proceeded on. Hawaii is where the heart is. The white Cadillac, bearing its discomfited load, cruised home.

Each day, or every other day, I checked the old woman's progress. Had she found a lawyer, or not? She was phoning, phoning — near and far, and the phone company was making a precise accounting of every call. It's hard to estimate what 8 hours of phoning a day would cost. Communication and transportation throughout the nation could easily be free, of course, but that would never do: if they were free everyone would want to travel and communicate. So the old woman would certainly be billed, and without a ringing victory would sink deep into the red. But she phoned, phoned, telling strangers about her poor dog, which died, the meanness of a nun in Fresno, some corner of buildings in L.A. and a menacing personage named Shocker. It was no wonder that she required many calls; most listeners probably got only pieces of the story, and no doubt she confused their identities. She must have called some of the same people twice; the yellow pages of her telephone book were crisscrossed with scribbled-in numbers or torn from one edge to another. One day Violet told me happily that a lawyer had agreed to take her case, but when we went to check the appointment date she could not remember which one.

At length, however, she scored a success: a lawyer in L.A. agreed to see her, and she had marked his name. I congratulated her and agreed to come by in the evening to look over the manila envelope and make sure everything was in order. She walked back to her apartment with her leisurely but steady pace, shuffling her zipped-up shoes and talking baby-talk to the cats running figure eights between her feet. I went in the other direction, toward the field, lurching forward at every step. As usual, across the street a gang of kids ran up yelling, "Wolf! Wolf! Wolf!" The dog let himself be petted and loved, then freed of his leash burst through the field with unhuman power.

After a fine walk, I knocked at the old woman's door. She opened it, and at that moment papers flew up like flocks of white Pigeons, lifting off the table in front of the window, which she had opened wide, and also off the piles of documents stacked in the chairs and the couch. She turned from the door, clucking "oh, oh," and feebly tried to swipe a sheet from the air. Her motion frightened Rocky, who loped over the back of the sofa, spilling a whole pile of explanations and life stories. I, hastening to get inside and close the door, dragging in the Wolf, who terrified the drowsy cats, at once was confronted with another problem: the smell of gas, the sight of two turned knobs on the stove, one lit burner. In a moment the place would explode. With three brisk

steps through the swirl of papers I turned off the gas. As simple
as that: her life and mine saved. But she meanwhile was
standing in place, half-turning, oblivious, as the fluttering pigeons
landed about the apartment.

THREE

THE GARGOYLE

"YOU KNOW, Gary," the old woman told me the next morning, "I had such a wonderful dream. I dreamed that Laurence came back to me. I knew he wouldn't leave me like that. He was sitting out here, right in my living room. I woke up and came out to see him. It was so real, I woke up and came out to see him. It was so real. Has that ever happened to you?"

"Yes, it happens to everyone."

"I almost couldn't believe he was here. I went back to my bed. It couldn't be just a dream. It was so real."

She extended the <u>so</u> in her ultra-rich fashion.

I had come over to check her out before her trip to L.A. To my disappointment, but not surprise, I found the manila envelope opened against instructions and the materials rearranged. This time I openly chided her, like a baby.

"Why did you open the envelope? I told you."

She babbled back pathetically: "I thought there were some things..."

I walked around, not concealing my impatience, searching for missing papers. Fluffy (I call him Savva) was persuaded to jump off page 2 of the freshly typed cover letter. Two legal documents were located next to her bed, beside back issues of <u>The Reader's Digest</u> and magazines on nutrition. A key item turned up in the middle of an old stack, and very quickly I had reassembled the materials reassembled the night before. Once again, the packet was ready. Now it would be up to her: she would have to drive to L.A. and present her case to the lawyer. I was not a legal advisor, and I had resolved not to waste another whole day on her affairs. By now I was desperately broke, and

I had to do something for myself, if only lie in a tub of hot water and read the want-ads.

The old woman set about pouring milk for the cats. The bowls, I noticed, were rather dirty. Crockery was boiling in great cauldrons on the stove — her way of doing the dishes. She seemed in no hurry. I impressed on her the need to get moving and promised to return in an hour to speed her on her way. I expressed my regrets at not being able to drive her.

When I returned she was indeed ready to go. She had fixed herself up in an old dress and coat, had a black bag swinging from her arm and a forced expression of eagerness on her face. I bucked her up with a few words of confidence, handed her the manila envelope (not touched this time) and showed her, once again, the order of materials.

"But where is the letter?" she asked in a rush of horror.

"Right here, right here," I showed her.

"Ah, good, good."

She looked around the apartment. I grabbed cats one by one and threw them out.

"They'll be all right," I assured her.

The bowls were moved outside, by the door. The old woman found it difficult to carry everything, so I volunteered to carry the package to the tank. She meanwhile became distressed again and looked around desperately.

"Where are my keys?"

I found them stuck in the inside lock; sometimes she left them inside, sometimes outside. I handed her the keys, she dropped them. I considered it best to step outside, to hasten her toward the car. But, after picking up the keys, she dropped them again. She tried to open her purse, then to slide the keys in her pocket. I stood there looking at her incompetence. Could I let her propel a white bomb down the highway? She might blow up any number of people, both innocent and guilty.

At the gas station the boy literally ran out of the glass office. He shined up the windows, the headlights, the side mirror. I tried to fill the gas tank myself, but couldn't fit the nozzle in the slot. The boy fooled around with the back trunk, and the lid raised automatically, like a garbage truck. The slot thus exposed, we got the nozzle in. The big car, a classic of kitsch, began to guzzle: the meter, already set on half-cost, spun around like a one-armed bandit. We had the oil checked, also the water. The boy was pointed to the old woman for payment. She pressed down the window automatically and laboriously took out her checkbook. The boy was left with a big smile on his face and a thin piece of paper in his hand that would bounce from city to city throughout the Inland Empire.

The bomb was smooth, however, and we reached our destination with minimal difficulty. The old woman got out and entered the tall office building, taller than I would have expected for an earthquake city, leaving me to find a lot large enough for the Cad. I tried my best to find a space on the street, so as to save her some money, but every inch of asphalt was taken and I regretfully slipped into an underground tunnel, which then spiralled upwards to the point of unconsciousness. That's where I parked. Mrs. W., I was informed by a secretary in the front office on the 71st floor, or 119th, something very high, had arrived and retired with Mr. S., the attorney, into the conference room. Since I had the package, I thought it best to join them. I left the front office and prepared for a grand experience, each step sinking in brown Orlon.

It was not my intention to control the old woman's life or to take over the management of her affairs. But I knew that for all practical purposes this was her last chance. If she failed to convince this lawyer, to hook him with the lure — if only by the upper lip, the alae of the nose, or the pinkie, she would be out of her fortune, another miserable old bag with a tedious story and no one to tell and no one willing to listen. And I knew that on her own she would fail, unless she behaved entirely differently from the way she did before me, or unless something in the documents I had not read would whet the lawyer's avarice. I decided the best thing I could do would be to sit in and insert help where needed — trim and stuff the carcass of the old woman's case, as it were, so as to make it as lifelike as possible.

Violet was seated in the middle of a prodigiously long table, a man seated facing her on the same side. I introduced myself, produced the envelope. The lawyer started browsing through the documents; he was actually able to read them. I gave him a brief accounting of the case as I saw it, since he did not bother with the painfully typed cover letter. The old woman, to my chagrin, seemed to be drifting mentally: her eyes were filmy, far away. It seemed she didn't care. The lawyer, an exceedingly ugly man with glasses, a bulbous red hairy nose and a chin that wobbled in progressively fatter layers into something supposed to be a neck, didn't notice. He was munching dockets. I waited in trepidation.

He looked up. It was hard to tell if he was recently bored, or his permanent boredom had been alleviated by what he had read. His first question concerned what, in fact, Violet hoped to recover. She began right away with an attack on Shocker: "He is so evil, he'll stop at nothing, and do you know, he forced my husband to drink in the hospital." I broke in that her case fell into three sections, etc. The lawyer, still addressing Violet, but responding to my comment, stated that it would be impossible to recover the property, since she had been divorced prior to her husband's death. Again, I interposed that she wished to contest the divorce. Violet contributed that she had never received the cash settlement. The lawyer's face remained impassive: perhaps this was a device he had practiced at the beginning of his career and his facial muscles had atrophied over the years. However, there was the slightest glimmer of puzzlement. He returned to the papers, leafed through them slowly.

"Ah, Judge B.," he said to himself.

"Yes," reacted Violet, "she's a judge now, but she took money from Shocker, the same as..."

The lawyer turned up his dead face and heard Violet out. She, poor thing, had no idea that she was destroying herself. She had somehow forgotten that she was speaking not to me, or to Angel, but to a tough, expensive Los Angeles attorney. Here, at the most crucial moment of her case, if not her life, she was

suffering a lapse, perhaps from the relief at having arrived at
this point. I could do nothing to save her.

"Judge B. is one of the most respectable..." the lawyer
remonstrated. "And she would never... blah, blah."

I followed with the observation that it was natural for one
to become suspicious when a victim of injustice: the old woman
had been treated harshly, that much was clear. And I directed
his attention to the flipflop of Shocker, from one client to the
other, simultaneously picking out the papers of his censure.

The lawyer examined them, his face unresponsive.

"Yes, this is a statement of censure," he agreed, "but it's on
a matter of..."

He made it sound as though Shocker had gone on vacation
at that time; it had nothing to do with this case. The lawyer
became interested in other papers, so I preserved silence. Violet
was declining badly; she understood vaguely the rebuff concern-
ing the judge and seemed mentally to have returned to the
sunshine, the cats.

"I see that you have sued every one of your lawyers," the
lips above the wobbling necks noted in passing.

"That Mr. J.," the old woman roused herself. "He told me: 'I
can get more money from Shocker than I can from you. I won't
go to court.' But he charged me, he charged me all the same.
Thousands and thousands," she drew out the words in the finest
opulent manner, "of dollars."

"Well, let's see," said the lawyer. "Here is a check for 2000,
another for 1375. This one is only for 325..."

"Shocker bought them all off," the old woman rattled on.

"Bought off Mr. J. and Judge B.? Hm, that's very interesting." The gargoyle permitted himself a touch of sarcasm, as if
only now forming the picture in his mind. Finally, he came to
the point. "There are only three weeks remaining for your final
appeal."

I rushed out the trump cards: the two wills. Whether they
had been considered in probate, I did not know. But the old
woman had never been notified of the death, and these two

documents alone deserved to be examined and checked against the record. On these alone she might have a case.

The lawyer looked at the original copies that Violet took, not without delays, from her purse. His face, of course, retained its immutable ugliness. He handed them back without a word. His mind was made up. But for some reason he did not hurry: possibly he had the hour to fill, or a portion of the next hour, so he could send the appropriate bill for consultation. He spoke about this and that, somewhat at a loss whether to address Violet or me, often inadvertently speaking of her as though she were not present. All the while she rolled her glazed eyes over the wood paneling and smiled an anile smile. I felt like a participant in a vile auction, rating the monetary value of a discarded old woman, dressed in an ancient dress and put on the block. How much is this old crone worth? She still has some juice in her veins. Maybe a pearl in her purse. Do I hear 1 hour? Do I hear 2? The lawyer took his time, then drew out the knife for slaughter.

"It would be impossible to bring this case to court in three weeks. You have to notify the other participants in advance, so they will have time to prepare their defense. Documents have to be drawn up, filed. No one would be able to do this in three weeks. Even if I filed the appeal, the court would throw out the case on the basis of insufficient time."

The old woman understood. And I understood that she could not be set adrift without hope, however flimsy the sail. I asked the lawyer if anything at all could be done, if any scrap could be saved. He responded fairly considerately, but still with the look of a stone freak, that we could write to the Clerk of the Superior Court of Fresno County for a copy of the probate proceedings and the final will of Laurence W., stating the year of his death and enclosing a self-addressed envelope. Depending on the information received, Violet might find a lawyer to take up this matter. I thanked him and made ready to leave. Violet woke up from her reveries, looked about her. The stone face mumbled a few words of standard condolence, the layers of neck wobbled. The odd couple stepped out into the plush lobby.

The parking bill for 2 hours was 10 dollars. Violet penned another shaky check. We loaded up at a gas station near the freeway; another check. I noticed that Violet didn't bother to enter the debits in her accounts. We turned down into the grand highway, joined the speeding shells of metal.

"Well, that lawyer wasn't much help," I offered. The old woman was silent. "He'll probably send you a bill, but there's no need to pay it."

She chuckled at this: "I have no intention of paying him a cent, not a cent!"

We glided along, and again she fell silent. I forgot about her for a while and then looked over. Her mouth was wrinkling, her eyes staring fixedly ahead and tearing: it was coming home to her. I looked back at the road, not wanting to invade her moment of grief.

A few minutes later I looked back: she had gone to sleep. She was old, old, and every wrinkle and vein, every furrow dug by the years and misfortune, every infliction wrought by the league of conniving advocates, with the maniacal Shocker at their head, was highlighted by the blazing sun, now beginning to fall. Her lips hung loosely, her eyelids puckered, her hands fell thick, purplish and edematous. I looked back at the road, fought against sleepiness myself. The miles rolled underneath the plump wheels; in the rear-view mirror I could see the great sweeping fin, as though the car were a rocket turned on its side: ordinary cars appeared magically to the right of the fin, then disappeared, then just as magically appeared in the side mirror. I glanced over at the old lady. She was dead. I looked back to the road. No, it couldn't be. I looked back at Violet. Nothing was moving: the veins and furrows had settled, become fixed. I looked for a sign of breathing, a pulse. Nothing. And I decided that this was proper, this was the best time for her to die. She had given it her best, she had lost. Why prolong the agony, slide into senility? I didn't relish my position: shooting down the highway in a Cadillac with its owner dead at my side, but I could just take her to the morgue and make my explanations. I was almost glad for her: she died a heroic death.

Just then the lips parted and the eyelids cracked. "You know," she mused, "I don't need a big house anymore. Just a little cottage in Palm Springs. That's all I need. With a garden. I lo-o-ove to tend the garden. And the sunshine."

FOUR

SATAN

THE CATS were meowing, rowring and sfitzing. I got out of my sleeping bag, slipped on some pants and went outside, around the corner of my apartment. They were all present: Demon, Savva, Rocky, Angel (or Two Face), the black Egyptian, the orange stray with patches of fur chewed out of his hide and the big bruiser himself, Nathaniel. He was creeping toward the stairs running up beside the former love-couple's residence, and the other cats were drawing back, circling and trying to sneak up behind him. They did not run at my approach, but freeze-framed, glared at me a moment, then resumed.

Under the first step I saw the point of the ritual: a silky longhair black Persian with a tiny face, a dot of a nose and huge, electrified yellow eyes. There could be no doubt that she was a bitch. Nathaniel crept under the stair; she half-rolled onto her side away from him, flicked her tail. He nuzzled up for a brute lick; she lashed out at him with spring-like speed, catching him off guard and chasing him out sideways. The other desperate males rushed in to take his place, but once again he crept forward in his deliberate way, and the underlings backed off. Savva and Angel, in fact, didn't even try: they watched and growled in surprise to themselves; they were still too young to know what it was about. Demon kept close, as close as audacity allowed, certain that he would win the fair prize. I knew it was useless to scatter them; they would immediately reassemble. So I returned to the floor and fell asleep to the pandemonium, occasionally punctuated by the cry of a tortured neighbor.

The Persian belonged to a new tenant, a somewhat chubby girl with black hair, a pretty face and a thin line of moustache. Violet was upset, because the girl lived with a black man.

"She just lo-o-oves him, can you imagine? She just lo-o-oves that black man."

I told her it was O.K. with me, but she countered: "But what about her parents? What do they think? I told her, 'Think about the rest of your life. All the troubles you will have, how people will treat you.' But she can't see it, she simply adores the man."

I apprized Violet that times had changed, that it was no longer unusual for a black and white to live together.

"But she wants to marry him. I warned her: people will treat you differently. And what about your baby? What is he going to be — black or white or brown?"

It was good to see the old woman taking an interest. Perhaps she had let the millions pass by and was settling down to a moderately happy present, with cats, sexual scandals and changing times.

But no, she hadn't given up. I discovered her at the phone, calling God knows whom and saying God knows what. She was giving 'em hell, demanding her rights — the person on the other end was probably a random number.

I decided to steer her into safer waters. The newspaper, I said, would probably print her story. Something might come of this, because you can never tell how the public will react to an item in print. She might not attract an attorney, but something else might develop. It was worth a try. And, as a back-up, I suggested that if all else failed, she could type up her memoirs, make the case into a book. It was an interesting story, many people would read it. She might help another old lady. What I expected, of course, was that nothing would come of the newspaper article and she would live out her days pounding the typewriter, adding page after page to the confusion. But she would have a purpose and pleasant intermissions. "Build long, my dear Fet," as Tolstoi told his friend, who was building a house, "or you may finish and fall into despair."

<u>The Press-Enterprise</u> sent over a beautiful young woman named Arlene. She dressed modestly but excellently in a vivid green dress with a diaphanous sash of lighter color about the neck. Her face was rosy and radiating the freshness of youth, unhardened by experience, though she must have seen a lot. She came around to my place to get the story in advance, and even took me to a Mexican restaurant on her expense account. I looked lousy, ragged; my apartment was a mess, and by habit, when I meet someone willing to listen, I blabbed non-stop. The whole story gushed out, with all my reflections, suppositions. She dutifully took notes, probably thinking I was madder than the old woman.

Then she went around with me to the apartment and was introduced. The apartment, woefully, was worse than mine: papers everywhere, piles of cat poop, boxes, trash, bowls all over the floor, clothes draped over chairs, telephone books, <u>The Reader's Digest</u>, the Sony television playing non-stop. I left the lovely thing in the old woman's clutches and went back to my armchair to daydream impossible dreams. Later I saw the reporter returning to her car with an armful of familiar folders and blue dockets.

By this time my poverty had reached such a pass that I was troubled by a library book that had come due. The bus fare to return it was lacking, and my bicycle had picked up its monthly nail. The old woman, it occurred to me, owed me: no cat food had crossed my palm for a long time. So I got the ring of keys and sailed downtown, taking twice the space of any mere Datsun or Toyota. The Cad, to be sure, was drinking down the precious fluid like a desert of sand, but I was saving myself a fine — 5¢. I pressed the buttons of the master control panel on the driver's door; the windows stopped in different places. The windshield wipers jerked on and off, water shot up at my face. This was so much fun that, before I returned, I drove to the house and picked up the kids. We went for a spin with the radio blasting hillbilly music and the windows running up and down. Clark was visited — he's a car buff, and the whole gang of us terrorized the neighborhood. Then everybody was driven home, and the white mammoth returned to its owner, the ring of keys put round her finger. The pleasure ride over, I settled down for my nightly rice banquet.

The self-addressed envelope came back from Fresno. Violet rushed it around to me. "No record of probate for Laurence W. in Fresno County for the year of 1978." We couldn't believe it. He had died there; Mildred survived there.

"It's Shocker," the old woman sputtered, "Shocker!"

That one word told it all. He had manipulated the records, perhaps invaded the files at night. Or one of his servants had done his bidding. His fingers were constricting around the old veiny neck, tighter and tighter. He was choking the old crone, he loved to choke old crones, to make them spit blood, to make their swollen tongues stop up their throats... I shook my head. There must be a reasonabler explanation.

"Perhaps probate was held in L.A., or in Palm Springs."

"Impossible!" she insisted, spraying saliva.

Soon after, Arlene left me a message. I phoned from a free campus location and received the bad news. She couldn't go ahead with the story. She had spent more than a week on it, revisiting Violet and reading all of the materials. The old woman, she claimed, was not telling the truth. She had understood the divorce, even initiated it. She had received the cash settlement, it had paid her legal fees. She had hired lawyers one after the other, then sued each one in turn. The woman was a virago, a blistering hellfire, only now declining in vitality.

"She brought it all on herself," Arlene told me, citing the materials she had read and adding details and arguments I have since forgotten. I came to the old thing's defense, asking questions and posing possibilities. But the reporter, while admitting there were curious features, stated a bare fact: the newspaper could not stand behind such a story. Besides, her boss had another assignment for her and told her to stop wasting her time.

"I thought the newspaper would be interested in the human-interest angle," I replied ruefully. "And the feminist angle."

The cub reporter set me straight: "That's all we have, women's stories. They're getting to be boring."

The old woman, it seemed, had outlived even this fashion.

"Shocker!" she spat. "Shocker, he knows what's going on. They're afraid of him. He has friends in the press, you know."

"No, Violet, you have to stop this. Shocker is just a lawyer. He's probably forgotten the case. He doesn't have any special power. He doesn't care..."

"No, he doesn't care what happens to me. He's got my millions, my millions and millions of dollars."

There was no talking to her. I left, but at 5 a.m. there was a rap at my door. The old woman was standing there with a foolish smile on her face.

"Do you know where the letter is?" she asked me.

What letter? — the cover letter, it seems. I asked her if she had any idea of the time; she had not. She had begun sleeping when tired and waking when slept; the old wind-up clocks in her apartment had stopped. The TV ran all the time: who knew whether it was day or night? I walked her back part of the way, since she tended to lose direction and circle my block of apartments.

"Laurence told me I should call Shocker," she said lightly. "He has some money for me."

Did I hear rightly? Laurence told her?

"You mean in a dream, Laurence told you."

The old woman looked up at me as if I were dim.

"No, he told me."

I was at a loss what to say. If she believed Laurence to be alive, it might be wrong to hit her with the blunt truth. So I persisted:

"You must have been dreaming. Violet. Remember, you have vivid dreams, and they seem real afterwards."

She looked confused. "Yes, yes," she agreed at last. "But they are so re-e-eal."

The next day I was called over again. She wanted me to check some number, but couldn't remember which. I observed that the cats had passed a milestone: a brown blob right on the silk couch. The bowls were empty, encrusted with bits of dried meat. I tried to clean things up, emptied the trash, put the jug of mountain spring water in the cooler for her — this was a recent accession. The telephone bill lay open on her desk: many pages of numbers, a figure over $200. Violet herself was shabby: the nightgown had become her daily garb, a pair of shuffle slippers her footwear. Her legs, remarkably swollen and pitted, resembled the soft underbellies of hippopotami.

She turned to me and asked: "Would you call Shocker? I don't want to speak to him." I had expected this turn; it seemed inevitable. But I didn't want to accept it. She had succeeded in infecting me with her fear; I knew my ignorance of law would put me at a disadvantage with this crafty adversary. Besides, I feared that Violet's paranoia would turn on me: I would be added to the list of henchmen, I would become Shocker's chief agent, the spy sent out to misdirect her and spoil her final efforts to regain her millions. On the other hand, I realized that I had become involved in her story, her fate, and this episode was an integral part. What to do?

I expressed my unwillingness: what was the point?

Violet for the first time became submissive. "There must be some money for me," she pleaded. "Ask him if he has any money."

I told her I was certain he didn't.

"But ask him if Mildred might share some of the estate. I'm an old woman," she moaned.

Touched by this confession, I agreed. But first I had to protect myself:

"Now, Violet, I want you to understand. I can't go on the attack with him. The best I can do is pretend not to understand and ask for his advice. Do you see?"

She nodded obediently.

"So don't think I am against you if I don't argue with him. I will pretend I don't know anything, understand? I think we can get more out of him that way."

"All right," she said.

I could tell she was already nervous, and I was not too confident myself. I phoned the L.A. operator, got the listing for Victor E. Shocker. His secretary put me through when I informed her the call was in reference to Violet W. I heard a man's voice stating his name. A nondescript voice, perhaps a bit more tenor than I had imagined.

I explained to him that I was a neighbor who had found Violet in sad straits; she had many bills, little income and memories of a rich husband. I understood that he had been involved with her case and wondered if he might know any way the woman could recover even a small part of her fortune. Violet, meanwhile, was prompting me with strenuous gestures and stern grimaces, having immediately been put out by my meekness. But it worked: Shocker did not hang up and started talking. I listened.

Yes, he said, he had vague recollections of the case. But there was not a lot of money there. Only 30 to 40 thousand dollars when Laurence died, and that was eaten up at once by his sister — there was a sister, he believed, up north — and the sons of the first marriage. It was a sorry sight the way the sons fought over the property; they were trying to get it while the old man was dying, and the judge took them into closed chambers and gave them a good bawling-out. They actually cried. Millions of dollars? No, that was back in the twenties, he believed. After that Laurence had only some stocks and a modest bank account.

Violet was motioning frantically as bits of this account were relayed to her through my replies. I waved back at her and encouraged Shocker to continue. Did he happen to remember the divorce? Violet claimed she had never received the cash settlement.

"Claims!" she grumbled out loud. "Claims!"

Shocker sounded tired. They had been through all that before, over and over again. She had received the money, about $10,000, he recalled, and it had paid for her legal bills. She had sued so many times for this money, which she had already received, that the judge took her aside and lectured her, and she was given written notification that the court would not hear this case again and would hold her in contempt if she attempted to pursue it.

"Oh, those lawyers," she interjected, "how they tied me up."

What about Mildred, might she be willing to part with some money, since the old woman was a relative, so to speak?

No, that was not possible, because she had no money. She had a house in Fresno, he now recalled, and she had built a wing on it with the money she had inherited. Yes, there had been an examination of wills at probate — the last one was written after the divorce.

"They made him write it!" the old woman ranted.

She was shaking her fist at me, as though I were betraying her. I held out the receiver to her: here, you tell him, if you like. She cowered from it like a lioness from the whip of her trainer.

It was really a shame, Shocker went on, she could have been quite happy. She had a little house in Palm Springs, the furniture and some valuables. All she needed to do was get a job to pay her expenses, but she chose to risk everything to get more money. No, no, there was no more money to be had. A sad story, he concluded, but there was nothing he could do.

At the risk of giving him the final satisfaction, I asked what action he would advise for the old woman to support herself — she couldn't get a job now.

He advised checking with welfare — "Never, never!" stormed the old woman — and social security. Although she received social security through Laurence, he believed. "But there's no point in going to lawyers," he added. "Why, she visited an attorney in Los Angeles just the other week."

I thanked him; we signed off.

Violet was exasperated. I was perplexed. The man sounded perfectly reasonable, and yet... he remembered the case awfully well more than 10 years later. A wing on the house in Fresno? Social security through Laurence? Our trip to L.A.? Did he know everything, after all? Violet was fuming, shaking; she didn't know what to do with herself.

"Welfare! He wants me to take welfare! It's hum... it's hum..." And now she broke down completely, she was screaming with rage: "No, never, never! I want my millions, I want my millions!"

She actually started jumping up and down, like a child throwing a tantrum. But she was too old to keep this up, and she stopped, contorting her face with hatred, spitting and slashing with her big yellowish horse teeth. She was trying to curse, but didn't know how. "Goddamned... hell damn bastards... nasty hell damn sth... sth..."

Her ultra-rich lisp completed her miseries.

The next time I saw her, she was calm, so I tried to talk sense into her. The final date for appeal had expired, I reminded her. The probate records were probably in L.A., but there was a final will, written after her two wills, so it was hardly worth the effort. Most likely there was no money left, as Shocker had said, or if there was it was all tied up, possibly concealed. It was time for her to decide: either to waste her life in a hopeless pursuit or try to make the best of what she had. Again I related the joys of leisure, the contemplative life, the purpose of writing memoirs. She listened patiently, with a soft smile. "I can't let them get away with it," she purred.

I took another approach.

"O.K., Violet, let's say you get your millions. What would you do with them? You're not a young woman, you know. You're not going to fly around the world, are you? Sure, you can buy a house, but do you really need more space than you already have? Are you going to eat more than you presently eat? Will millions buy you more sunshine? Do you need more cats? Just tell me, why do you need a million bucks?"

The old woman was dumbfounded. She searched about herself with vacant eyes. The question, quite obviously, had never entered her head in all of these years. She had simply taken it for granted that she needed millions of dollars, millions and millions of dollars.

"Why I, I... I want to buy some clothes," she blurted out with a toss of her head, as if the question were too trifling to consider beyond a moment.

I got a job. My debts had piled up, my prospect dropped down. Step by step I was drawn into a job I had originally refused: day care of a quadriplegic. Almost immediately Violet dropped out of sight. I had to bicycle to the job five times a day, bicycle back, and that alone was tiring. The emotional demands of the job, for me at least, were draining. I had no time for the old woman, her molasses movements, her mad conversations, always sticking on the same point. I told her in advance, of course, that I would not be around anymore, and again advised her to take care of her daily matters and leave Shocker to Judgement Day. But she gave me the same answer. I avoided her, to tell the truth. My rest-time was now precious: I couldn't squander it on the same old story. When I saw her standing outside her apartment, or in one of the walkways, I took a different route, or sped by and called out hello. She looked around, wondering where the voice had come from.

Still, she felt free to rap on my door at any hour. Sometimes I would answer, sometimes not. If she stood there a very long time I would feel sorry for her and admit her. She would come in almost apologetically, have nothing to say, or give me a patently phony excuse. On one of these occasions I learned that her neighbor was leaving with her black boyfriend: Violet would be all alone. At the supermarket I happened to see the couple, and it turned out, to my way of thinking, that the girl had got the better deal: the black man was light brown, athletic in bearing, alert, while she was already beginning to blimp out and her moustache was visible three aisles away.

The Persian longhair, as might be expected, was left in the old woman's care. Or rather, abandoned. In the following days, I saw her slinking around the bushes, her belly distended with babies. Little demons, in fact, for Demon alone managed to stride up behind her and manfully nip the back of her neck. She was starving every time I saw her, and I fed her when I could. Nathaniel, however, was even more pitiful: he showed up one morning with a whole patch of scalp, from his right eye to the back of his right ear, torn off. The raw white flesh was stippled with red dots of capillaries. He was timid, skittish. The bowl had to be left at some distance, and when other interested cats approached it, he packed off.

So, as in the beginning, my contacts with the old woman were made slapdash in the midst of other concerns. Looking back, I now realize that I should have foreseen the catastrophe, but while I saw every sign I did not know where it pointed. Life had not presented me such a vista as yet. When Violet continued to talk of Laurence, as though he were in touch with her, I let it pass: I simply looked deeply into her eyes. Perhaps she was pretending? The eyes, however, did not permit penetration: they were opaque. A pasty film lay over them, yet in the centers little flecks, like little sparklers, signalled great delight, gaiety — a private celebration. I wondered if I was seeing the real thing — or was she imitating a movie. But she didn't go to the movies: their madmen imitated people like her.

Once I mildly suggested: "Violet, do you remember? We have the death certificate. Laurence, you know, is dead."

She paused over this item of news.

"But he came into my living room."

No, I assured her, that could not be.

Another pause, then the answer: "Shocker, he forged the death certificate. He wanted to fool me. But Laurence found out. He wouldn't leave me alone like this."

Shocker had been promoted, his powers had expanded. Now he no longer contented himself with strangling old women and controlling their lawyers, bribing judges and silencing the press, watching, watching everywhere and knowing every move, every thought, every breath of his enemies; now he assumed command over life and death. He could make a living person disappear and all the records declare his death; he could abscond with millions of dollars and not leave a blot in the books. Behind the scenes, with supernatural powers, Victor E. Shocker moved men and money and defied the glory of God.

"Violet," I tried one last time, "you are dreaming all this. Laurence is dead, and you want him to come back. You dream that he does, then you forget it's a dream. But you have to keep the two separate. When you're awake, he's dead."

She stopped and looked at me. The gay light went out of her eyes for a moment, and she examined me very seriously.

"What an odd idea!" she giggled. "I know he's alive. I see him, I talk with him. If it was only a dream — oh, that would be horrible."

I had to give up, pedal away. She was now alone with her delusion, living among the dead, at the mercy of a malevolent spirit. And the arguments of reason, the assertions of the quick, the convictions of society — these were odd ideas.

The next time I saw the old woman I didn't want to. I had just prepared myself for a night with Shakespeare, the last televised play of the season. A scrape at the door: it is she. I knew at once that she was pathetic, desperately lonely. I couldn't refuse her entry. But at this time I was absolutely exhausted, thirsting for my leisure like a man who has slogged through swamps and mine fields with a piece of shrapnel in his head — he sees the compound, he lets his last energy go in anticipation of the bed, takes another step and... a babbling old crone pops up in front of him. She muttered something about a piece of paper, shuffled in and sat down when I stepped aside. <u>The Tempest</u> was in progress, and Violet proceeded to expatiate on her love of Shakespeare, and the prowess of Laurence in the arts and sciences. She spoke of him in the past; this Laurence, the historical one, was evidently separate in her mind; the new, revived one did not make his appearance. I strained to hear the TV. Yare, yare! — someone was yelling. I consulted my pocket edition of the work, acquired at the university book exchange in return for a useless Russian volume, hoped the woman would shut up. She kept on babbling: "Oh, how I love Shakespeare!"

Patience was wearing thin, but I had the presence of mind not to be rough with her. She smiled at me blissfully, her eyes completely fogged; she was lapsing into a happy vision, perhaps a slip back in time to our earlier, less troubled conversations. I could hardly stand to look at her, yet I was mad. She dropped her keys, shattering the queer dialogue. I held my breath, tried to attend, but I could not help but see how she feebly lifted the ring between her thumb and forefinger: it dropped again. She smiled, picked it up. I smiled politely, but not very graciously, turned back to the set. But I could see her, of course, leaning over, trying to pick up the ring, getting it up to her waist, shaking it for the pleasure of the sound, dropping it again. Let others judge me who have endured such a nuisance: I announced that the Wolf had to go for a walk, stood — and she obediently rose to leave with me. I watched her wander back to her apartment: it was a straight line from the point where I left her, but she made it look like a maze.

The last time I saw her before the end I was on my way to work: the afternoon check. Violet's car was clogging the entrance to the parking lot. She thrust her white head out the window: "What's wrong, what's wrong? Why won't it go?" I stopped my bike, asked her to get out. A quick check confirmed that the car was overheated. The hood, looking like the carapace of a huge prehistoric tortoise, was raised, releasing puffs of steam. Fetching a scrap of trash from the back seat, I covered the radiator cap, screwed it off; a geyser shot up in the air. Wolfgang, I and the bicycle danced backwards. Leaving dog and bike at a safe distance, I ran into Violet's apartment for a pitcher of water. The sink was stopped up with dirty pans, putrid dish water and floating chunks of food. I thought to phone Darwin, in case I'd be late: the line was dead. Bills scattered over the desk, the Sony playing an educational children's program. I managed to get some water, passed Violet on her way in. She was carrying a bag of groceries — someone had accepted her check. I poured a little water in the radiator; it shot back out, boiling. This I repeated a few times, because the car had to be cooled quickly, as it was blocking the driveway. Water ran from the bottom of the radiator, trickled from the hose running under the motor. Eventually the needle went down: I was able to start the motor and drive the car haltingly to a parking space, where it died. The great white mammoth had finally succumbed, pouring water from its punctures, dropping globs from its joints, too weak even to close its eyes. Did I kill it, or Violet, or the both of us together? Or was it the victim of an evil design? No time to think: a man in a wheelchair was waiting.

FIVE

HELL

IT WAS time to tell her the bad news: I would be moving. Jean had decided to go to San Diego for two years, where she would study, and I was permitted back in the house with my daughters. In fact, I had already moved everything and had one night remaining in my apartment. My job had also come to an end; for two months or more I had slighted Violet. I felt sorry for her, but now could make it up, spend some time with her.

I rapped on the door: no answer. I knew she was inside: the white bones of the mammoth gleamed in the lot from the floodlight attached to the building. She would be riding no more. But her inside light was off, as was her outside. This was unusual. I knocked again. Something scraped within at the bottom of the door — a cat. I knocked again — with force. All was still, the cat whined. I banged, banged. A shuffle, the door slowly opened. Rocky ran out. Violet's face appeared in the dark, long and tired.

"Oh, I was just going to sleep. I'm so tired."

The odor of gas hit me, I pushed past her and stepped to the stove, knocking against things. The vent was wide open: no flame. I turned it off, saved her life. By the light of the flipping TV, I made my way to the window and opened it. A fluffy white body crept over the furniture, languid pigeons slipped to the floor. I told the old lady the news; she went back to bed, uncomprehending.

The next day I phoned the rental office from the house, announcing myself as Frank Smith. I could not give my true identity, since I had moved out without notice, evading the dog fee. The old woman's stove was defective, I informed the landlady, the pilot light kept going out. If it wasn't repaired, there might be a serious accident. The water heater too was deficient: she had no hot water. The landlady offered excuses, but promised to send someone over for the stove. She didn't want a corpse on her hands.

And who was I? A friend from out of town, who happened to have stopped by. Did I know the old woman's husband? No, I couldn't say that I did. The landlady wondered, because Violet was a week behind in her rent. She said her husband would pay it, but the husband couldn't be found.

"She looks kinda funny sometimes," the landlady observed. "Do you suppose you could talk to her husband?"

I promised to do what I could.

Afterwards I went over on my bike. Violet was up and about, but not fully coherent. I told her about the stove; she complained that they would never fix it.

"About the rent, Violet. Do you have the money to pay it?"

"I don't have to worry about that. You see, Laurence is going to pay it."

"Laurence?" I inquired, wondering if he could make things materialize.

"Yes, I told him: 'If you're going to live here, you will just have to pay the rent.'"

Perfectly logical, I had to admit.

A day or so passed. Unpacking books, setting up house. Still, I worried about the friends of my former life: Demon, Darwin, the old woman. The first, I should mention, preferred to stay — to fight the bully (who had grown a new scalp), to love the Persian (who had birthed in the bushes) and to pick up foxtails and weeds in his wanderings. Today, as I write, he is alive and well, having charmed the new tenant of my apartment, who leaves big bowls of cat food outside the door.

Darwin had hired a new attendant; he welcomed my visits for conversation, but didn't require my services anymore.

The old woman, once again, had not turned out her lights. I found her inside, behind an unlocked door. The cats were running wild over the furniture: they wanted their supper. Violet sat slumped in her armchair; she couldn't rise. The Sony in front of her was playing a program in Japanese: she didn't notice the difference. I switched the channel, asked her how she was doing. She mumbled something about hunger. I checked the refrigerator: the door was weighed down with bottles of vitamins, bags of soya powder, bone meal — products of Lindberg Nutrition. On the racks were cans of oysters, bottles of pickles, relics of ancient meals. She had nothing to eat.

"When was the last time you ate, Violet?"

"I had something the other day, soon."

What did she want? Ice cream, she had to have ice cream. With my petty cash (the only kind I had), I bought a short order from a nearby restaurant. Violet's dry old face took in the nourishment, the hamburger and milk, like slow quicksand wrapping around a fallen lump.

"Mmm, mmm," she moaned.

A small portion of milk was poured into the dirty bowls for the cats: they climbed over each other to get at it and licked it up like flies.

The situation was desperate, I finally realized. My mind had been diverted — or rather, had never concentrated on the old woman. She had always been a sidelight, an accidental acquaintance, never the central focus. But now, without daily attention, she would fail. She could no longer function for herself. Yet if I telephoned anyone, any authority, she would without question be committed. The world doesn't like people who speak to the dead, unless they charge for admission. Perhaps if I fed her a few good meals, helped clean up her place, she could be persuaded to pay her rent from her social security, and then she might locate a suitable home with funds from welfare. After all, she was harmless, and a fairly likeable old cuss when dispossessed of her mania. Why should she be locked up, treated like a nuisance, a non-human, just because she believed she had lost a million dollars?

The next day, after breakfast, I went around to her place. She had managed to get herself into bed. Angel emerged from under the covers, jumped over her open mouth. I threw the cats out. Violet was famished. I made her some oatmeal, some tea with things I had brought: her sink was a cesspool. She sipped, chewed, wanted it hotter. She was freezing. I found another cover, a thick, expensive, woolen one. Her big teeth were chattering, they were really her own. I spooned up the stuff: she wanted, didn't want every other mouthful. Her whole body started shaking, letting out moans. She was passing beyond my ability to help her: I tried to ask her — what should I do?

"Don't take me to the hospital," she screeched, straining to kindle the old fire.

"But you're sick, Violet, you need medical help."

She mentioned her doctor, mumbling the first sounds of his name, losing the last sounds in faint raspings. I rounded up some vials from her bathroom, her clothes cabinet, read her the names from the labels. She recognized one, I hurried across the street to phone. The doctor's secretary informed me, by return call, that they were sending a paramedic and that, if she so advised, Violet would be taken to the hospital. There the doctor would treat her.

The paramedic was a brown girl pleased with her training: she pulled down the covers and examined Violet, making a point of stating the medical terminology. The elephantine legs, mottled with pits, were such and such a condition, indicative of heart trouble; the blood pressure and auscultation confirmed the diagnosis. The girl looked in Violet's mad eyes, took her temperature and did other small things, recording each result on her clipboard. She checked underneath Violet to make sure the bed was not soiled: I held my breath, hoping I would not be called upon to perform that disagreeable task, since I had done my share with Darwin, and for that matter with Wolf, who had been suffering weak bowels of late. Fate smiled on me: the bedding was clean. A chunk, without toilet paper, was discovered in the toilet: I flushed it down.

The paramedic decided that Violet needed emergency treatment. It was a good thing, she hummed, that I had called the doctor. Once again I had saved the old woman's life, but I was beginning to doubt my good service. Might she not better die in

her bed, petting Angel and conversing with Laurence? Now she
was headed God knows where.

A dinky ambulance, looking like a milk truck, answered the
paramedic's call. Two men rolled Violet onto a stretcher, paying
no attention to her arms, legs or anything else. She was shoved
into the back like a big loaf of bread. A few feeble protests rose
up from the stretcher, but the girl and I assured her that her
own personal doctor would attend her. A little purse with as
much identification as I could find was placed on her stomach.
The ambulance took off; no one stopped to watch. It was a sunny
afternoon: the joggers were coursing the field, the tenants
passing by on their way to the pool or getting the coals ready in
their hibachis for the steaks they would cook by their doors. The
brown girl suggested I keep Violet's keys, in case her mail
needed to be forwarded: she herself was not permitted to take
anything or even to enter the apartment. We petted the cats,
which had all congregated, and the girl took her leave.

Violet would be in intensive care for the next three days,
incommunicada. During that time my function would be to feed
the cats and keep an eye on things. The first thing my eye fell
upon was a bill in her mailbox, arriving the day after her
departure, from the Goodhew Ambulance Service. Probably it
was mailed before the sheets were turned down on her bed. At
first I was puzzled, but then I understood: they were billing her
next of kin. The next day a yellow notice was scotch-taped face
down on her door: pay up or ship out. The landlady, who had
told Frank Smith on his last phone call, "I don't want to throw an
old lady out on the street, but (sob) I want my rent!" — had given
up on Laurence.

I decided to send Frank Smith out of town and in my own
name phoned the city's ombudsman, obtaining the number from
Arlene at the paper. It turned out to be an ombudsperson, Janet
Goesky by name, and she was swamped with emergency calls
for aging women: Violet was by no means an isolated case.
Goesky promised to phone and placate the landlady, and to keep
in touch with the hospital. She expected a Public Guardian
would be appointed over Violet from the Adult Protective Service

— an institution unknown to me. She would try to jawbone them into sending someone to clear the apartment, but, she said frankly, don't expect much. Often she had to spend her own money and find her own volunteers, though hers was an unpaid position. The notice from the landlady, she informed me, would hold for so many days and then, if not answered satisfactorily, be followed by an eviction notice. At that time the landlady would have the legal right to seize property in lieu of rent. If the Social Services paid the rent, and Violet recovered, there was a chance she would return to her apartment. Meanwhile, Goesky advised, I should go through Violet's things and forward any important papers, including bills, to the Social Worker stationed at the hospital. As a private citizen, I had more freedom in this matter than officially appointed persons. Goesky herself sounded quite old. She was active and hardy, but so too was Violet once upon a time.

On the third day, after dumping a tin of oysters in front of the starving cats, who ate a few bites with revulsion, I rummaged through the desolate apartment. Clothes littered the furniture, the floor. Bureau drawers had been pulled out and dropped: the old woman had lacked the strength to put them back in place. A shoe here, a slipper there. Half-empty bottles, empty bottles, vials, medicines, magazines of various dates, a tinted photograph in a frame of a World War I soldier with a moustache and leather wraparound flyer's helmet, glass jewelry, safety pins, big blankets, broken wooden chairs, cardboard boxes of china, pencils, staplers, desk calendars ten years old, thirty years old, hand mirrors, little boxes that rattled, clocks not ticking, defective lamps with Japanese designs and square pagoda shades, dirty spoons, balls of trash, egg shells, empty egg cartons, huge plastic jugs of spring water, dry piles of cat droppings. In a bottom drawer of a bureau in the bedroom I came upon a last will and testament: it was dated 1962, or was it 1967, and named the sister of a brother or sister, or cousin, as beneficiary — Violet probably survived whoever it was. From diverse piles of papers I paused over a neatly typed parcel of small-sized stationery: "This is the story of my dog..." The writing was cute, house-wifey. Additional chronologies turned up. I skimmed a few, resisting the temptation of others. Bills were pouring in with each day: first notice, second, third. I put them with the will in a large discolored manila envelope. Going through her purses, of which there were three or four, I came upon a curious item: a little red wallet.

Inside, I thought, might yet be some document that would help her — identify a living relative, or entitle her to welfare benefits, insurance. I looked through the slits for cards: not a stitch. I flipped the transparent plastic holders: not one photograph. The lengthwise section for currency was empty, but on pulling out the flap to the secret compartment I detected a little piece of paper rolled up in the corner. I took it out, unravelled it and read the pencilled reminder:

Satan is a legalist.

Violet recovered physically. I phoned her a number of times over the days and listened to her ravings. The nurses weren't feeding her, she insisted; they wanted to starve her. When she begged them for food, they stood around laughing.

Why did I almost believe her? — I could visualize orderlies amused by the mad woman, grinning and cracking jokes in her presence. I spoke to the head nurse of the floor, a very reasonable woman, and learned that Violet had eaten heartily at the last mealtime — though the diet was limited. Tomorrow she would go on solids, and I could tell her so to reassure her.

"She is quite confused," the nurse told me, and every other person in the hospital used the same word — "confused." It was clear the shrinks would be summoned.

Violet meanwhile cried and groaned on the phone, describing the most horrid scenes of persecution. I listened with remorse, because they were real for her. She was living in absolute hell.

But one fine day there was a change: Violet was happy. The people were kind. She had never been treated better. In short, the right drug. As for me, she didn't know who I was. I had to identify myself by reference to Wolf, whom she unfailingly remembered. The cats too were vague: she spoke of Angel, but tended to confuse him (whom she always considered a she) with Fluffy (that is, Savva) and a cat from the epicene past. Our conversations thus reverted to their initial subject, only now in infantile/senile form. I scheduled my phone calls for five minutes to nine, beyond which calls were not permitted.

During these same days I repeatedly phoned Goesky, who repeatedly phoned the Adult Protective Service, which repeatedly failed to materialize. I carried out trash and straightened a few things, but otherwise left the mess in place. Why bother, if Violet might not return? And, of course, I continued to feed the cats, now bringing my own supply of food, paying back the fee I had once earned. Neighbors occasionally stopped and remarked on the cats, but when I mentioned their status interest dropped and conversation evaporated. There was no one I could even ask to put out food, the bastards.

Since the days were passing and nothing was being done, I began to fear for Violet's possessions. The landlady had already demonstrated her priorities, and only I, as Chief Private Citizen, could ward off the pillage of the unguarded apartment. On the other hand, I didn't relish the prospect of removing things from the premises, pushing the Cadillac into the street — what would I do with the corpse if I managed to impound it? Each day as I sneaked into the evil-smelling place, I agonized: should I take anything, or not? The Sony TV, probably the only thing of value, stared at me mutely each day. Finally, I resolved: take the set for Violet. I opened the door and was stunned: the spot was empty. On the very same day the landlady had snapped up the goods.

This broke the seal. I took the Olivetti typewriter, typing supplies, sterling pickle forks, flashy jewelry that was certainly glass, the metal swinging bar. I also loaded a jug of spring water for myself on the back of my bike. The tap water of Riverside has more sediment than the phlegm of a consumptive, and I can't afford a high-powered filter. Most likely, I reasoned, the company would write the bill off. Anyway, why should they own the spring? The vitamins, I figured, would perish: they couldn't be resold and would therefore be junked, no matter who took them — landlady or social service.

Immediately after removing these items, I learned from the hospital social worker that Violet would not be returning: she was mentally incompetent and would be placed in an old-age home. If I would turn over the keys to her apartment, he said, the social services would, in good time, sell her possessions to help defray public expenses.

With this piece of news, I resolved to take for myself. More water, more vitamins, odd pieces of furniture — whatever would fit on my bike. Hauling cardboard boxes of china, electrical appliances and strange odds and ends (e.g., the correspondence for the year 1957, hideously maudlin Christmas cards, spices) out of the closet, I caught myself in time. My purpose was not to loot, not to tear the last shreds of tight skin from the dry bones, but to take what she herself would probably give me, could she understand the situation, and what others would probably discard. This was not stealing, was it? Later on, after my visit with Violet, I took the pickle forks to a pawnbroker. He offered 12 bucks. I accepted, since I felt like a criminal who could not haggle about a hot item. No one would buy the jade earrings. All the other jewelry was glass, a dealer told me with an outright sneer. I type with the typewriter, as you know. I swing, ourang-utan-wise, from the bar at the entrance to my room. The old woman's things live on.

Mr. Bussell, the Social Worker, was a diminutive old man in a fusty, baggy suit who had the relaxed manner of one who has endured misery and the stained teeth of one who cannot break a habit. I took him for an alcoholic, but he spoke soberly and was not chewing gum. I turned the manila envelope, now containing the keys and latest bills, over to him, and he, speaking without hurry, expressed his sympathy for Violet and others like her. In his baggy eyes I could see years of miserable old women passing through the wards, some to the plot, some to the home, some to the place whence they had come — a rotting apartment, with cats. And also, old men.

Leaving Bussell in his basement office, I took the elevator to the second floor and proceeded to the desk, which looked every bit the same as its replica on television programs. A nurse, in answer to my inquiry, consulted a chart and pointed me down the shellacked spacious hall. At each alcove, not closed off by a curtain or door, I saw sick old people, who didn't look back. Violet was visible from the hall, lying in the first bed of her room, flat on her back, with an open mouth, sound asleep. Her face appeared to have shrunken and the skin to have tightened over her cheekbones. From the neck down she was covered by a sheet, which clung close to her body and accentuated its puniness in the broad bed. The far bed was empty, the TV above it silent. But above the foot of Violet's bed, mounted on a metal plate right under the ceiling, the set was playing: a daytime serial or soap.

I stepped up close to Violet, watched her innocent breathing, her shiny forehead. Regretting the necessity of waking her, I shook her arm lightly. She went on sleeping, until by stages I was forced to give her a good tug. Then she looked up smiling, willing to do whatever. I asked if she remembered me, she didn't.

"Wolf?" I said, "the big black and white dog?"

Her smile changed from emptiness to content — additional wrinkles appeared about the mouth.

"O-o-o," she exclaimed in rising intonation, "Wo-o-olf. How could I forget?"

"Well," I continued, "I just stopped by to see how you were doing."

"I'm fine, I'm really..."

She paused, as if seeking the best word, but this intention slipped from her face and left unveiled a blank panic. Time began to be measured, to slide like mud. The droning voice of the television, reproduced in thousands of hospital rooms, prison cells, nurseries, gave sound to the enduring mindlessness. Violet, having dropped into a hole of silence, struggled suddenly and with a spasm of her cheek and nose forced to the surface: "...good, you know." She repeated the word a few times, to make sure she had retained it, and, having saved her mind from nullity, smiled peacefully.

I asked if she was getting enough to eat.

"Oh, yes, yes. They feed me so well. They are all such nice people, you know. Why shouldn't I get enough to eat?"

"You complained once."

"Oh, no, I'm feeling really, really... good, you know. I went to see him just yesterday. He's a fine man. He's a fine, fine...(again the eyes swirled around in horror)...man. Sarah and I, we were there. And you know, we had a picnic!"

"Who was the man?"

"The man? He's... you know, he's...(her eyebrows knitted, she felt like giving up, but then retrieved a word)...good. He runs everything, he controls the whole operation, everyone does what he says. And we went to see him at the little house."

I imagined a psychiatrist, but said: "You mean the head of the hospital?"

"Yes," she began, but then puzzled over something. "He runs the hospital." She paused, as if this matter had been firmly settled and could safely be let go. "He was so nice to me. And he's such an important man. He runs it all, you know, absolutely al-l-l-l-l!"

"And what did he say?"

"What did he say?" She fell into silence. The lovers on the soap were embracing, the woman confiding her problems. The scene changed, two women were talking. The hall was empty, clean. The air-conditioning was running.

"He... he..." Violet aspirated, stopped. Her eyes registered the utmost desperation, but also the unconsciousness of it. This was the final struggle, the claws scraping at the wall above the pursuing jaws. She had to climb, to reach. "He..." she repeated, her voice rising to a terrified squeak, "he..." The pupils fluttered briefly, then fell and stared into space, as if shocked.

"Well, I'd better be going, Violet. I'm glad you're feeling all right."

"Yes, I... am."

"And I want you to know, I'm taking care of your cats. Angel, remember? The white one with different eyes?"

She searched, found nothing. Bit her lips with her old teeth, the same despite many trials. Suddenly she remembered: "There were kittens at the picnic. Julie had them. So cute. He lives in a cottage, a beau-u-utiful cottage. Yesterday I went to see the King!"

I shook the bony hand, smiled at her uncomprehending smile. She was happy, she was with the King. But as I left I remembered a scene from my years as a professor. The empty classroom: the blackboard is erased, and only parts of words, smears of white chalk, stand out clearly at far removes from one another. Between them, on the slate, a landscape of faint squiggles.

EPILOGUE

ow that my typewriter has been repaired, I may swiftly report the fate of the cats. Since it was easier to feed them at home than at Violet's, I removed them to the house. They regained their health, lost their fleas and became a nuisance. Every time you stepped out the door, a cat would whine and trip you up. Inside, they were useless, peeing instantly upon contact with a rug. And, of course, they kept on eating, crapping all over the lawn and spraying the bushes. Savva was lush and beautiful, Rocky exotic, Two Face bizarre — but none of the three had much personality: they were grown-up babies. After a time, when I failed on my own to find them new homes, I called a place known as *The Cattery* and asked the woman if she might take them for sale. She agreed to come up the next day.

Ann Baker is a bit of a character. An old woman with wild grey hair and gaps between her teeth, she stands a few inches from you and shouts for all the world to hear about her business and yours, how she feeds her cats cheese and cream from Alpha Beta by a special agreement: she buys her hard cat food there, and they give her the outdated dairy products; how to treat ear mites; how bandits and nefarious dark people make raids on her cages. She was delighted to see Savva, whom she claimed was not a Himalayan, but her own patented breed, a Ragdoll. Without giving him a second look, she described to me all his physical features and habits — she knew him perfectly. When I stalled in my decision, since he was so handsome, she implied that he had been stolen: she never let Ragdolls out of her compound without fixing. (The young Hawaiians, I thought to myself, could well have picked up a stolen kitten.)

She then related a horror story about competition in the cat business — thefts from her premises, attempts to mix her pure breeds and outright assaults on the cats and slaughter. She produced photographs of dead cats, quasi-legal papers, and described a woman who collected giveaway cats and the sums of money frequently provided for their care, and then used these cats to train her pit bull dogs, which ate the remains. A vision of feline Armageddon arose before my mind's eye, but no worse than the routine execution of 15 million dogs and cats in the USA each year. She spoke, in passing, of the Riverside Humane Society, where I had done a stint of work: they were now putting 75 to sleep each day, 25 more than in my time. The bodies, as I recalled, were frozen and taken by a company that ground them up for fertilizer; the fertilizer nourished plants that fed animals destined for pet food. Thus the dogs and cats were recycled, if not indirectly eaten by humans. Wolfgang was marked for such a destination when I first saw him. Anyway, we talked about such delightful subjects in my driveway next to the hag's old car, she shouting blood and guts up and down the street.

Her offer was to take Savva and Rocky, but not for sale — rather for breeding. Savva, who in fact was a genetic freak, a sort of docile, retarded, extra-fluffy baby, she considered a stroke of good luck, though his eyes were slightly crossed. She hoped to enrich her new strain with him, the old strain having been massacred, and I could hardly refuse him the pleasure, let alone the cream, butter and cheese. Rocky was pure stuff: he'd have a sweet life too. But Two Face — well, cats don't sell well from summer until Christmas, and he was puny and strange. I would have to keep him, which wasn't so bad — he has come into his own without the others around.

We put Rocky and Savva, both bawling, in a cage the woman had brought and stuck it on the front seat. She went on screaming about her troubles, including an injury to the head that may have affected her brain, while I reduced my input and waited for her to leave. At length she ran down, left off the cat talk and climbed behind the wheel on her way to Alpha Beta. I waved a little wave as she started to pull out, but then suddenly sensed...

The car was big, white — without tails fins, true, but could it be? I stepped up, leaned over and spied the insignia in the hubcap: *Cadillac.*

POLYGLOTTOS

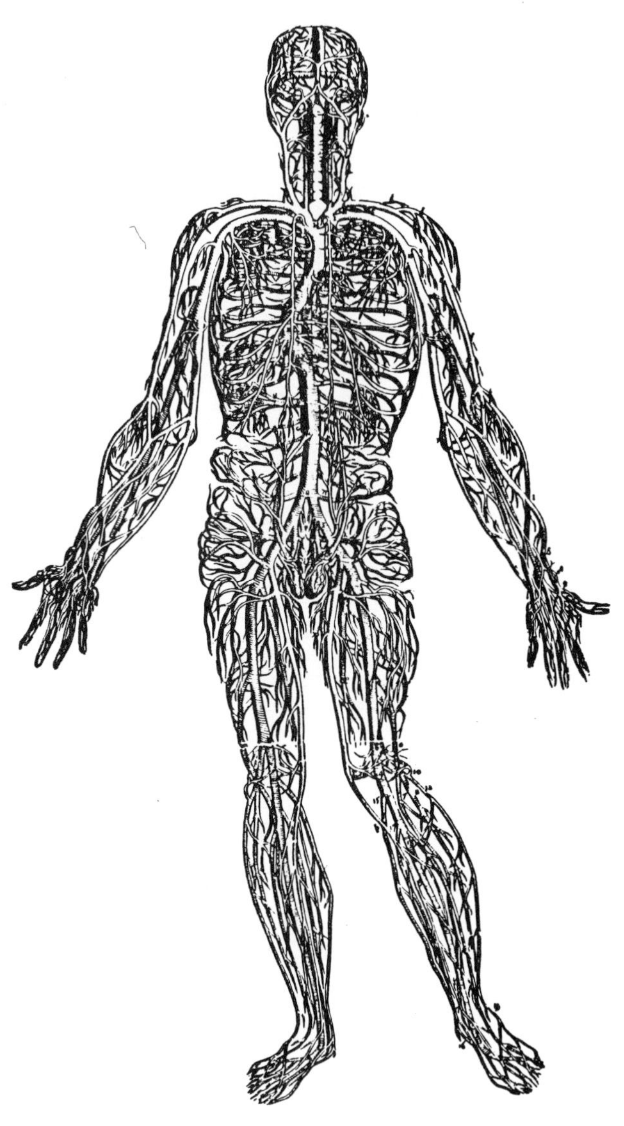

ONE

DOWN FROM THE MOUNTAIN

It was dark, but still early in the night. I was lying under an antenna station, eyes wide open. The floor of the station provided my roof, the concrete foundation and hard dirt mounds blocked off the chill breezes and needling rain. I tried to burrow my back in the crusted earth, to warm the spot at the base of my spine that registered warm and cold sensation, but the earth would not give way. From inside the mounds, farther back, where the sloping dirt joined the foundation, I could hear rustling, scuttling, squeaks. Every now and then something clicked above me, and I detected garbled radio voices in the hiss relayed over the mountain. Probably a red light was blinking at the top of the antenna, high in the sky, but I could not see it.

I lay in the dark and looked far below, over shapes of hills, boulders and valleys, at the double lights of isolated cars snaking down an invisible road. Farther out, past the silhouettes of mountains, a stream of dots poured down a grand highway. It was a private show: the lights reminded me of lives different from mine, different destinations, different stories, yet indicated a commonality. Where might that car be going, and what are its passengers thinking? Might they be a young man and his wife, early in marriage as I once was, and might not this trip be better than the place they have left and the situation upon their arrival? The mystery of night, imagination... But I felt no identity with them. Alone, teeth chattering, aware of my failure in life, I expected never again to take a trip, to have a destination or to converse with a friend. I looked at the lights with dumb wonderment, like a wild animal on the verge of extinction, catching sight of a passing machine.

My method of suicide was a poor one. Somehow I imagined that if I went up in the mountains and lay down, the days would pass and I would die. Starvation seemed the best way, or at

a way I could endure. My habits of exercise and careful
ting did not permit me to take poison, to make an actual
assault on my body. My body, after all, was not at fault.
Besides, I didn't have poison, or know how much to take. And
I was afraid to jump: mangled and gory, I might not succumb,
but instinctively try to crawl back. I might spend ten more
years not only as a failure, but as a cripple besides. The knife:
I had touched the point to my flesh between my ribs before I
left home. I knew it would hurt and make a big mess; I couldn't
take it seriously. I was a coward, afraid to take the honorable
way of Shakespearian heroes and disgraced Japanese. Then
again there was the probable effect on Jean and the girls, and
the life-insurance policy to worry about. Would it pay in such
an instance? I didn't want to leave things like my friend Steve,
who couldn't help it. No, starvation seemed best. Someone
would come across me after the event, my wife would have to
suffer only the moment of identification in the morgue, my
daughters would be spared, and the insurance company would
cough up, since the *corpus* was not *delicti.* I would leave no note;
besides I had burned up the pages of my pocket notepad trying
to start a fire with soggy matches and damp sticks. Those
concerned would assume I had fallen ill, exhausted myself —
slowly died.

But I hadn't counted on the cold. Whenever I started to go
to sleep, the temperature in my spine dropped like the mercury
in a thermometer, and the increased bundle of cold woke me up.
The whole day, after dawn, had been spent this way: finding a
place to curl up, trying to sleep, waking up, walking or running
to regain heat, finding a new place. The torment was imperson-
al, yet seemed spiteful: the elements would not permit me to
die. Actually, I now realize, I probably would have died from
exposure if I hadn't suddenly jumped up, shaking away the tears
of aggravation and clinching my galloping teeth, flung myself
out from the antenna station and started running like mad down
the mountain, zipping and rezipping the slipping zipper in my
sweatshirt. Over rocks, across streams, down deer trails, past
a surprised, alert and nasty-looking opossum come out to hunt
in the dark, all the way down the foothills and past the secluded
houses to my own house that I would be leaving, where I prepared myself some hot cereal and toast and consumed it with
nothing but the knowledge of need. The warmth rose in my
spine and with it the bitter truth: failed suicide.

So then, life would go on. But not as before. I had dumped everything from my mind, or almost everything. The moments of that dawn before the damp and cold sliced into me were resilient with spring-clear thought. Pushkin was right: *Proyasnilis' v nyom strashno mysli* ("Thoughts terribly cleared in him"). Things previously important flitted away — mere trivialities. The ways of the world, society, conventions — a little joke. The woman I had loved so desperately, the obsession that had ravaged me for years and tortured my wife, the great saga of my life that would be retold through the ages — a bitter anecdote. Of course, I had called her up long distance before I left, to give her the news and hear her predictable revilement. "If you're going to kill yourself, then you don't deserve my sympathy. I'm not going to mourn for you." And so on — she thought I was trying a new ploy to win her. It made me laugh, up in the mountains, when my thoughts terribly cleared. She ceased to matter, as did almost everything else.

What bothered me was that I hadn't had time to finish things, to leave behind a neat package of polished works. Such a package would not change the world, it would surely be kept in the garage, or a closet, perhaps eventually be turned over to a publisher who would perform the task of disposing of it. But all the same, I wanted to leave it. And I owed work to two others, both Russian. The first, Lev Lunts, the subject of my dissertation, whose posterity needed a book in English; the second, Lev Kopelev, still living, whose autobiographical account, *I sotvoril sebe kumira,* I had only half-translated before Jean told me to get out. Leaving home was one thing, leaving life another, but both belonged to me. Walking out on needy Russian writers, however, wasn't fair. I knew, in the spring clarity of my thought, that if I completed the two books they would simply slide into slots on the shelves of the libraries and unite indistinguishably with other books, but this was precisely the neatness I craved: to slide those books in, to label my box of manuscripts and to close up my life. Clean, perfect.

Further: though I intended to waste away, new seeds of life were planted. The clarity of thought was exhilarating, creative. Dawn, spring water — which I scooped up in my crossed palms, a place away from all offices: the rejection of all the people below in the city, their interests, their ideas — this was exciting. I wanted to capture that moment of mental clearing, when the babble of men ceased in my head and the stillness set in like the resounding chord of a grand instrument, when the sky asserted its everlastingness and rested content in its law. I wanted to shoot this moment through the flabby body of everyday wisdom, cut through the billows of platitudes like a bullet through clouds. So much was contained in that moment! – but I was no Bodhisattva, no Moses, the thought of turning back to better the world was a delusion. I smiled, kept my head clear and continued my ascent… But now the cold had driven me back down, and since I was to stay, I could live on that moment: revise old works, begin my attack on the triumph of the philistines and do the two translations. The Kopelev book would even pay money.

That is, three cents a word. It's the standard rate offered by the major publishers, though they like to cite it as "thirty dollars per thousand words." It sounds more that way. And it really isn't bad if you have another job, for example, that of a professor. You do some translation at night, work during the summer, and by the end of the year you pocket an extra thousand, or two, or more depending on the size of the book. In other words, the university subsidizes the publisher – or in other other words, the students pay for books they never see, give presents to the prof whether they like him or not. In my time I had received such benefits – on a reduced scale, since my publisher was a small one. For six to eight months spent on a translation I had picked up six to eight hundred dollars, spread over three years. It was great, since I had done the work for the love of it. Jean and I were able to pay off old bills and still have enough left over for Moo Goo Gai Pan one evening.

But things were different now: I had no other work. 3¢/word – that comes to \$9/page @ 300 words/page. If the Russian is easy, you might knock out three final pages a day; if it's difficult – less. Kopelev was difficult, as I already knew; but he was long, and this meant I might earn enough to survive for a time on my own. Jean let me go with 600 bucks to get set up; half of this went for rent and a bogus "holding fee." I had some money coming in from articles on science fiction, so I would make it until the second half was done. There was more reason to hope. If I could impress the publisher (that is, the editor-in-charge) with the quality of my translation, I could then submit my own writings (the least experimental). Perhaps, after my suicide, I would be a success.

I moved into an apartment with my dog, fed a stray cat and sat down at once to my typewriter. From now on, no two or three drafts: I would try for one, with corrections neatly typed above deleted alternatives. If the page got too messy, I would type it over. But the main thing — no lingering, no fond dreaming over poetical renditions. Stop reconstructing sentences. Maximum speed. Money. I had come down from the mountain for three cents a word.

TWO

OY, LYSHEN'KO!

I sotvoril sebe kumira — the title itself posed a problem. It refers to the second commandment (Exodus 20: 4): "Thou shalt not make unto thee any *graven image.*" Thus reads the King James English version (with my italics). But the Russian Synodal version has a different sense, whereby *ne delai sebe kumira* means "Thou shalt not make unto thee an *idol.*" Or even better: "Thou shalt not make unto thee a *living idol.*"

The problem is that the word *kumir* stresses not the gravenness or woodenness of the image, but rather its lifelikeness, its exalted stature, compelling idolatry. In English the phrase "graven image" may designate only a representation, not a living man. In Russian the word *kumir* may apply alike to a graven image or to a living man. It derives, according to the etymological dictionaries, from the Finnish *kumartaa* — "to bow down, pay obeisance, worship," etc., and hence means anything or any person one may glorify. *Kumir* occurs in Old Church Slavonic, the Biblical language of the Slavs, and Pushkin, with customary genius, applies the word to the statue of Peter the Great that comes to life in *The Bronze Horseman.* In Kopelev's title the word has an *a*-suffix in the accusative case, which means it is treated as a noun denoting a living being. The Russian reader understands that a Soviet idol is intended — Lenin, Stalin or any number of lesser tyrants — and that this idol is linked to the second commandment.

So then: neither *graven image* nor *idol* will work when translating *I sotvoril sebe kumira.* In the first instance, "He Made Unto Himself A Graven Image" retains our Biblical association, but loses the vitality of the Russian *kumir,* plus the Soviet associations with the word. In the second instance, "He Made Unto Himself An Idol" — or "He Created Unto Himself A Living Idol" — retains the sense of *kumir,* but loses the Biblical association for the English reader.

Another problem is the choice of the verb — the second word in the title. The author uses *sotvorit'* ("to create") instead of *delat'* ("to make"), the latter word occurring in the Synodal version of the Bible (the one in my collection). Later, toward the end of the book, I discovered that Kopelev quotes Vladimir Korolenko, who himself quotes the commandment with *sotvorit'*, apparently from a Bible other than the Synodal. I might have done some Biblical research at this point, but the university library had no Russian Bible different from my own, writings on the Holy Synod, established by Peter the Great and abolished by the Bolsheviks, were abstruse, and I would have been hard-put to depart from the King James "make" in any event.

Further, the verb in this form, without a noun or pronoun subject, does not tells us whether it is "he" or "I" who makes the *kumir*, only that the subject is masculine singular. The other two words in the title — *i* and *sebe* — also pose little problems. Those who know Russian will recognize them and those who do not will find explanations tedious. Suffice it to say that all four words in the title are refractory, and my various compromises came out looking lousy in English:

I Made Unto Myself a Graven Image
He Created for Himself a Living Idol
And Yet He Worshipped a False God

Perhaps I should have taken warning from the title that the book would be a bummer to translate, but as it happened, Carl Proffer, who had obtained the unpublished manuscript from the Soviet Union, printed it in America in Russian and made arrangements for its publication in English, recognized the unsuitability of the original title and dreamed up an entirely new, English one:

The Education of a True Believer

This title was excellent, incorporating a readily grasped English expression ("true believer"), yet capturing the overall sense of the text. The author, I was told, had sanctioned the new title, so I was spared a decision on the old one, which might have taken a long time and yet been painful. (My choice would probably have been the first of the three variants above.) For all that, the old title remained important to the viewpoint of the book, so I added the second commandment in the King James version as an epigraph. This prepared the reader for the pages at the end of the book, where I translated *kumir* as "idol" outside the Korolenko quote and as "graven image" within the quote, and I rejoiced that Kopelev also wrote *zhivye bogi* ("living gods") in one sentence, so that all the meanings of *kumir* were revealed.

The title decided, I turned to the first chapter. Here Kopelev relates his first political impressions and the impact of the Revolution. His family and relations in Kiev are presented, including a colorful Great-Gramps, who runs through the rifle drill with a stick:

> "Shoulder h-arms! One-two! Order h-arms! One-two!
> Pre-e-sent h-arms! Hwon-two-three!"

The Russian in this case was spelled as befits shouted military commands, so it was easy to find the correct equivalents of brutalized English. But Great-Gramps goes on jabbering, and the Russian becomes markedly defective, evidently under the influence of enfeebled pronunciation, obsolete forms and Ukrainian. The meaning was fairly clear, but what was the English equivalent? I opted for standard old man, with a few old-fashioned words:

> "Kerensky's a bum, a loafer, an out-n-out swindler. I
> been alive for five tsars, been born when the blessed
> one, Alexander First, was tsar. Went in the service
> under Mikola, took me away to Muscovy..."

And so on. The fellow sounds perilously close to a crusty old prospector in a cowboy film, but I depended on the Russian references to save me. There was no other way I could think of. How do you indicate Ukrainianized Russian in English?

A couple of pages further, only four pages into the text, a village woman runs out proclaiming the Revolution: *"Oy, ly-shen'ko, tsarya skinuli."* The meaning was clear: the Tsar had been overthrown. Only a couple of words were tricky — the second and the last. The last is the verb: the woman says *skinuli* — it means "throw down, toss off" and might better be applied to an overcoat than to a tsar. Evidently it is colloquial for "overthrow," so I translated: "Oy, … they've thrown off the tsar."

Oy is known to everyone; *tsarya* too. So the second word alone stood out: *lyshen'ko.* I assumed it was related to *lishat',* meaning "to deprive, divest, rid." The reflexive form *lishat'sya* means "to lose, be devoid of, be deprived of." The woman, therefore, was screaming something like: "Oy, what a loss, they've thrown off the tsar." No problem here, I'll just look up the precise meaning of *lyshen'ko.*

However, Kopelev spelled the word лышенько and in Russian лы- (*ly-*) does not normally change to ли- (*li-*).

Here I must stress that we are speaking of two separate letters, two separate vowels and two separate sounds. The first — ы — is transliterated into English as *y*. Its name is the yery and its sound is approximately that of the *i* in the word *milk* when spoken by an Alabaman. The second — и — is pronounced like the *e* in the word *legal.* In Russian it causes the middle of the tongue to rise to the roof of the mouth and to "palatalize" the preceding consonant. The difference, then, between лы (*ly*) and ли (*li*) is something like the vowel sounds of *lug* and *league.* The ы is found toward the end of the Russian alphabet; the и toward the front. With this little excursus we can proceed.

Possibly the woman, in her distress, I thought, had failed to palatalize, or maybe she used a dialectical form; then again the word may be related to another root beginning with *ly,* though the only thing that came to my mind were words for baldness: *lysyi, lysina,* etc.

Following my usual practice, I wrote the word in Cyrillic letters on the page of my rough English draft and circled it with red ink. Later I would visit the library with the pages bearing red circles and try to find as many as possible in the dozens of Slavic dictionaries not in my possession. With Kopelev, nearly every page had a red circle or two. Searching for лышенько (*lyshen'ko*), I consulted all the dictionaries of literary Russian, both Soviet and foreign, both Russian-English and Russian-Russian, looking under both лы and ли. To my amazement, there was no entry. I then went through the interpretive and dialectical dictionaries, pre- and post-revolutionary. Nothing. I looked through sets of encyclopedias, compilations of scientific terminology, stray books lying on tables. The word must not be Russian.

But Ukrainian, I checked again for myself, does not have the letter ы in its alphabet: it has the и and i — a dotted *i*, just as in English. Russian does not have the dotted *i.* Well, then, it must be that Kopelev, expecting his text to be printed in Cyrillic type — that is, in Russian — did not expect the typography to include the Latin letter *i,* even though the dotted *i* is part of the Ukrainian alphabet, which is otherwise Cyrillic. Russian writers often transliterate from other alphabets into Cyrillic, just as we transliterate from Cyrillic into Latin letters, to save money on type and typesetting. Therefore, лы really means лi — *l-dotted i.* Enheartened by this calculation, I attacked a small blue Ukrainian-English dictionary. No luck, only лiщина *lishchina* — "hazel, hazel-tree." "Oy, hazel-tree, they've..." But that's impossible, besides щ (*shch*) is as different from ш (*sh*)) as ы from и.

I proceeded to the larger Ukrainian dictionaries, both Ukrainian-English and Ukrainian-Russian, to no avail. There remained the multivolume State Academy of Sciences edition of Ukrainian-Ukrainian. Zilch. Fingering my way through the tomes on the shelves, I discovered packets of papers tied together with string — preliminary studies toward Ukrainian dialectology. Incomplete, of course, since Slavists have a habit of dying early in the alphabet of Old Church Slavonic and dialects of Pskov and Novgorod, not to mention Lvov and Kharkov. This poor pedant didn't make it to Л.

O.K., I still had the dictionaries of foreign words in Russian; the academicians have produced quite a few, ranging from little guides for schoolchildren to thick maroon volumes of Turkish words in Russian. I checked them all. I knew what it meant, all right, but I had to be sure, to verify my choice by something in print. Translation is creative, but not free. You must either know as a native or find an authority.

Having exhausted the labors of the compilers of words, whole decades and centuries of lexicographers working unremittingly through day and night, in fierce Turkish afternoons and frozen Siberian dawns, passing on their boxes and drawers of cards, slips of paper, scribbles on napkins, scratched out in Turkish, Mongolian, Armenian, Kazakh and Azerbaijan languages, transmitted in Latin, Cyrillic and Georgian scripts, possibly Sanskrit and Arabic as well, to their long-nosed, pin-eyed offspring blinking behind spectacles thicker than shot-glasses, who in turn sort the cards, add to them, reach a higher level of the alphabet and then expire, passing on their work to the modern professors, who obtain grants and get their students to complete the task, I turned to living bearers of the Russian language in my quest for *lyshen'ko*.

They responded: "It must be related to *lishat'!* But why is it spelled this way, with a yery?"

"I don't know, I was hoping you could tell me."

This, in English, Russian or half-and-half. The Russian scratches his or her head.

"Could it be Ukrainian? I know I've heard it."

I recount the story of my search.

The Russian: "Hm, strange."

Obliged to leave *lyshen'ko* circled in red, I passed on to the second chapter. Chapter Two finds the young Lev taking his first steps in German culture. The nursemaids, or "bonnes" as his mother calls them, are all German and teach him and his brother to read, write and speak the language. His family spends two years on a sovkhoz (state collective farm) run by the former landowner, Karl Mayer. His wife is Grossmutter Ida, her mother-in-law Grossmutter Maria, who speaks no Russian, save occasional cursing: "bastart... zon of bitch." The daughter of the Mayers is Tante Lucy, her husband Onkel Hans and their children Lily, Erik and Buby.

And, naturally, I had to check all these spellings in German dictionaries and encyclopedias, even though most are foreign names in German, just so I would know the proper spelling with Latin letters. Onkel Hans's last name is *Spanbrucker*, which I believe eventually was confirmed in a dictionary of German surnames. Young Lev begins reading in German literature and history, and the names are given in Cyrillic: *Karl May, Friedrich Spielhagen, Lützow's Black Jägers.* The first two were listed in a German encyclopedia of novels, the third in a multivolume set of world history written in German.

But, all in all, the German element in Kopelev's book was not overly large, though the name Willi Husemann, the newspaper *Rote Fahne* and the German-Soviet firm *Derunaft*, among other words, took a little time to verify in the later chapters.

After the Spanbrucker episode, Kopelev introduces Lidiya Lazarevna, a private tutor and Populist, who brings eyes slanted by *bazedovaya bolezn'* — Basedow's disease — and a huge reading list of revolutionary poets and theorists, fortunately mainly Russian. She is an *intelligent* — that is, a member of the *intelligentsiya.* The collective noun has come into the English language (from which it originally derived into Russian), but not the singular representative thereof: consequently, one must translate "member of the intelligentsia," "intellectual," etc. She is also a *Bestuzhevka* — that is, a graduate of courses for women established by K.N. Bestuzhev-Ryumin, about whom I might have made a note, had the publisher shown any inclination to pay more than 3¢ a word. But my tentative proposals were rebuffed, and so hundreds of references were allowed to sink into the text.

After Lidiya Lazarevna, Lev becomes a boy scout and learns about the founder of the scout movement, Baden Powell. Amusingly, Kopelev provides a footnote on Powell, after neglecting to identify dozens of other figures. Since the footnote was in Cyrillic, I had to look up the man's name anyway in the Soviet encyclopedia of Russian history, which gives foreign names in their native spelling in parentheses after the Russian entry.

The kids in the scouts sometimes wear something called an *apashka.* Assuming the word to be commonplace, I circled it in red and nonchalantly consulted the Russian-Russian dictionary of standard literary language the next time I went to the library. No dice. The Russian-English dictionaries, the Ukrainian, dialectical, etc. I could find no entry for *apashka,* not even in the dictionaries of foreign words, to which I had turned on the premise that the word might be based on "Apache." But this time I got lucky. My living bearer of the Russian language replied off-handedly, "Oh, that's an open-neck shirt." An everyday word, yet I had never heard it in three trips to Russia, thirteen years of college and eight years of teaching. Perhaps a Russian would have trouble finding "shades" in an English dictionary.

For the summer of 1923, the Kopelev family stayed in the village of *Sobolevka* to the west of *Vinnitsa.* Both names had to be checked in the atlas, since the first might better be transliterated *Sobolyovka* and the second *Winnica.* The first was not found, the second showed up in the fifth or sixth atlas. In Sobolevka, as on the sovkhoz, Lev's father worked as an agronomist, boarding his family in the house of the sugar refinery's manager, Pan Tadeusz Waszko. The manager's children are Każik and Zosia, whose friends are one-legged Zbyszek and "ruddy" Każik, Jadzia, Halinka, Wanda, Zbych. These Polish kids, as is to be expected, go to the kościoł every Sunday and speak a Polified Russian. Confusion arises between the tongues. Writes Kopelev:

> Until I understood that the Polish *żyd* was not the same thing as the Russian *zhid* [Yid], but rather the same thing as the Russian *evrei* [Jew], we had a number of fights.

A local tough calls out to the new boy:

> "Hey, you, sonny-boy, who d'ya belong to — the Polaks, Russkies or Yids? Come on, say this: *kukurudza s grechkoi* [corn and buckwheat]. Or this: *palyanytsya* [white cottage loaf]."

Kopelev explains:

> It was assumed that Jews were unable to pronounce the sound *r*, and Poles and Russians couldn't pronounce the soft, scrumptious-smelling word *palyanytsya*.

At this point the reader might have questioned Lev's nationality himself, if not so uncouthly. He knows quite well what will follow: Lev's enthusiasm for Polish history and culture. Sienkiewicz, Pan Wolodejewski, Mieszko, Boleslaw the Mighty, Kosciuszko, Dombrowski, Brżozowski — they're all listed, and every one required checking, since they were all spelled in Cyrillic. I discovered that Polish names are often spelled in English in a modified way, so that Jan Henryk Dąbrowski is also spelled Dombrowski.

In Polish matters I turned to a former student of mine named Vickie Kosowicz, who turned to her parents when she was uncertain of spellings. Children of Russian émigrés, Poles, Czechs, Yugoslavians in America very often major in Russian at the university, since they have a great advantage over native English speakers. They make the other students feel dumb and the non-Slavic teacher feel incompetent, and the best way to deal with them is to ask them questions.

Several versts from the village is a little town, where the Kopelev and Waszko families stop one Sunday after a hunting trip. What happens there may best be quoted:

> The carriage was surrounded by barefooted boys in caps with broken visors or crumpled little hats and with ringlets hanging down beside their ears. They hollered, laughed, poked us with their fingers. My short knee-length breeches obviously amused them. They all wore cuffed or three-quarter length pants, like the country or refinery boys. The shouts *kirtze khayzelekh* (short pants) had a sarcastic ring. I tried to converse with them in Ukrainian and German, changing the *a* sounds into *o* so it would seem like Yiddish. The boys a bit older answered in a mixture of Yiddish, Polish and Russian-Ukrainian words. There were no scouts or Young Communists among them. When I told them that I too was a Jew, they made disbelieving and hostile noises. The loudest and most frequent words heard were: *khaz'r* (swine), *apikoyres* (non-believer) and *mamz'r* (bastard). One curly-headed, wide-eyed youngster in a huge crushed bowler asked spitefully: "Do Panicz eat *khaz'r?*" I admitted that I did and tried to explain that the ancient prohibition was suitable for hot Palestine, but here pig was not dangerous.
>
> Several voices broke out: "You pig yourself... *khaz'r...* *mamz'r... kush in toches!* (kiss my ass!)" Heavy lumps of dirt started flying, and only the intervention of the longbeards standing nearby warded off a big tussle.

Here Kopelev provided the translation (into Russian) of the Yiddish words, but once again not the English spelling. Consulting dictionaries at the library, I discovered that Yiddish has no standardized spelling — it grows on the soil of other languages and incorporates their alphabets and spellings. At least, so it seemed to me from the variant spellings in the books I could find. Some words cited in this passage, moreover, were from Hebrew, if I am not mistaken, but after riffling through a few Hebrew dictionaries backwards — that is, the right way, I gave up and settled for one of the Yiddish spellings.

In the first two chapters, then, I encountered Russian, Ukrainian, German, Polish and Yiddish, plus assorted words from other languages, such as the name of the French revolutionary Delescluze (spelled in Russian *Deleklyuz*). There was a goodly amount of Russian slang, plus Ukrainianized Russian and obsolete Russian — *e.g.*, the names of the various currencies of revolutionary times. Yet, strange to say, I liked it. What galled me was the payment: the price fixed on *khaz'r, mamz'r, kush in toches!* (15¢). Had I been working for free, as I had done in my previous translations, I would have been challenged, intrigued and proud of every success, and I would have taken my time. But here every success mocked me with a paltry sum, and I had to go faster, faster, losing money with each trip to the library.

Of Chapter Three I will complain only about the Grandmother, who earlier was heard to remark:

"Ta ne troskochi ty po katsaps'ku, ya zh tak ne rozu-miyu. Yak ne znaesh' ridnoi movy, ne loshen keidish, ni idish, to khoch' govor' po-lyudski, a ne po-panski..."

This gobbledygook (Ukrainian + Yiddish) I rendered thusly:

"Now don't you be chattering at me in Russky talk, 'cause I don't ken it. If you not know your mother tongue, or Kaddish, or Yiddish, leastvise speak like person, not like pan..."

Typing it now, I see that my attempt failed: the first sentence is Tennessee twang, the second is New York Yiddisher Mama.

In Chapter Three Grandmother steps forward as a main character, berating the family of her son, Lev's father:

"U vas zhe vse tref... Vy i svinyu iiste. Vsya posuda ne chista, peremishana..."

Which came out in translation:

"Ev'ryting you haff be *treyf* – not kosher... Pork you
even be eating. All your dishes be unclean, all mixed
together..."

Whether anyone speaks this way in English I hesitate to
say, but this version is more consistent than the first attempt.
Yiddish, Ukrainian and the words of Jewish ritual become
prominent in this chapter, as Kopelev recounts the religious
crisis of his youth, precipitated by his inquiring mind and the
unequal struggle between Bolshevik romanticism and parental
(and grand-parental) conservatism. In the next chapter, the boy,
now free of Tsar and God, enters the mysteries of teenage sex
with his Red girlfriends. His family moves from the environs
of Kiev to Kharkov, and references to places abound. I consulted a Baedeker circa 1930 for maps of the cities, but they really
didn't prove helpful. All the same, despite the unrelieved
peppering of Ukrainianisms, the language brightens up a bit –
there is more and more Russian, and I could begin to breathe
more freely. Toward the end of the chapter, the boy studies
the party struggles after the death of Lenin, and I am in my
element. The pages fly by.
Till Chapter Five – "Esperanto." Lev is introduced to the
artificial language by his new teacher of Russian literature:

"The grammar of Esperanto is ingeniously simple,
easy, within the reach of any memory. Sixteen rules
in all – they can fit on one blotter. All the nouns end
in -*o*, all the adjectives in -*a*, all the verbs in -*i*. Only
one conjugation. No exceptions. Distinct endings...
Paroli – to speak, *parolas* – I speak, *parolis* – I spoke,
parolos – I will speak. The simplest rules of word
formation: *lerni* – to learn, *lernejo* – school, *lernilo* –
textbook, *lerneanto* – student."

Unfortunately, this exciting lesson is delivered in Russian,
hence transcribed by the author in Cyrillic. Esperanto, although international, makes do with Latin letters, not Cyrillic.
Therefore: back to the library, to check out a little grammar,
crusted with dust, bearing a red stamp on the return slip for a

month in 1953. At home I ran through the book, trying to find the correct Latin spellings in the glossary at the back and the examples in the text. Happily, most were found — but they were spelled noticeably differently from the indicated Russian. Evidently Kopelev had quoted from memory and made a few mistakes.

The chapter moves from the international language, which Kopelev recognizes is "a paper plant, not a branchy tree whose roots are hidden in the depths of the national soil and subsoil," to internationalism — a tie between nations, all with their own multifarious customs, colors and ways of speech. As a natural polyglot (the word comes from the Greek: πολυγλωττος — *i.e., polyglottos,* "many tongued"), Kopelev rises above the baffling babble of his background, condemns every expression of ethnophobia and espouses receptivity, tolerance and universal brotherhood: "I knew, I believed, felt while still a child that all nationalities, all religions and all languages were equal." He reaffirms the hope that there is no Hellene, no Judean, and adds:

> In youth I believed that this hope had taken flesh in the call: "Proletarians of all countries, unite!" Later I became convinced that it lived in many other expressions as well. And for me today it sounds most clearly in the Pushkin speech of Dostoevsky: "To be really a Russian — this means to be a *vsechelovek,* a universal man."

These lofty sentiments carried me on, though I could not help wishing that this particular Russian had absorbed one or two languages less. They may all have been equal, and they all brought me the same recompense, but they did not convert into English with identical speed.

I went up in the mountain at this point, possibly after the next chapter — a short account of school chums, made difficult only by geographical and historical names. The check for the first half of the translation was left heroically endorsed in my wife's desk. Upon my return, some of the money was allotted to me to set up my apartment, where I could press through the last chapters. Glancing ahead, I could see that the seventh chapter dealt with a group of Ukrainian poets, the eighth with a Ukrainian newspaper for the Kharkov Locomotive Factory, the penultimate and longest with the forced grain collections of

1933, and the ultimate with the author's ideological doubts, the arrests of his friends and other misfortunes. This last chapter, entitled "The End of Youth," leaves Lev on the threshold of the purges, the Second World War and a ten-year term in Gulag.

But before sending in the first half, I had to solve all the words circled in red. *Oy, lyshen'ko!* persisted as an ever-recurring refrain to my library vigils, renewed with each chapter, sung with new hope as I picked up a dictionary, believing I had absentmindedly overlooked the word the last time, groaned with new despair when the word once again failed to appear. The solution was right there in front of my face, and yet I failed to see it. Only when I pondered how best to transliterate the Ukrainian word *palyanytsya* did I see the light.

Kopelev had spelled the word in Cyrillic паляныця, that is, with a yery — the ы — after the *n*, but the Ukrainian dictionary had the letter *i* — the и — in this place: паляниця. I had found the word without difficulty, since not many words begin with *palyan...* Now why had Kopelev insisted on the ы when this letter is lacking in Ukrainian, and the word properly spelled in its native tongue has a и — a word, moreover, which Russians were considered incapable of pronouncing?

Ah, what a bonehead! Of course! — the Ukrainian и is pronounced like the Russian ы. Kopelev did not want to use the и so as to avoid confusion with Russian pronunciation of that letter. However, by inserting the yery for pronunciation purposes he distorted the true spelling, which I should have realized from other examples, as well as from Ukrainian words with the dotted *i* left intact. I picked up the blue Ukrainian-English dictionary at the library, opened to лишенько — *lishen'ko*, not *lyshen'ko* — and found the word "woe."

No problem, the word had been there all along. And in the next dictionary, the next, and the next. I found *lishen'ko* in every bloody one of them, every Ukrainian knows the word, every Russian can figure it out. The word is universal: *Oy, lishen'ko!* is bawled by babies the world over when they want to suck, and I had been bawling for months.

So there it was. All this work for a lousy *lishen'ko*, for one word, for 3¢, and the word turned out to mean "woe." But I had the last laugh. I translated the woman's cry: "Oy, woe is me..." That is, the one word of the original is represented by three words in the translation. Thus I tripled my profits.

THREE

BANANAS AND KVAS

As I labored, the image of Kopelev came frequently to mind. I had met him in the summer of 1972 while in Moscow on the cultural exchange. The stated purpose of the exchange was to train teachers of the Russian language, but the daily grind of courses on fine points of grammar in actuality militated against the real learning experience, namely speaking the language in the wider society. The idea seemed to be that we teachers of Russian should forsake contact with living Russians in order to prepare other Americans for such contact. But, of course, if any of our students ever did make it to Moscow, they would surely not speak as well as we, and they would have obligatory tours every day as well. So what was the point? To keep us in check.

My body was in bad shape from the bad food, not improved by the excellent vodka. My mind was exhausted by the flow of foreign language processed through it each day; it would periodically shut down, first by faltering over every word, then by creating no thought. Even if I turned to another of our group and spoke English, my speech was awkward, unwieldy — a partial translation from half-Russian. But suddenly, after this standstill, the machine would accelerate — Russian words, phrases, puns and metaphors would stream through me, I couldn't speak fast enough, I chattered. My tongue would tingle in the middle from palatalization, while the tip would go numb from jabbing the lower alveolar ridge. The momentum would carry me to a peak of verbal ecstacy, from which I would plunge even deeper than before, scrape around for words, drag my mind after me, or simply sit glassy-eyed at night, silent, bolting vodka and emitting waves of smoke. The Russian students considered me moody, a figure out of Dostoevsky, and I played the role to the hilt. It saved me from having to speak.

After a month or more of this nonsense, I started missing classes, visiting writers and collecting materials for my critical work back home. I saw Veniamin Kaverin, with whom I had corresponded, a former Serapion Brother and close friend of Lunts. I visited the kitchen of Mme. Mandelstam, who was so bitter she took even me for pro-Soviet, mainly because I attempted to defend the Serapions against her charge that they were all *govno*. Tamara Ivanova proved to be a surprise, for she had been married not only to Vsevolod Ivanov, but also to Isaac Babel, but she was rather reticent. Vyacheslav Vsevolodovich, Ivanov's son, dropped by — a refined literary critic. And so on — I saw my share.

Everywhere, of course, I was known as the writer on Lunts and publisher of letters to him in a Russian-language émigré journal — letters from Gorky, Zamyatin, Ehrenburg, Chukovsky and all the Serapions. I enjoyed a sort of minor celebrity, meanwhile sharing the concerns of honest Russian writers — themselves a minority. Yet always I had the sense that literature was important, people were following it — there were real events, the human spirit was struggling against the bureaucrats, the censors, the hypocritical critics and plodding toadies, the loathsome yes-men, and this distinction from the situation in America, where literature is a gala parade of best-sellers, movie-stars and television promotions, and all are yes-men, imparted a melancholy sweetness to my summer in Moscow.

Kopelev I saw three or four times. First, at his apartment on Krasnoarmeiskaya (Red Army Street). He appeared as I might have imagined — big, burly, with a black beard, now streaked with white. His presence was enormous, his erudition instantaneous and imposing; I felt dwarfed and stupid. His living room was packed with books and, as with many of the intelligentsia, papered with photographs and paintings — a melange of literary notables and personal friends. I spotted Solzhenitsyn right away, standing out like a challenge to the visitor, and yet, for all that, domestic — as if the newspapers were not filled with invective against him and anyone might put him in the glass of the bureau.

We spoke a bit of the photos, then slipped, as I recall, into the subject of communication. Lev Zinovievich was irritated by the press's failure to report the swamp fires outside Moscow; smoke was pouring into the city and stirring up rumors. He had already heard talk of saboteurs, foreign agents and explosions, and all this folly could be stopped with one factual news item. I proposed that the good citizens, habituated to false news, would misinterpret a factual item, and Lev, taking me up, expatiated on Russian obscurantism, as if he would change the order of things if given only half a chance.

His wife, Raisa Davidovna, a woman of classical beauty, frowned throughout, mindful of the listening walls. But Lev merely waved his broad hand and laughed at such pranks; he was amused by the same cars with the same license plates parked outside his door every day. The meeting was cut short by the arrival of a German girl with glasses and a satchel. Lev switched to German (did the eavesdroppers switch?) and gabbed with gusto. The girl was evidently expected, just come from abroad, something like that. He drew me a map of directions to his dacha in Peredelkino, replete with bus numbers, and advised that I had best wait a while, in view of the suspicion of foreigners in the outskirts at present, then I left.

A few weeks later I set out for Peredelkino. It was fairly late in the evening, and I had not bothered to phone in advance, but at any other time of day my stomach was undependable, and all the phones were bugged anyway. Things were going bad for me, my brain had taken another dive, and I was trying to force it up. I missed bus after bus, then luckily grabbed a taxi heading straight for Kopelev's corner; the women passengers knew him and gave me specific directions from the road. They asked no questions of a foreigner visiting this man. I walked up to the dacha, beloved possession of Russian writers, the scene of Chekhovian romances and the pride of theatrical designers — a little shack set off from other shacks by a wooden fence. There were people within: noise and spicy smells came out in the summer air.

I entered in the midst of a birthday celebration for a relative, a son-in-law, who was Italian. There were Russian-Italian foods, a dry-looking cake with decorations and yellow frosting. Women were chattering, Kopelev was wielding a skillet. I glumly handed over some books and magazines, which I always brought for writers, and Kopelev took a keen interest in them, then tossed them on a huge pile of papers I had not noticed before. They seemed to be mostly in German. The party proceeded, Italian was spoken, while I retired to a couch and played my Dostoevsky role, hoping no one would pay attention. But Kopelev, for some reason, asked me about Marshall McLuhan and the technological revolution; then upon learning of my course in utopian literature he cursorily ran through the tradition, recalling details from Sir Thomas More's work. Finally I was left alone.

Later on the couple went to visit another dacha, and Lev Zinovievich and his wife accompanied me to the train station. Both were apologetic for neglecting me, not suspecting that I was in no mood to talk. But in these last moments I forced myself to sound intelligent and spoke of Solzhenitsyn and my understanding of *The First Circle.*

Lev, as the prototype for the character of Rubin, naturally had much to say on this matter, and he started talking about Stalin in a loud voice, as if he were strolling down a street in New York, and not down the narrow pathways of a resort in Sovietland. Raisa Davidovna was again perturbed and kept trying to shush him. His view was that Solzhenitsyn had drawn a caricature, not a faithful portrait of his life, though in some chapters the details were unerringly accurate, as for example "The Trail of Prince Igor." But there was one major fact that Solzhenitsyn had cut out, which would change the whole complexion of the portrait, and here Lev told me a big secret. I nearly gasped, and Raisa hastened to remind me: "Not for publication." She repeated the reminder a couple more times and once more as I boarded the train.

(The secret has since been published. It was that the opening scene of Solzhenitsyn's novel was based on a factual event — a telephone call to the American Embassy in Moscow from a Soviet citizen reporting that Julius Rosenberg had given the secret of the atomic bomb to the Soviets. By eliminating this detail, and in fact changing the call to one of warning to a wrongly denounced doctor, Solzhenitsyn took away "Rubin's" legitimate reason for cooperating with the authorities in attempting to identify the caller.)

The Italian lad was returning with me. We sat on the wooden benches, and he lit up. His Russian was not really good, though fluent. We might have spoken a bit in English — I can't recall. My impression was that he was too sympathetic to the Soviet regime, he was an opportunist — some sort of business deal was in the works, Fiat or something. Suddenly a pair of Soviet militia flatfooted through the door in the back and caught my companion with a lighted cigarette. They came down hard on him, stating the law in a menacing tone and delivering a lecture on social order — one of those nauseating "social-consciousness" lectures intoned by boneheads and bullies from the petty ticket-tearer to the bureaucrat with the power of life and death. The Italian was scared, apologized obsequiously, promising never to repeat such inconsiderate behavior. They left, he found it difficult to recover face and we travelled in silence.

Remembering Kopelev during the translation, I invariably called to mind bananas and kvas. It happened early one sunny afternoon. I had taken the metro — the subway — to the Krasnoarmeiskaya stop, when I noticed a young man with a big smile and a jaunty step sporting a bunch of bananas. At that very moment Soviet citizens in the environs perked up: their eyes, as mine, darted behind the man to the next smiling citizen with bananas, and the next. We streamed in that direction, joining the side flow from adjacent streets. The people converged on a little park, directly in the line to Krasnoarmeiskaya, where a booth had been set up, behind which a couple of surly saleswomen were handling the goods from cardboard boxes marked *Ekuador.*

We fell in line, which at once extended out of the park, around a corner and probably to the city limits. Lively conversations developed over the unaccustomed dainties, and a hum of approval went up as a buyer passed with a bunch. Since I always had trouble with the names for foods and could be bullied by the notoriously irascible saleswomen, I inquired of those near me whether a bunch was *gvozd'* or *grozd'.* The first word, as I feared, was "nail," the second — "bunch," but to my surprise the Russians began debating the best way to designate bananas. They were not used to talking about them, evidently.

As I neared the promised spot, it became clear that supplies were dwindling; the patient consumers were losing their good humor, their holiday mood, and beginning to chide those making the purchase.

"Hey," they shouted, "don't take all the good ones!"

The younger saleslady caught on, and dished up a pile of brown bananas to the woman before her. The woman objected, only to be told: "What am I to do with the ripe — *spelye* — ones? I can't sell them afterwards!"

The crowd chimed in: "Yes, you should take some ripe ones with the good."

A rule was established, soon to be applied to the fresh – *svezhie* – green bananas. Within a half-hour my turn came: I accepted some green, some brown and made off with a few yellow besides, comporting myself with maximum civility, though the older, tougher saleslady must surely have thought: "Why should he have good Russian bananas, he's a foreigner." Gleefully I made my way out of the crowd, pitying the latecomers running up to the end of the line, for whom there would not be one *shtuka.*

Arriving at the Kopelev's, I immediately brandished my present – a mix of bad, good and promising – to Raisa Davidovna, who was happy to receive it, but not as thrilled as I had expected. In turn, she set a big jug of apple kvas in front of me, fresh from the country. She poured me a little glass – noticeably little, then left the room, saying that Lev Zinovievich would come out shortly – he was in poor health. I could appreciate the difficulty of fetching goods from the country: in Russia everything is difficult. But I was sorely parched. Smoking, speaking Russian and weeks of diarrhea had taken their toll, besides which I love apple juice.

I polished off the glass and filled up another. This I tried to sip, but it was soon gone. Raisa Davidovna came back, and I asked for a bit more; she consented with controlled reluctance and remarked that she was sorry there was not more – the kvas was intended as a gift for some old relative, a grandmother or other. I felt like a rat, but couldn't help thinking to myself: Damn it, I brought you bananas, you can spare a few sips – mash granny a brown banana. Naturally, such selfish calculations made me feel even more guilty. And this guilt lasted all the way through the translation, all the way up to today.

Kopelev came in. I gave him some books, we began talking. After a time, the conversation turned to language and concepts. The Russian language, I asserted, had no word for "privacy." *Lichnaya zhizn'* ("private life") was immediately ruled out, for I had in mind not the way an individual lives, but the concept of privacy, the right to it. How could Russians fail to meddle in each other's lives, I asked, if they lacked the basic understanding – the very word – of a person's right to be alone?

The Kopelevs were amused. "What else?" they inquired.

"Efficiency – the Russians have no word for efficiency," I said, pronouncing the English word in the midst of my Russian.

"Aha," they answered, and sought a Russian equivalent. *Effektivnost'* was ruled out — this was more like "productivity," as was *proizvoditel'nost. Deistvennost'* was closer to the concept, but this suggested speeded-up activity, not intelligent management.

Lev Zinovievich couldn't stand it — he pulled out a dictionary. "Here it is — *koeffitsient poleznogo deistviya!*"

The textbook definition — we all laughed.

"And?" they wondered, beginning to suspect that my list contained personal grievances against the Russians.

"Sophistication," I declared, "the Russians have no word for it."

Here the Kopelevs were not sure what the English word meant. After a time spent in explanation, I felt the need to even the balance, so as not to be rude, and remarked the English lacked some concepts of the Russian. "*Bezalabernost',* for example." The word means something like "being willing to do whatever anyone else wants to do." I sometimes liked that quality of the Russians, but the term can have a negative connotation, and the Kopelevs were not cheered.

The buzzer rang, and a German girl in glasses, carrying papers, was admitted to the apartment. She was not the same girl as the first one, but she blabbed heartily in German, Lev joined in, and it was time for me to leave. I left with all these details in mind, but also with the odd notion that I had been sitting at a piano, which could not have been the case.

The first day I returned home to Rochester, I had to go to the supermarket for groceries, and there, in the first aisle from the entrance, was a sumptuous display of bananas. Bunches and bunches were stacked upon bunches on a low open table, and all were firm and yellow. Yet, to my surprise, no one was rushing to grab up an armful, the aisle was perfectly desolate. As I watched, a lady took a cart and rolled by, casually glancing at the heaps of golden treasures, transported, no doubt, from the very same *Ekuador.* I stood looking at the bananas and felt very sad. Then I took a bunch.

Looking back on my meetings with Kopelev, I could hardly say they were auspicious. We had no thrilling conversations, no special friendship developed between us. I came to visit a noted literary figure, to speak with the real-life Rubin, keeping in mind that I could regale my students back home with the account: these were the days when students read Solzhenitsyn and even made an attempt to learn Russian. He granted hospitality to a student of Russian literature and a foreigner, and also received some hard-to-get publications. And that was that.

A few years later, when a translator ran short on a deadline for Kopelev's *Khranit' vechno (Preserve Forever)*, he sent sections of the book to friends for on-the-spot literal versions, including me. From these he would make an artistic rendition, or find someone else to do it. He paid, I accepted: a chapter on the transit camp. It was loaded with camp slang, almost impossible to translate. I hated it, though some parts were colorful, such as the account about an obsessive masturbator. And only when all other possibilities for making money had failed did I accept the present job, which proved to be even worse.

To tell the truth, I wanted nothing to do with Kopelev. He was too hard to translate, I did not like his style, and the hardships of his life were too complicated, too foreign, for me to feel a kinship. He was an important man, but not a great writer, whereas I was something less: a measly translator, who would have to moil and toil for what small repute he might win, all the while knowing that he had moiled and toiled more than I ever would. Hobbes put it best, in his preface to Thucydides: "For I know, that mere translations have in them this property: that they may much disgrace, if not well done; but if well, not much commend the doer." And to top it off, I had imbibed too much of the ailing man's kvas. But the contract was signed, the first half was finished: I couldn't go and die before the next chapter like an old etymologist, somewhere in the middle of a vowel. Besides, I had not come down from the mountain for this book alone.

I persevered, through memories of kvas and Polish words, and now I can write about it. Just the other day I learned that the translation had been published and reviewed this past summer. That is, several months ago. The publisher forgot to notify me. The reviewer, a university professor with tenure, recognized the problem of indicating Ukrainian Russian in English, and said that I had solved "some of the problems brilliantly," but for many more lines cited a series of mistakes — obvious oversights caused by haste. I suppose I shouldn't complain about this — for him to list the successes and only mention the goofs would be against the rules.

On the same day I received this information, I came upon the following item in the newspaper:

Soviet dissident starts year-long trip abroad
New York Times News Service (13 November 1980)

MOSCOW. — Lev Kopelev, the last giant of Moscow's dissident fraternity, left his beloved Russia yesterday with his wife, three suitcases and two return tickets to Moscow — hoping desperately that he will be allowed to come back.
"We go only to return," the writer and literary scholar said at the airport customs checkpoint, presenting two Soviet passports validated for a year's stay in West Germany, where he has been invited by several German sponsors to pursue his research projects.

The unnamed correspondent knew the best way to write his story — between the lines.

FOUR

PUSHKIN

I am writing about the difficulties associated with one book: my personal problems, the peculiarities of the text, the life of its author. And likewise the joys and especially the miseries of translation. These miseries were not exhausted by the variety of languages, but were multiplied by the many epigraphs, citations and poetical extracts with which the book is ornamented. I would gladly enumerate the instances, and expound the theoretical principles in each, but the several readers of my first drafts have pronounced a unanimous verdict: it's boring. Even a friend who can read Russian and does fine translations herself has said: "I can't stand it."

I had hoped that my literary woes might give me some literary mileage, if only at a ratio of 10 to 1. But, alas, translation is too tedious, or at least an explanation of it, and so woes score a victory, 10 to 0.

Above all, I had hoped to show why Pushkin is the greatest poet of all times and peoples. If for no other reason than to read Pushkin, it would be worth the years of agonized study necessary for a mastery of Russian. Those who have not made this study, nor come by the language naturally, are poor, sad things deprived of the clearest, most perfect expression of thought, just as those who have never heard Bach, Mozart, Beethoven, never looked at a painting of Da Vinci, a woodcut by Munch, never read a line of Plato, are underdeveloped creatures, mere potential human beings.

But why is Pushkin so wonderful? How can one make such a claim? After all, there are translations of his works, and they don't seem so great — rather singsong and banal, in fact. You can't expect people to read every great writer in the original. Who has read Homer, Omar Khayam, Lao Tsu, Kierkegaard in their native tongues? We need translations, else we would be thrown into confusion: each person would know only his own language, suspect every other; there would be no communication between peoples, only ba-ba, bo-bok, bab-ble. Why must an exception be made for Pushkin?

The answer is simple: he is untranslatable.

And here I myself must act as censor. In my original draft I related that Kopelev in Chapter Four of his book had quoted from Pushkin's *The Bronze Horseman*:

> *I pered mladsheyu stolitsei*
> *Pomerkla staraya Moskva,*
> *Kak pered novoyu tsaritsei*
> *Porfironosnaya vdova.*

And I then subjected the presumed reader to five pages of my various attempts to translate this quatrain, winding up with this pale simulacrum of verse:

> Before the younger capital
> Old Moscow seemed to lose her glow,
> Just as before the tsar's young bride
> The royal-purpled dowager.

But looking over those five pages now, I see that they fail to make the point. They show only difficulty, difficulty, whereas Pushkin is ease and light. No, the best way to prove Pushkin's genius and my — rather, everyone's — hopeless inability to translate him is to throw those pages away. To dedicate this chapter to him, but not try to prove anything about him. Let the mystery remain. The reader must find out on his own. Pushkin is as fine as clean air, but you can't catch him in a jar.

In the second half of the book there were quotations from Pushkin, Shevchenko, Christa Wolf; epigraphs, slang, Soviet acronyms (*partkom, gorkom, raikom*), Yiddish, Polish, German, even a word in Romanian (*siguranta*—the Secret Police). Chapter Seven was devoted entirely to bad Ukrainian poetry — that is, the literary groups that young Lev encountered, filled with bombastic hopefuls. My task was to make equivalently bad English verses — but would the reader understand? Chapter Eight was loaded with locomotive vocabulary, Chapter Nine with peasant speech and new Sovietese. The final chapter, at last, was pretty much straight Russian. It concludes with the hope that the memory of people will "sweep clean all the temples of graven images," counteract the idols of our time — Ho Chi Minh, Che Guevara, Nasser, Castro, Kim Il-Sung, Idi Amin. The admonition of Korolenko is repeated: "Conscience is the only master of your actions, and graven images are not needed."

The Education of a True Believer took its author seventeen years to write, from 1960 to 1977. I could imagine the interruptions, the hardships, the secrecy, the partially written manuscript, the fear of disclosure, the bad food, the illnesses, the sad memories and the joy of releasing them onto paper by means of a rickety Russian typewriter. And the relief when once the work was done, safely received in the West, published, disseminated, taken for translation in many tongues. But, of course, the author would not relax: "We cannot escape the past."

The translation took me from August 1978 to June 1979, including a few weeks lost on other matters. The second half went faster than the first, despite my uncontrollable musings, my unavoidable rough drafts. I worked furiously, ten to twelve hours a day, taking time out only to eat, walk Wolfgang, feed the stray cat, talk to an old neighbor and smoke a cigarette in front of the poster given me many years ago by my first Russian teacher, the vivacious Helen Yakobson. She placed high hopes in me...

Pushkin strides down the high road, his cape flying out behind him, his head cast up to the right, his curly brown hair and full sideburns glinting, his gaze fixed afar. He was hounded by the Third Section, humiliated by the Tsar, tied down by petty financial and marital problems, and yet he strode and looked ahead and conceived perfect verses...

No, I didn't delude myself: I would never be Pushkin. He created the Russian language himself, out of a bewildering jumble of Slavic words, dialects, Church Slavonicisms and Gallicisms. Whereas I had a few masters before me, somebody named Shakespeare, for example, and the English language might possibly survive without my conceits. But I took heart from the eternal youth of Pushkin; I felt that I was emerging from my troubles. The work was done — 455 typed pages. I turned my gaze to the future.

FIVE

THE LIFE PLAN

In my youth I had conceived a life plan. I didn't want to go to college, because I didn't believe others could teach me how to write. At the same time I knew perfectly well that the things I wrote would not sell: they were so brilliant, so unprecedented, editors would not know how to read them, would certainly reject them. Perhaps, even then, I had an inkling of what I know now: the pieces were pretentious take-offs from Kafka, with a hypertrophic growth of adjectives and an undernourished plot. While seeking daring flights of imagination and setting off verbal pyrotechnics, they betrayed their immaturity. Nevertheless, though I protected them with trumped-up bravado, I did not miscalculate their effect: the responses from editors were painfully blind — this was back in the days when editors actually read manuscripts and wrote personal responses, rather than skimmed two pages and slapped on a form letter. So I would have to find another way, and since no one could teach me about literature I would have to take something that someone could teach me — a science, a language, a skill.

Helen Yakobson could speak Russian; I could not. I signed up. In a short time I had worked out this plan: become a translator, win a reputation for your work, submit your own writings. People will want to read the original creations of the gifted technician, you will have contacts, and so on. Naturally, working a regular job as a lifetime profession was out of the question.

Over the years I got sidetracked — studied, taught and wrote critical articles. The original pieces that I could submit became fewer. And more rigid, calcified by academic training, a critical reaction in advance of every word. Still, I loved to translate; it seemed a shame to read a whole work in Russian and then leave it as a cipher for others. One by one my versions of stories and poems found their way into print, and then when Carl Proffer founded his own press and opened the gates to translations from Russian, heartily despised hithertofore by the musty pedants, I flooded the field. I created a name for myself — but, alas, one not quite monumental enough to hold back the economic debacle of the seventies, when we all began to pay for the Vietnam War. Last hired, first fired: the University of Rochester, following a masterful policy of beheading all vulnerable faculty in the humanities, cut me in 1976. (My senior professor told me I had published too many translations, and he actually persuaded me to write an apology to the dean. It didn't matter — the axe was economic.) By now I was married, with children.

A phone call from Riverside, California. Would I be able to teach a seminar in Bulgakov? Of course, I had read practically all of his works, seen his plays staged in Moscow, spoken with his widow. Well, someone was needed for such a course. What, I exclaimed, can there really be such interest in Bulgakov on campus? After all, he's not the best-known Russian writer. The answer, which I now know was thoughtless, came back: he's the author of *The Master and Margarita,* so there should be some interest. Fine, no need to haggle. The woman they had first hired, to satisfy the demands of Equal Opportunity, had suddenly changed her mind, so they permitted themselves to ask me, a male. We moved to Riverside, hoping to take a new lease on life.

I spent the summer studying Bulgakov, reading his novel about Molière in Russian, making notes. The first day of class: a skinny boy with glasses sat at the long table. We waited ten minutes, no one else showed.

"Well," I said at last, "at least you're here." He looked at me sheepishly. "Why do you like Bulgakov?" The boy could not manage an answer. "You know who Bulgakov is, don't you?" He shook his chin once to the side. "Then why did you sign up for this seminar?" He mumbled that he was a linguistics major and needed a course in the language to complete his credits. I knew my fate lay in his hands: I would have to please him, keep him, so at least I could get paid. But my days were numbered, and each class with this ninny would be an exercise in humiliation. Somehow I managed to smile and ask all the questions and supply all the answers in this first class (and all succeeding classes). Afterwards, as we left the building, the student deferentially stepped back to let me pass through the door, but as I did he opened it with ill timing and caught my shoe with the sharp metal corner, effectively slicing it in half.

"Uh, sorry," he smiled helplessly.

All talk about tenure was dropped, the "one-year renewable" was not renewed. I drew unemployment compensation, began to write in earnest again. A translation was done on speculation; Macmillan picked it up: *The Second Invasion from Mars* by Arkady and Boris Strugatsky. It was easy, the 3¢/word didn't bother me. Trying to follow my lead, I submitted an introduction. Macmillan, however, was committed to Theodore Sturgeon for introductions to its science-fiction series. They returned my analysis, published his three pages of pap. And probably paid him.

But I plugged ahead. Sent in a wild short novel. The editor, Roger De Garis, liked it, but unfortunately didn't tell me so for over a year, and then only after vigorous prodding by mail. It turned out he was in the losing minority; the other editors didn't think it would sell. Clearly, this De Garis must be strange, if he liked my writing. More recently I sent him another short novel, *The Mad Kokoschka*. He returned it with the note: "Shortly after talking with you, I found out that Macmillan was letting me go. Needless to say..."

The Kopelev project came up: the first translator had backed out, due to other commitments. I hesitated, then recalled my old plan. I would take on this uneasy load, accept the light payment, grumble not. I would type a neat copy on my IBM Selectric, paying for paper and film ribbons; I would pay for the Xerox copy, the First-Class postage. I would make correct estimates of the number of words, even modest estimates. And then, when my work was done and approved, I would submit my own writings.

The time was at hand. The ms. received, the check in the bank. Half of the total $4000 — it didn't look small, until one figured the time it took and the time it must last. Jean was reminding me of child support: I wrote a check. Now the trick was not to let myself be forgotten. I inquired about a translator's preface. The editor couldn't promise anything, but she'd consider whatever I had to offer. I set to work.

The chief question raised by Kopelev's book, as I saw it, was this: How could a smart, inquisitive boy like Lev, who spoke several languages, read German publications from an early age and actively studied the newspapers in an attempt to formulate his political convictions, become a true believer? How could he fail to hear the warnings of his parents, the promptings of his conscience? How could he participate in the forcible seizure of property and grain from the peasants, when he understood perfectly well that the directors were ignorant fanatics and the peasants were doomed to starvation? And how could he go on believing in the cause through the Stalin years, the pact with Hitler and his own imprisonment in Gulag?

The answer, arrived at rather hastily, was that there are periods when the external influences swamp those of the home, when parents are discredited by the spokesmen of history, the Zeitgeist. The young Lev goes through the same stages as most boys, only the material is different. When he daydreams himself a hero, it is as the leader of a Red Cowboy Regiment sovietizing the USA. He wins the personal commendation of Lenin, upstages Trotsky and walks off with the girl, whose breasts he will squeeze. Lev goes from the cub scouts to the Red pioneers, from tying knots to political agitation. Intelligent as he was, open as he was to foreign perspectives, he could not resist the great sweep of the time, and only in old age could work out his redemption.

But what then, I now asked, of our own youth, who did not read at all? I cited figures on literacy, mass media, 20 thousand commercials viewed each year, etc. Could we expect our children, who could not speak their own language, let alone three, four or five languages, many of whom had no native language, but only a moronic mix of mispronounced words, could we expect them to withstand the pressures of the time? Would they fail to make graven images, not worship at the feet of empty idols? Given the proper catalyst, would the youth of America not become true believers, and would they not trash all opposition?

I asked these questions directly, without hysterics. The concluding words touched on the difficulty of the translation, without whining. All in all, I was pleased: the preface was sharp, but diplomatic. It gave the publisher the chance to say something about Russia, but also about America. Also to chicken out, which is what it did.

In a gracious note the editor expressed her dismay that she could not use it, and hoped that I could find a place for it elsewhere as an essay. She even regretted that I had written it without pay; I answered that I had received many rejections,

and not been paid for a one. (I could never have guessed that
the Kopelev part of the preface, minus the American lesson,
would be plagiarized for the blurb on the flyleaves of the
cover.)

So, taking advantage of her charm, I put in a word for my
own works. Would she, could I…

Indeed, she would be glad.

I set to work. But on what?

The moment of clarity had not passed away; it had only
waited its time. I recalled the other tasks that, aside from the
cold, had brought me down from the mountain. It was too late
to revise my juvenile stories, but I could sort them out, label
them "juvenilia." And other things could be put in order, made
more distinct, so the hypothetical reader of the future would
consider me more intelligent than I was in the past. As I came
closer to the present day, I saw more and more the need for
revision and dreaded the time required. But on picking up the
play, *The Mad Kokoschka*, I saw at once that conversion to a
novel would be simple. I put the play to my right, sat at the
IBM and typed the finished copy. This method guaranteed that
I would not get too clever, too unorthodox, for the editor and the
millions behind her. I permitted myself a few tricks, though, so
as not to waste my time.

The editor turned it over to her assistant — *i.e.*, a sub-editor,
whose appraisal was forwarded to me. It was positive. The sub-
editor missed the point, but she was a nice person and read
niceness into the work. Only one problem: the novel was too
short — a mere 118 pages. This was as far as I could stretch the
play, and still many of the pages were white with dialogue.
What to do? The foot was in, the leg was in, the body was still
out the door. I replied that I would like to submit a second
piece to fill out the volume, but should this piece be unsuitable,
I would send another. The idea being to preserve the Kokoschka acceptance, not risk it on the next piece. The editor
agreed.

Searching through my archive of rejections, I plucked out
two possibilities. The first — the wild short novel, the second
— a longish story based on my obsessive love. Neither fit well,
but the story drew its title and some of its material from the
Solzhenitsyn novel about Ivan Denisovich: it was called "The
Warm and the Freezing." Perhaps this would find a warm re-
ception with the editor, or sub-editor, or sub-sub-editor.

I sent it.

Months passed.

During these months I embarked on other projects, eventually returning to the second Lev of that morning, Lev Lunts. It was hard to go back to the subject of my graduate study, a subject that had been close to my heart. Lunts had died at an early age; his sister had preserved his effects. I had visited her in London, witnessed the opening of the old suitcase, packed with unpublished materials. Letters to Lunts from Zamyatin, Chukovsky, Gorky. We — Genia, her husband and I — had lived through the emotional discoveries, the intrigues of others to acquire the letters, the sadness of Lunts's strange sickness. With a peculiar shift of the spirit, we had returned to the twenties (though I had never been there), to cold Petrograd, to the inextinguishable excitement of literary imagination. And then she had died, to reappear in my dreams, when I would visit an old house and discover one more letter of Lunts. Now I had to run through it again, be re-amazed at the erudition of this vibrant young man and to weep once again as he died in Germany, longing to return to his beloved city and the circle of his literary "brothers."

At the end of October, I devised a new tactic: make a proposal in advance of the answer. This way I would remind the editor of my languishing manuscript, and should it be rejected, I would already have another foot in the door.

(The danger of crashing backwards from pushing both feet forward at once did not occur to me at the time.)

And so I mailed off a "project proposal." The title: *Great Deaths.* The idea: to describe the last moments of famous and not-so famous people, with an eye toward colorful endings and curious last words. Without much subtlety, I pointed out that "books of lists" were in fashion, and so was the theme of death. Why not combine the two in a fascinating book, a sort of guide on how to die? Copyrighted material was no problem: it could be paraphrased, or discarded. Fifty subjects were planned, to include Julius Caesar (*"Kai su, teknon!"*), H.L. Mencken ("Well, bring on the angels."), Gustav Mahler ("Schöner Mozart!"), C.G. Jung, Iosif Stalin, Buddha, Franz Rosenzweig, Yukio Mishima and many, many more. As I reminded the editor, there was no end of people who had died.

Just to show that I wasn't fooling, I prepared a sample packet of six deaths: Charles-Valentin Alkan, Ludwig van Beethoven,

Gary Gilmore, Velimir Khlebnikov, Gertrude Stein and Leon Trotsky. Naturally, I did not take this non-book seriously; it would be a parody of our sub-literature, the abysmal sensationalism of the pulp trade, yet perilously close to the real nonthing. I didn't know that Norman Mailer was already hard at word securing copyright for Gary Gilmore material, nor that Leon Prochnik had written a book called *Endings: Death, Glorious and Otherwise, as Faced by Ten Outstanding Figures of Our Time*, including good old death-loving Mishima. Nor that two writers, Scott Slater and Alec Solomite, were looking forward to the publication of their work, *Exits: Stories of Dying Moments and Parting Words*. Nor that an apparent man and wife team, Norman and Betty Donaldson, had happily produced *How Did They Die?* Nor, finally, that many years later a multimillionaire would get into he act: *They Went That-A-Way* by Malcolm Forbes. You can't kill a good idea.

The shot was fired. Silence — week after week. Rice entered my life, food stamps. I tied knots in my broken shoestrings, waited. No need to prod, to push my luck. Let the editor take her time, or the sub-editor. I don't want to blow my life plan with haste. And so I studied Greek, cultivated the life of leisure — *i.e.*, poverty. The days hobbled by — hard days, but with them I was winning back self-esteem. The poorer I got, the more determined. As my motto I took the stand of Karl Kraus: *No compromise!* True, Kraus had inherited a fortune from his father's paper mills, so he could print whatever he pleased, while fortune granted me no money. But I felt I could withstand the endless wind of rejections, clutching to a precious metal, which no longer had any currency.

Still, it was difficult to believe that for every evil there was a corresponding good. That, as Emerson put it: "For every grain of wit there is a grain of folly. For every thing you have missed, you have gained something else; and for every thing you gain, you lose something." It was easy enough to recall Schopenhauer, who refuted the notion of a just universe by asking us to consider the respective thoughts of two animals, one of which is engaged in eating the other. Nevertheless, in my hardship, I could not help feeling the touch of grace. My mind was free — to think, to dream. No one had to be satisfied — save philosophers long dead. I did not have to play a role — except perhaps to myself, but this was a life role, with immense flexibility. Besides, I was gaining experience: something was seeping into my heart, and though the details of my life might find disproportionate and unfair expression on paper (one month to one paragraph, for example), I was becoming a writer. The role of professor was removed from me, along with the actor's salary. Alone in the fields, in the mountains, as Wolfgang went running, I felt communion with the greats of the past. They had been published, I was their posterity. Perhaps I was capable only of scribbling, the rejections were right — no posterity for me. But, ah! the passion.

The New Year 1980 came, no word from the publisher. Finally, in February, reduced to the lowest level of want, I put in a call (reverse charges) to New York. The editor accepted: I popped the question. What did she think of the story I had sent? Did it make a volume with the Kokoschka? The sound that I heard in reply made me wince, I had to hold the receiver away from my ear.

"Gar-r-ry," came the drone in a powerful voice, a New York voice of big-business importance. "I'm terribly sor-r-r-ry for the delay. We've been so busy…" I could hear the last word reverberating in her nostrils. "Let me see," she continued, "you mean the second story."

I muttered an "un-huh," but was spoken over.

"It real-l-ly doesn't work. It's crudely written, too obvious. Don't you have something else?"

This riled me. She obviously held the mistaken notion of editors — namely, that they can judge literature better than writers. Right away I knew she did not understand the story: it was emotional, too subjective, a failure on many counts — but not crude, not obvious. I stifled my outrage, politely asked: "Didn't you like the time sequence? The convolutions of circles corresponding to the theme that love is a ring? (Pause.) I admit that the piece is too subjective…"

"It just doesn't wor-r-rk for me," came the nasal verdict, as if quality were determined by what worked for her. The spontaneous reflexes of her nervous system were the instrument that registered the vital signs of literature — only her reflexes weren't spontaneous, they were controlled by commercial instincts, and her nervous system was not of flesh, but a grid, a mesh for sifting the formula.

I did not reply. The subject of Kopelev came up — plans for publication, news of his condition.

"You know-w-w," she intoned, "we paid you peon wages for that translation. I just happened to look at the contract recently, and I was amazed."

"I know."

"Well, why didn't you say something? You could have called us."

"I understood it was the standard rate, and in fact Macmillan paid me the same for another translation."

"Thirty dollars per thousand words?"

"Three cents a word."

"Well-l-l," she drawled, "I don't know about Macmillan, but around here we usually pay..." And she cited a figure so astronomical that to this day I can't remember it. Somewhere between nine and eighteen cents a word.

Good thing I had kept my cool. Now I could put in: "In that case, is there any chance for restitution?"

"No!" shot back the answer, neat and clean. No extended vowel, no nasal reverberation. Almost a ring of horror — sharp, urgent. A no that told the whole story, ripped the mask off this corpse, powdered and prettied for her daily funeral.

"The Great Deaths," I ventured, "what do you..."

"Gar-r-ry, Gar-r-ry," the drone had returned, "I just don't know. There's something wrong about this thing. One dead person, two dead persons, three dead persons — I just don't know-w-w-w."

Good thing she was paying for the call, with those drawls. But then, hadn't I already paid? And others like me — the conned, the plagiarized, the underpaid? She could drawl long distance; I had to spend a food stamp to get change for a local call.

"There's a touch of humor in it, you know."

"I know-w-w, I know-w-w. But it's no good to laugh at the people you want to sell books to. You can't be subtle with the public, you can't sell a book with problems."

"There's room for literature, don't you think?"

"I know what you're saying," she huffed, "and we publish literature too. Just last year we published two or three novels that we knew wouldn't make money, just because we thought they were good."

"That's a small percentage, wouldn't you say?"

"If a book is good, we will publish it."

Here I forgot my tactics, unfurled the scroll of woes. *Ordinary People* by Judith Guest — the first unsolicited manuscript published by Viking in 27 years. At about five to ten thousand mss. per year, that's... And the recent experiment, when Jerzy Kosinski's novel *Steps* was sent to publishers without his name. All rejected it.

She interrupted: this proved nothing.

Oh, no, it proved...

But she didn't want to hear. Some remarks were spoken away from the phone.

"I'm sorry, Gary, there's a call from London, I'll have to call back."

"All right," I agreed, recollecting myself.

She took my number.

I sat in silence, hunching my shoulders. What a fool, after all this preparation. She's dealing with big business in London, I'm a nobody. But maybe not everything was lost (I knew it was). I might sign off amicably, keep my face in the window, after my second foot was brushed out the door. Other translation projects might come up, I might ask for the newly stated rate. It was drizzling outside, the radio station from which I had placed the call was unlit. Gloomy thoughts.

The phone rang. She actually called back. Maybe the call from London wasn't fake, or maybe she recovered her cool.

"Listen," she resumed abruptly, "I didn't call to argue about the publishing business. I just want to know how you're doing." The solicitude slayed me, but she went on. "Have you tried sending the Kokoschka to a magazine?"

"No."

"Gar-r-ry, Gar-r-ry, you're going about this all the wrong way. You've got this hostile attitude toward publishers, but you're not sending your things to the right place. Besides, the Kokoschka thing isn't really that compelling."

"What magazine do you recommend? The only one that publishes serious literature is *Harper's*, and I heard it's going out of business."

"Why not *The New Yorker*?"

Because it has its own stable of writers, you idiot, the same as most magazines, journals and small presses. This is not the twenties when it sought new authors, new forms. But I decided to compromise and thanked her for the suggestion. *The Mad Kokoschka* was out on the street.

"No, Gar-r-ry," she went on, definitely piqued, "you have the wrong attitude. You concentrate too much on the negative side. Things aren't so bad. A good writer can find a publisher. It's not hopeless."

"On the contrary," I replied through gritted teeth, "I am aware of my good fortune. I am permitted to talk directly to you, and I know that many writers will never have the chance. You, or rather your secretary, has read my novel and given me a personal response. This is a rarity that I appreciate. I enjoy a privileged position, and I am only too grateful, though it has taken me years of study and work, and also the translation of a difficult book."

"Look," she said, not heartened by my humble acknowledgement, "we publish a lot of books that bring people a great deal of pleasure, and many people here make a good living — editors, secretaries and book designers, so the business is not entirely despicable."

Taken aback by this unexpected eloquence, which had the ring of a prepared speech, I could only stammer in agreement. Finally I was beginning to understand the desperation of my position — no income, no prospects, rice. The phone call was over-extended, only seconds were left. I inquired about the possibility of future translations. I had heard about Shostakovich's memoirs...

No, they had already come out.

Anything else along that line?

Nothing on the horizon, she answered. Russian projects were few, no new ones anticipated. She wished me luck. Click.

In the dark room I looked at the phone, the dismal sky in the window. The meekness I had shown made me sick. A failed compromise tastes pretty bad. I said it out loud: "Yes, it is despicable. Entirely despicable." And I cursed myself for lacking the heart to shout it at her, to shove her self-justification up her reverberating big-business nose. Then I snitched the station newspaper, to check the want-ads.

Outside. Take the Wolf for a walk. What will I do? Where will I go? I'm broke.

AFTERWORD

THE MISFORTUNE MENTALITY

The answer was nowhere. The answer was, nowhere. I would stay right where I stood. Clark Pryce, moved by my plan to search for a cave in the mountains, got me a CETA position at the station. From a picker of mushrooms in the fields I became a programmer of classical music. A radio personality. Not much pay, little respect, but plenty of leisure. I could continue my pursuits.

A contest was held for original plays. I entered *The Mad Kokoschka* and won. I had the joy of seeing my vision take flesh on the stage. As for publishers, I scored a modest success here and there, but generally speaking my foot — both feet — remained well outside the big door. The part-time job became full-time. I stayed in Riverside, nowhere.

O.K., I've made my complaint. So what? Did I really have things so bad? Compared to others, no. Sometimes I think my misfortune was more of an attitude than a situation. I see guys walking down the street talking to themselves, grumbling out loud or even snapping at others. I recognize their state of mind. I was almost there. I know how you become a homeless bum, a street freak, an untouchable. You take a loss and can't get back. Your credits start to run out. You learn that your promise has been spent, and your prior achievements have a short shelf-life. If not soon replenished, they get stale. Then time clears the shelf. People get used to you in the lower position. It's the best you can do to hold it. Thinking you deserve a higher spot doesn't win you any friends. Without good luck, the only way to go is down. You wind up on the street — a deadbeat, a lifetime loser. People who knew you when can't understand how it happened. But mostly they don't think about it. You played your hand; they're still playing theirs. I recognize those grumbling guys: they've got the same attitude I had. The misfortune mentality.

On the other hand, maybe they really did have hard luck. Nothing special, nothing personal, just a random shot. Which comes first, the misfortune or the mentality? No one knows, but one seems to feed off the other. It's a downward spiral.

So I wrote about it, as a sort of literary experiment. My feeling at the time was that my troubles would be relieved if I could convert them into print. I feel relief now when I read about them, but mainly because they're back there, not because my writing spared me anything. In that sense the experiment failed. It was impossible to detail every little aggravation, every choking slight. I had to think of the reader.

Why should he suffer all of my gripes? Why should he share my misfortune? I lived in a dream world where my miseries would be observed by a great unknown future reader who would understand, commiserate and make them all worthwhile. Obviously I can't ask such a thing of the person reading these lines. You've got your own troubles. Why should I give the miseries, you — the sympathy, and not the other way round? Why, in fact, should I write, or having written, publish? The attempt is unfair, unequal, unless I suffer more, or make my sufferings pleasurable. Then again, I can't determine how you will react — with concern, reproach, amusement. The reader makes up his own mind. The writer has already written: he's dead, he can say no more.

Yet just as I had a chance to participate in the lives of Darwin, Violet and Lev without having to suffer their fates, so you have had a chance to experience a period in my life without having to pay my rent. I suppose I shouldn't have made such a big fuss about myself, but other writers do the same thing. They dream of a great future reader who will make everything all right. Whether it be their sorrow, their passion, their view of the world, they try to trade it off to someone else, and they assume that the bargain is fair. They're wrong, of course. They must live their own lives; no reader can redeem them. And so I shouldn't feel guilty. They call it literature.

OTHER BOOKS by Gary Kern

Translations

Before Sunrise by Mikhail Zoshchenko (Ardis, 1974)
Snake Train by Velimir Khlebnikov (Ardis, 1976)
The Second Invasion from Mars by Arkady and Boris Strugatsky (Macmillan, 1979)
The Education of a True Believer by Lev Kopelev (Harper & Row, 1980)
This I Cannot Forget by Anna Larina (Norton, 1993).

Anthologies

The Serapion Brothers: A Critical Anthology of Stories and Essays (Ardis, 1975)
Zamyatin's WE: A Collection of Critical Essays (Ardis, 1988)

Creative works

Marchenko, a play in 13 scenes (*Mosaic*, Riverside, 1984)
The Mad Kokoschka, a play in 3 acts (Xenos Books, 1986)
The Last Snow Leopard, a novel (Ghost Dance Press, 1996)